Cranr

Cranmer

A living influence for 500 years

A collection of essays by writers
associated with Durham

Edited by

Margot Johnson

Durham
Turnstone Ventures

Acknowledgment is due to the following for permission to reproduce material listed:
SCM Press for permission to quote from John Cassian in Owen Chadwick's translation of *Western Asceticism*, Library of Christian Classics, Vol. XIII (London, 1958); Hodder & Stoughton for permission to quote from Beside the Bonnie Briar Bush by Ian Maclaren; the Cambridge University Press in respect of A.E. Housman's 'The Name and Nature of Poetry', printed in A.E. Housman, *Selected Prose*, edited by John Carter; Faber and Faber Ltd. in respect of the Introduction to *The Festal Menaion* by Mother Mary and Bishop Kallistos Ware; Epworth Press for permission to quote from 'Charles Wesley' by W.F. Lofthouse, in *A History of the Methodist Church in Great Britain*, Vol. I, edited by Rupert Davies and Gordon Rupp (London, 1965); Collins Fount for permission to quote C. S. Lewis's 'On a Vulgar Error', in *The Oxford Book of Twentieth Century Verse*, edited by Philip Larkin (Oxford, 1973); and The General Synod of the Church of England for use of Professor Henry Chadwick's speech in the Crockford debate of February 1988. Every effort has been made to trace the literary heirs of the Geoffrey Bles, the publishers of M. V. Woodgate, *Father Benson of Cowley*. The author and publishers wish to record their acknowledgment to the work in question.
Quotes from the New English Bible © 1970 by persmission of Oxford and Cambridge University Presses.

Turnstone Ventures,
37, Hallgarth Street,
Durham. DH1 3AT

British Library Cataloguing in Publication Data
Cranmer, Thomas, *1489–1556*
   Thomas Cranmer essays.
   1. Christian doctrine
   I. Title   II. Johnson, Margot, *1921–*
230

   ISBN 0–946105–08–1

Text Set in Baskerville by Selectmove
Printed in Great Britain by Billing & Sons Ltd, Worcester

CONTENTS

Preface   vii

Contributors   ix

I   Thomas Cranmer: A Biographical
        Introduction
        David M. Loades   1

II   After Cranmer
        John R.H. Moorman   25

III   Liturgical Language and Devotion
        Gerald Bonner   30

IV   Cranmer and the Daily Services
        Anthony Gelston   51

V   Cranmer's Pastoral Offices: Origin and
        Development
        Kenneth W. Stevenson   82

VI   'And with Thy Holy Spirite and Worde':
        Further thoughts on the Source of
        Cranmer's Petition for Sanctification
        in the 1549 Communion Service
        Bryan D. Spinks   94

VII   The Worthy Communicant
        Hugh Bates   103

VIII   Cranmer's Baptismal Liturgy
        Stephen W. Sykes   122

IX   Music and English Liturgy
        Margot Johnson   144

X   Prayer Book Catholicism
        Sheridan Gilley   167

XI   Cranmer and the Evangelical Revival
        James P. Hickinbotham   190

XII   Charles Wesley's Hymns and the *Book of Common Prayer*
J.R. Watson   204

XIII   One Dissenter's thoughts on the *Book of Common Prayer*
Charles E.B. Cranfield   229

XIV   The Prayer Book Outside England
Richard F. Buxton   240

XV   Some Reflections on the Theology of Thomas Cranmer
Peter Forster   253

XVI   Modern Ordinands and the *Book of Common Prayer*
Michael Vasey   273

XVII   The Church of England and the *Book of Common Prayer*
Douglas R. Jones   291

Preface

This collection of essays originated in two proposals: to preserve, in printed form, the texts of several excellent talks given to the Durham diocese branch of the Prayer Book Society and not published elsewhere; and to seek a means of celebrating the 500th anniversary of the birth of Thomas Cranmer on 2 July, 1489. It seemed a natural step to suggest a book of essays which would fulfil both objects.

A small, independent, ad hoc steering committee was formed, consisting of Mr K.T. Cummings, Mr J.H. Macartney and the present editor, and it was agreed that further authors should be invited, the choice depending on their academic suitability and their past or present Durham connections. The original authors, Emeritus Professor the Rev C.E.B. Cranfield, Mr Gerald Bonner, Dr Sheridan Gilley, Bishop J.R.H. Moorman and Emeritus Professor the Rev D.R. Jones, agreed to the proposals; and the first four, still easily accessible in Durham, suggested possible writers or approached others, bearing in mind the need for a balanced volume which would cover Cranmer's life, various aspects of his liturgical work, their outcome in the centuries following his death, and their place in the modern church.

The response was most encouraging, although, with less than a year's notice, a few authors declined because of prior commitments. Two names are missing for other reasons. Mr Richard Lloyd, organist of Durham Cathedral before taking up a similar post at Salisbury, was to have contributed an essay on Cranmer's services and the music of John Merbecke and his contemporaries; but owing to a serious illness had to withdraw, with regrets. The other is Canon Geoffrey Cuming, formerly Vice-Principal of St John's College, Durham, and later of Oxford, a member of the Liturgical Commission, and an eminent writer on liturgy who has been quoted by several authors in this book. His death in the spring of

1988 has left us the poorer. His literary executor, the Rev Dr Kenneth Stevenson, although not a Durham man, very kindly offered to contribute an essay, and pleads a personal connection through his sister, married to the Rev Dr Peter Forster. His grandfather, the Bishop of Århus, Denmark, once preached in Durham Cathedral. Dr Stevenson was able to persuade the Rev Dr R. Buxton to fill a gap by writing on the Prayer Book outside England.

The resulting rich mosaic displays a wide variety of material, coloured by divergent views, which should stimulate further studies and discussion.

As editor, I should like to thank all who have contributed to the volume, especially for their patience and courtesy in enabling the material to be ready within a very tight schedule. Grateful thanks are due also to the other members of the steering committee, and to Miss Marjorie Dickinson for her expert secretarial assistance.

Margot Johnson

Cranmer Essays
Contributors' CVs

WILLIAM HUGH BATES was Tutor and Librarian, St Chad's College, Durham (1963–70); curate at Horsforth (1960–63); Vicar of Bishop Wilton (1970–76) and Pickering (1970–76). He is now priest-in-charge of Crayke and three other parishes; tutor, North Eastern Ordination Course (1979–); contributor to five theological journals; and *The Sacrifice of Praise* (1981).

GERALD BONNER, Anglican layman and former church-warden, served in the Royal Armoured Corps in World War II; was Assistant Keeper, Dept. of Manuscripts, British Museum (1953–64); Lecturer (1964), Reader (1969–88) and is now Reader Emeritus in Theology, Durham University. A specialist on St Augustine and the venerable Bede, he has published three books, edited another, and contributed articles to four lexicons and nine journals (six abroad), besides reviews. His wife Jane is Secretary to the Durham Council of Churches.

RICHARD F. BUXTON, former chemical engineer, was ordained in 1968; research student in theology and assistant chaplain, Exeter University; tutor, lecturer, and later Vice-Principal, Salisbury and Wells Theological College (1973–77); Careers Adviser Manchester University (1977–) and honorary lecturer in liturgy (1980–). He has produced one book, contributed to another and to a liturgical dictionary and reviewed for three journals.

CHARLES E. B. CRANFIELD, a minister of the United Reformed Church, and Emeritus Professor of Theology, was successively Lecturer, Reader and Professor at Durham University (1950–1980). He is Joint General Editor of the *International Critical Commentary* (1966–), and has contributed the commentary on Romans to the series. He has written several other books and commentaries, besides articles in composite works and journals. He was an army chaplain in World War II.

PETER R. FORSTER, a Church of England clergyman, has been Senior Tutor at St John's College, Durham, since 1983, and represents the Universities of Durham and Newcastle in General Synod. He has specialised in the work of St Irenaeus, and contributed articles to several composite works and journals, besides reviews.

ANTHONY GELSTON, twice Oxford prize-winner, was ordained in 1960, and in parish work before becoming Lecturer (1962–76) and Senior Lecturer (1976–88) and Reader (1989–) in Theology, University of Durham. He has written about and edited the Syriac text of the Twelve Prophets, besides contributing to seven journals. He has a forthcoming book on the East Syrian Eucharistic Prayer.

SHERIDAN W. GILLEY, Anglican layman and Senior Lecturer in Theology, Durham University, formerly taught Ecclesiastical History at St Andrew's University. He gained six prizes and awards in the University of Queensland, Australia (1963–67), and five in Cambridge University (1967–72). A prolific writer (over forty articles, and reviews in seventeen journals), he has specialised in nineteenth-century Anglo-Catholic and Catholic history (particularly Irish topics); is preparing two books; and has broadcast on Radio 3 and 4.

JAMES P. HICKINBOTHAM was Hon. Canon of Durham (1959–70) and Proctor in Convocation (1958–1970). After curacies in two parishes, he was Chaplain, Wycliffe Hall, Oxford (1942–45), and Vice-Principal (1945–50); Professor of Theology, University College of the Gold Coast (1950–54); Principal of St John's College, Durham (1954–70) with Cranmer Hall, Durham (1958–70); and Principal of Wycliffe Hall, Oxford (1970–79). He was the author of two books; and died 26 April, 1990.

DOUGLAS RAWLINSON JONES, Residentiary Canon of Durham Cathedral (1964–85), and now Emeritus, is also Emeritus Professor of Durham University, where he was

Lecturer in Theology (1951–63), Senior Lecturer (1963–64) and Lightfoot Professor of Divinity (1964–85). After ordination in 1942, he was a Bristol curate for three years, then at Oxford Lecturer, Wycliffe Hall, Chaplain, Wadham College, and Lecturer in Divinity until 1950. He was a member of General Synod (1970–80 and 1982–85) and Chairman of the Liturgical Commission (1981–86); D. D. Lambeth 1985.

MARGOT JOHNSON, theologian and historian, is part-time Tutor in History, Department of Adult and Continuing Education, Durham University (1966–). Formerly of Hull University Library (1938–39); East and West Riding County Libraries (1941–43); Durham University Library (1950–52, 1956–57); Deputy Librarian, Durham Cathedral Library (1961–63); Library Association Senior Examiner in Religion and Fellowship Thesis Examiner (1963–76); Lecturer (in Bibliography), Newcastle Polytechnic (1964–65). She has published numerous articles and short books, has three books in preparation, broadcast on radio and television, and led a church choir for ten years.

DAVID LOADES is Professor of History, University College of North Wales, Bangor (1980–) and Visiting Fellow, All Souls College, Oxford (1988–89). At Durham University he was Lecturer in History (1963–70), Senior Lecturer (1970–77), and Reader (1977–80). He was previously Lecturer in Political Science, University of St Andrew's (1961–63); and is the author of numerous books and articles on Tudor History and Reformation studies.

JOHN R.H. MOORMAN, Bishop of Ripon (1959–75), retired to Durham and died 13 January, 1989. After curacies in Leeds (1929–33) and Leighton Buzzard (1933–35), he was Rector of Fallowfield, Manchester (1935–42); Examining Chaplain to the Bishop of Manchester (1940–44) and to the Bishop of Carlisle (1945–59); Vicar of Lanercost (1945–46); Principal of Chichester Theological College and Chancellor of Chichester Cathedral (1946–56) and Prebendary of Heathfield (1946–59). He was Delegate-Observer to the Second Vatican Council (1962–65); Chairman,

Anglican Members, Anglican-Roman Catholic Preparatory Commission (1967–69); and member of the Joint International Commission of the Anglican-Roman Catholic International Commission (1969–83). He served on the Advisory Council for Religious Communities (1971–80); and was President of the Henry Bradshaw Society (1977–89). He specialised in Franciscan studies, and wrote fifteen books and many articles.

BRYAN D. SPINKS is Chaplain to the Chapel, Churchill College, Cambridge (1980–), School Master Fellow Commoner there, Michaelmas 1988; and part-time Lecturer in Liturgy, Cambridge University (1982–). He is a Durham graduate and D.D. After ordination in 1975 he served in the diocese of Chelmsford (1975–79). He is an F.R.Hist. S. (1985), Chairman, Society for Liturgical Study (1986–); corresponding consultant, Worship and Doctrine Committee, United Reformed Commission (1986–), and a member of the Church of England Liturgical Commission (1986–). He visited Lebanon as personal guest of the Maronite Patriarch to study Maronite Liturgical manuscripts (Summer 1987), and was Visiting Lecturer at three American Lutheran Seminaries (Autumn 1988). He has written three books, contributed articles to thirteen journals, and reviews in three.

KENNETH W. STEVENSON is Rector of Holy Trinity and St Mary's, Guildford (1986–). After ordination in 1973, he served in Grantham and Boston parishes (1973–80); was part-time Lecturer (Liturgy), Lincoln Theological College (1975–80); Chaplain and Lecturer in Liturgy, Manchester University (1980–86); and was Visiting Professor in Theology, University of Notre Dame, Indiana (Spring, 1983). He is Secretary of the Anglo-Scandinavian Theological Conference (1985–); has published eight books and articles in ten journals (for which he holds a Manchester D.D.), and reviews in seven; and is a member of the Liturgical Commission (1986–).

STEPHEN W. SYKES is Bishop of Ely (1990–); and was Regius Professor of Divinity and Fellow of St John's College, Cambridge University (1985–90); Honorary Canon of Ely Cathedral (1985–); and President, Council of St John's College, Durham (1984–). He was formerly Canon Residentiary of Durham Cathedral and Van Mildert Professor of Divinity (1974–85); and previously, at Cambridge, Assistant Lecturer in Divinity (1964–68), Lecturer (1968–74), Fellow and Dean, St John's College (1964–74). He was Edward Cadbury Lecturer, Birmingham University (1978); Hensley Henson Lecturer, Oxford University (1982–83); and Chairman, North of England Institute for Christian Education (1980–85). He is author or editor of a number of books on Anglicanism and on modern German Theology.

MICHAEL VASEY is Tutor, St John's College, with Cranmer Hall, Durham University (1975–), following a curacy at Tonbridge Parish Church (1971–75). He is a member of the Grove Group for Renewal of Worship (1976–); Grove Spirituality Group (1980–); Director of Grove Books (1985–); and on the Editorial Board of Alcuin/Grove Liturgical Monographs (1986–). He is a Church of England representative on the Joint Liturgical Group (1986–); attended the First International Anglican Liturgical Consultation at Boston, USA (1984) and the Second at Brixen, Italy (1987); and is a member of the Liturgical Commission (1986–). He has written a number of studies in the field of Liturgy.

J. RICHARD WATSON is Professor of English, Durham University (1978–) and a Methodist layman. He represents the Free Church Federal Council on the Archbishops' Commission on Church Music. Previously he taught in the Universities of Glasgow and Leicester. He has written or edited a number of books and has a particular interest in Romantic and Victorian poetry, with special reference to landscape and hymnology; he is currently engaged on a critical study of the English hymn.

I

Thomas Cranmer:
A Biographical Introduction
David M. Loades

> I would you should well understand that I account my
> Lord of Canterbury as faithful a man towards me as
> ever was prelate in this realm, and one to whom I am
> many ways beholding, by the faith which I owe unto
> God . . .[1]

This rare and apparently sincere tribute from King Henry
VIII at the time of the Council conspiracy against Cranmer
in the spring of 1543, provides the key to his remarkable and
controversial career. He was the King's man. As such he was
brought out of the academic obscurity of Cambridge and
promoted to high office. As such he survived every hostile
assault, and was perfectly placed to exercise the maximum
influence after Henry's death. And for the same reason he was
pursued to death by a vengeful Mary, intent upon obliterating
her father's achievements. At the time of his execution, on 21
March, 1556, he was four months short of his sixty-sixth birth-
day, an old man by the standards of the time, but in full vigour
of body and mind. Had Mary lived, or borne an heir to continue her work, he might have been no more remembered nor
respected than Miguel Servetus or Reginald Peacock.[2] But
Mary died in November 1558, and her successor Elizabeth
was very much her father's daughter. Within five years, John
Foxe had published *The Acts and Monuments of the English Martyrs* and Thomas Cranmer had become the founding father of
an enduring and immensely influential tradition.

He had been born at Aslockton in Nottinghamshire,
probably on 2 July, in the year 1489. His father, also
called Thomas, was a minor gentleman in terms of

wealth or local power, but the bearer of an ancient coat of arms.[3] Young Thomas was the second of three brothers, and seems to have been brought up with more aptitude for the rural pursuits appropriate to his status than for academic learning. Like many boys of his condition, he was taught his first letters by the parish priest, and afterwards seems to have attended a grammar school in the vicinity. This experience he later claimed to have blasted his youthful enthusiasm for letters, but it would be more accurate to say that it gave him a permanent distaste for traditional educational methods. In 1501 his father died, and two years later his mother, perhaps perceiving talents which were not obvious to others, entered him at Jesus College, Cambridge. This was not the orthodox course for a young gentleman, as it would have been a hundred years later, and suggests that he was already marked for an ecclesiastical career because of his position in the family. If that was the case, it was slow to develop. For eight years, according to an anonymous biography written shortly after his death, he was '... nosseled in the grossest kind of sophistry, logic, philosophy moral and natural, not in the text of the old philosophers, but chiefly in the dark riddles and quidities of Duns and other subtle questionists ...', which simply means that he followed the normal arts curriculum of the period – long since discredited by 1559.[4] When he took his BA in 1511 it was without any particular distinction – he was ranked thirty-second out of forty-two successful candidates – but having independent means was able to continue his studies. By this time humanist influence was gaining ground at Cambridge, and Cranmer began to familiarise himself with the works of Erasmus and Faber. By the time that he took his MA in July 1514 he was well read in the Latin 'new learning', and had begun to study Greek and Hebrew. At about the same time he became a Fellow of his college, and was moving somewhat belatedly towards ordination and a benefice.

Within two years, however, he had apparently jettisoned his entire career by marrying. Very little is known about this episode, beyond the fact that his wife's name was Joan, and that she died in childbirth less than twelve months later. Cranmer's enemies subsequently claimed that she was a barmaid at the Dolphin Inn, and that he had been compelled to marry her because she was pregnant by him.[5] These two charges are not really compatible, because if the 25-year-old Cranmer had really forced a local barmaid he would certainly not have married her (or been expected to) because of the difference in their social status. Joan was probably the daughter of a bourgeois or minor gentry family, and the immediate sequel makes it unlikely that there was any scandal attached to their union. Having lost his Fellowship (which could only be held by a celibate), and being past the age at which he could look to his family for further support, Cranmer was temporarily reduced to poverty. He was appointed to a Readership at Buckingham College, which probably provided him with little more than bed and board since Joan lived at the Dolphin, supported by her family. It was from this circumstance, and from his frequent visits there, that the stories later told against him derived. He was even reputed to have been an ostler, when the northern rebels were particularly incensed against 'low born councillors' in 1536. Her death a few months later may well have been a great blow to the young man, but it would be stretching the evidence to find any indications of that in the writings of his mature years. Quite exceptionally, he was then re-elected to his Fellowship at Jesus, a clear indication that he was held in very high regard there. By 1520 he had resumed his ecclesiastical career, having been ordained priest and licensed as one of the twelve preachers permitted to the University by a Papal Bull of 1503. In 1521 he was admitted to the degree of Bachelor of Divinity.[6]

However, no benefice was bestowed upon him, perhaps because he did not seek one, or endeavour to attract the attention of a patron. Instead he devoted his time to the careful and methodical study of the

Scriptures. He was a slow reader and a copious note-taker, but his reputation for learning began to spread. In 1525 Cardinal Wolsey offered him a foundation Fellowship at his new college in Oxford, but Cranmer declined the honour, preferring to remain at Jesus, where he shortly after became Reader in Divinity. Unlike his near-contemporary Hugh Latimer, there is no evidence that Cranmer held heretical or unorthodox views at this time, or that he had any connection with the so-called 'White Horse group' of crypto-Lutherans. His commitment to biblical scholarship, and his willingness to read banned Lutheran books place him clearly in the reforming camp, but it was the catholic reformation of Erasmus and John Colet which attracted him when he finally disputed for his Doctorate of Divinity in 1526. Even such a moderate position could be highly controversial. As an examiner in divinity, he would not allow candidates to proceed to their degrees if they were not sufficiently familiar with the Scriptures, and this aroused the fury of those conservatives whose staple academic diet consisted of scholastic commentaries; but he was fully supported by the University authorities, and was in no sense *avant garde*.[7] His attitude to the Papacy, soon to be a matter of such importance, is harder to determine. No recorded opinion or gesture before 1529 suggests that he had abandoned the orthodox position, but, like most Englishmen, the Roman jurisdiction probably sat lightly upon him. When he was given good cause to think seriously about the matter, he found that the Holy See did not engage his conscience, and that made him a useful man to the King. By 1529 Cranmer was forty – well advanced in middle age – and had enjoyed no career worth speaking of. In spite of his learning, and the respect with which he was clearly regarded within the University, he had written nothing and had held no administrative post more responsible than auditor of the proctorial accounts. The vast majority of graduates of his age and standing would either have become senior University officials, or would long since have moved out into lucrative preferments. That Cranmer had done neither of these things is a mystery. Later his admirers were to praise his extraordinary humility and zeal for study, but in fact he had done little to make his learning effective or available, and seems to have been simply unwilling to take any initiative upon his own behalf.

The event which finally shook this comfortable and obscure don out of his seclusion was the King's divorce. In the summer of 1529 there was plague in Cambridge and Cranmer had taken refuge with the family of two of his pupils at Waltham, when Henry decided to visit his nearby residence. As was customary when the court was at a small house, several of the courtiers and servants were billeted on neighbouring gentry, and Cranmer found that he had two fellow guests. Edward Fox and Stephen Gardiner were old Cambridge acquaintances, now rising rapidly in the King's service, and deeply pre-occupied with the 'great matter'. Exactly what passed between them is uncertain, but Cranmer seems to have taken the view that the issue was one of theology rather than canon law, and could only be resolved by scriptural authority.[8] Since Henry was already convinced that his case, based on lack of sons, rested upon a text of Leviticus, this line of argument may well have appealed to him, but what he really needed was a means whereby to elevate an Old Testament prohibition above all ecclesiastical authority, including that of the Pope.[9] Such a theory lay ready to hand, but its provenance was dangerous, and the Lutheran doctrine of *sola scriptura* would need to be carefully wrapped up before the King would be ready to make use of it. It seems that Cranmer was sent back to Cambridge with instructions to research such a possibility, and within a few months had become an enthusiastic advocate of the King's cause among his sceptical and sometimes hostile colleagues. Reports of his success in this context reached Henry some time during October, thanks no doubt to Gardiner and Fox, whose own careers stood to gain immensely from a breakthrough, and before the end of the month he was summoned to see the King at Greenwich. When he left the royal presence, it was with a commission to write a learned treatise justifying Henry's position, and orders to take up residence with the Earl of Wiltshire at Durham House while he did so.

This task he had completed by the end of December, and although the text does not survive, we know that the King was very pleased with it. At the end of January 1530 the Earl of Wiltshire was sent to represent Henry at the Imperial coronation in Bologna, and Cranmer went with him. The latter's mission, however, was to the Pope and to the Italian universities, not to the Emperor. Contrary to what is sometimes alleged, Cranmer did not introduce the idea of obtaining *censurae*, or judgements, from the universities, but he was obviously an ideal man for such a business.[10] He remained in Rome from April to September 1530, with the official status of Penitentiary. This title was conferred upon him by Clement at Henry's request in order to give him access to the Rota, and other means of discharging his mission, but it had no financial or political implications. Cranmer was unable to obtain the disputation of Henry's cause which was one of his objectives, but he did manage to persuade the Pope not to inhibit the judgments of the universities, and was instrumental in obtaining favourable responses from Padua and Bologna.[11] Meanwhile Wiltshire had been instructed to warn Charles V that the King had a new weapon in his armoury, a 'wonderful and grave wise man' who was convinced, and was convincing others, that his marriage to Catherine was invalid. Such notoriety was not, however, immediately translated into reward. No wealthy English benefice awaited Cranmer when he returned to England in October 1530. Instead he went back to Durham House, and to the service of the Boleyns, although whether as chaplain to the Earl or to his daughter, Anne Boleyn, is not clear. By the summer of 1531 he was at Hampton Court, having probably accompanied Anne when she took up residence there, and was clearly acting as one of the King's theological advisers. By January 1532, when he set out on his second foreign mission, Cranmer was a Royal Chaplain and Archdeacon of Taunton.

As a novice in diplomacy he had done well in Rome, dealing with an exceptionally subtle and slippery potentate, and his appointment as resident Ambassador with the Emperor was a recognition of that achievement. The date of his provision to Taunton is not known, but he is not alluded to by that title before 1532, and the status would have been an appropriate one for an ambassador, so it may well have been connected with the Imperial mission.[12] The nine months which Cranmer spent tracking the Emperor around his vast dominions were among the most momentous and adventurous of his life. For the first time he came into contact with secular politics at the highest level, and also with Lutherans on their own ground. In addition to his declared instructions, he had a number of secret objectives. One of these was to put pressure on the Emperor over his support for Catherine by manipulating the Turkish threat, and Charles's evident need for support, both within the Empire and from the rest of Christendom. Another was to persuade the Lutheran princes and theologians to change their minds. Luther himself had made no secret of his disgust at 'Junker Harry's' behaviour, and although his followers had their own quarrels with the Emperor, they had no intention of collaborating with the King of England.[13] In neither of these directions did Cranmer make any significant progress, in spite of numerous discussions with Granvelle, Charles's principal adviser, and a secret meeting with John Frederick of Saxony at Nuremberg. Instead, the Ambassador's own convictions seem to have taken a considerable battering. Like other Englishmen before him (and since), he had gone out with a very insular set of priorities, and although well prepared to refute the kind of canonical arguments with which he had been assailed in Rome, he lacked the maturity and sophistication to influence the politicians of Ratisbon and Nuremberg. Whether or not he actually confessed his unease to Granvelle, as the minister later alleged, he was certainly given an opportunity to see Henry through different eyes. It was the Lutherans, however, who moved him most. He had never before seen a reformed church order, nor a vernacular liturgy, nor married clergy. There is no evidence that Cranmer ever accepted the Confession of Augsburg,[14] and it was to be many years before he embraced the Reformed doctrine of Justification by Faith alone, but in other respects he was deeply affected.

In the first place, he already agreed with the priority accorded to Scripture in the Evangelical Church, but may never have considered the value of vernacular translations. He must have been aware of the popularity of Tyndale's English New Testament, printed in Antwerp in 1526, but having worked in an academic environment would have seen little of it at first hand, and would not, in England, have seen such Scripture put to public use in worship. More immediately important, however, was the fact that he married again. In the circumstances, this can only be described as a most extraordinary step to have taken. At the time of his first marriage he had been an obscure young academic in minor orders; but now he was a priest with a promising career in the King's service, and in the middle of a conspicuous mission. He can have known the young woman and her family for only a few weeks, and it is very unlikely that they spoke a word of each other's languages. Although the marriage was to endure for the rest of Cranmer's life, and as his widow she was to re-marry twice after his death, very little is known about his German bride. She was named Margaret, and was a kinswoman of the Lutheran divine Andreas Osiander, who probably performed the wedding ceremony.[15] There was never any suggestion of constraint upon either party, and Margaret was to be as faithful a companion over the ensuing twenty-four years as her husband's public position permitted, so a mere vulgar intrigue can be ruled out. So also can Cranmer's 'conversion' to Lutheranism. Presumably, like Thomas More, he recognised that he did not have the gift of chastity, and finding himself in a community which accepted the marriage of clergy as not only permissible, but even meritorious, he took advantage of the situation without too much thought for the problems which the future would bring. If he had been an unscrupulous man, it might have occurred to him that, whereas Margaret could be his wife in her own eyes, and in those of her family, she could be his mistress in England without seriously impeding the type of career upon which he had now embarked. Such deliberate cynicism would have been out of character, but Cranmer was not the man to make a demonstration of his convictions over clerical marriage, and his wife was to remain unacknowledged until the laws of England in that respect were changed in 1547. Within a few weeks they were temporarily parted, as Cranmer made a hazardous journey in pursuit of the Emperor, first to Linz, then to Vienna, and finally to Mantua. By the middle of November he had been informed that the King was recalling him, and Margaret seems to have gone straight from Nuremberg to England to await his arrival. Where she stayed and who cared for her during that interval is not known.

The death of the Archbishop of Canterbury, William Warham, in August 1532, and Anne Boleyn's increasing frustration, had forced Henry into an opportunist move. The King's advisers, particularly Fox, John Stokesley and Nicholas de Burgo, had been urging him for some time to challenge the Pope by seeking a solution to his problem in England.[16] To their voices had been added that of a rising new recruit, Thomas Cromwell. The obvious agent, however, was the Primate of All England, and Warham had been a prelate of the old school: loyal to the King, but totally opposed to any unprecedented or unorthodox course of action. The vacancy at Canterbury thus presented a chance which had to be seized. The new Primate must be a man wholly committed to Henry's cause, and preferably one whose conscience was genuinely engaged. Cranmer was not the only man who satisfied these conditions, and certainly not the most obvious, but he may have seemed the most suitable. Henry knew nothing of his recent behaviour in Germany, and never suspected the doubts which his Ambassador seems to have revealed. As far as he was concerned Cranmer was a loyal and able servant, who had been conspicuously successful in attracting academic support. Moreover he had the full confidence of the Boleyns,[17] whose star was pre-eminent in the court at that time. Cranmer himself was scarcely over-joyed to receive the news; '. . . there was never man came more unwillingly to a bishopric than I did to that', he later declared. This was not the conventional *nolo episcopari*, but a genuine expression of self doubt. He had no experience of high office, and no training for it; he had just married in defiance of the canon law; and his convictions had been unsettled by recent experience. He must also have known that Henry was not a man who could be lightly cheated of his expectations. No wonder Cranmer dawdled on the way home! Quite apart from the bitter winter weather, once he crossed the Channel the die would be cast, and he would be occupying what promised to be one of the hottest seats in the Western Church. He reached London on 10 January, and his appointment was announced almost at once.

After so many years of delay, matters were now moving at breakneck speed. Within a few days of Cranmer's return, Anne was discovered to be pregnant, and before 26 January Henry had secretly married her. The Archbishop-elect did not perform this ceremony, and did not know about it until later, but it put him firmly on the spot. As soon as he was consecrated he would have to annul the King's first marriage, so that the expected heir could at least present an appearance of legitimacy. Consecration, however, was no mere formality. Not only did it involve obtaining the appropriate Bulls from Rome, but also the swearing of an oath of allegiance to the Papacy which Cranmer knew perfectly well he would have to break at once. In spite of numerous warnings, and of his own personal knowl-edge of Cranmer's views on the divorce issue, Clement granted the Bulls immediately and without difficulty. He probably had a very shrewd idea of what was about to happen, and was not averse to precipitating a crisis so far away.[18] If Henry appeared to get what he wanted, he might stop badgering the Curia, and disrupting its delicate politics with his endless feud. It might be necessary to excommunicate him, and his new Archbishop, but that would be a short term problem, a move in the diplomatic game. The Pope had neither the knowledge nor the imagination to perceive that his action might result in a schism of indeterminate duration.[19] So Cranmer was duly consecrated, with all the traditional ceremonies, at Westminster on 30 March, 1533, having first read out a formal protestation that the oath which he was about to swear would not bind his conscience against the laws of God, nor against the laws and prerogatives of the realm of England. He was later (understandably) charged with hypocrisy over this protestation, or rather over the oath which followed it, but such moral evasions were frequently used when the oath was a political weapon. Unknown to the Marian clergy who so bitterly denounced the fallen Archbishop in 1555, their own King Philip had made an exactly similar protestation before swearing to uphold and respect the terms of his marriage treaty with Mary.[20] In 1533 Cranmer had no choice. The King would have insisted upon such a caveat, because he had no desire to find that he had another Thomas Becket on his hands.

With an Archbishop of irreproachable legitimacy and unprecedented docility, Henry could proceed to action. There was as yet no Royal Supremacy, so the Metropolitan Court, convened at Dunstable on 10 May, was theoretically independent, but the great care which he took over his own citation shows that the King had no intention of allowing Cranmer to forget that he was also a subject.[21] There was no serious pretence of impartiality, and Catherine duly obliged by ignoring the whole procedure. She was declared contumacious, and her marriage invalid. On 28 May, just three days before Anne's scheduled coronation, the Archbishop also gave judgment that, as the King had had no lawful wife since his accession, he had been perfectly free to marry at any time. Consequently his union with Anne Boleyn having been lawfully solemnised, it was a good

and valid marriage. In all this, Cranmer was obviously
an instrument of the King's will, but there is no evidence
that he did violence to his own conscience in the process.
His guiding principle was, and continued to be, that the
monarch's authority derived from God and was answerable only to heaven. He was, in a sense, the keeper of
the King's conscience, but it would never have occurred
to him to contradict any settled conviction which Henry
might develop. Such a conviction, however improbable
it might seem, had to be accepted as the will of God.
Consequently in 1533 Henry and Catherine had never
been married; and in 1536 Henry and Anne had never
been married either, in spite of his earlier pronounce-
ment. It is not surprising that Cranmer was represented
by his enemies, both at the time and since, as a mere time
server. However, the accusation was not justified. Like
Stephen Gardiner, with whom he disagreed on so many
points, Cranmer was Henry's man, and his conscience
was committed to the Royal Supremacy. It was only after
Henry's death that each of them was to demonstrate
that he possessed an alternative moral principle, when
Gardiner fell foul of the Protectorate government, and
Cranmer fell foul of Mary.

Paradoxically, it was Cranmer's honesty, not his malle-
ability, which retained Henry's confidence throughout
the vicissitudes of the later part of his reign.[22] In spite
of his secret marriage and his enthusiasm for Scripture,
he was not a Lutheran, and in the one theological area
which really mattered to the King, the doctrine of the
Mass, he was at this time entirely orthodox. Consequently he was able to disagree with Henry, and to
give him unpalatable advice, in a manner which even
Thomas Cromwell envied. It was he, for example, who
had to break the shattering news of Catherine Howard's
misconduct in 1542, a blow from which it took the King
many months to recover. At the same time he did not
have, and did not aspire to, political power. His horrified
but compliant reaction to the fall of his former patrons,
the Boleyns, was a reflection of his impotence rather
than the flexibility of his conscience. Unlike Wolsey

he cannot be reproached with having surrendered his moral autonomy, because he never believed that he possessed any. His first crisis as Archbishop came in 1539 when Henry, alarmed by evidence of radical preaching in the London area, applied sharp brakes to the process of religious change. Cranmer's anonymous biographer linked this to his disagreement with the King over the dissolution of the monasteries.

> . . . the king taking displeasure with the said archbishop and other bishops (as they term them) of the new learning, because they would not give their consent in the parliament that the king should have all the monasteries suppressed to his own use, but would have had parts of them to have been bestowed upon hospitals, bringing up of youth in virtue and good learning, and other things profitable for the commonwealth . . . in the next parliament made six new articles . . .[23]

Modern research does not support this simple view, and it was probably Cromwell rather than Cranmer who was principally under attack, but the Act of Six Articles represented a serious setback.[24] His support for the English Bible, simplification of the calendar, and the destruction of pilgrimage shrines had placed the Archbishop firmly on the reforming side of the Henrician church. But in 1539 Stephen Gardiner and his allies demonstrated that there could be a much more conservative interpretation of the Royal Supremacy, which was equally acceptable to the King. Cromwell's fall and execution in 1540 represented the peak of conservative success, and left Cranmer as the next obvious target. The northern rebels in 1536 had branded him as a base-born heretic, and had demanded his death. After 1540 the conservative faction in the King's Council took up the chase, and several attempts were made to persuade Henry that the Archbishop's doctrine was unsound.

The King, however, refused to be moved. By the summer of 1541 he was encouraging Cranmer to appoint reforming preachers at Canterbury, and took a certain perverse relish in defusing the Prebendaries Plot which resulted two years later. It is now known that this was not merely a clerical conspiracy, but involved a powerful faction of the Kentish gentry, who were opposed to the Archbishop for a variety of reasons.[25] When their complaints reached the King, probably through Gardiner's mediation, Henry sent for Cranmer and, according to Ralph Morris, greeted him with the words: 'Aha, my chaplain, now I know who is the greatest heretic in Kent!' Whether or not he adopted such a light-hearted attitude, he committed the whole matter to Cranmer himself to investigate. This not only sent the conspirators running for cover, it left the Archbishop in no doubt about the strength of the feelings which he was arousing. Undeterred by this fiasco, within a month Gardiner and his allies tried again, this time using a direct approach to the King as they had against Cromwell. Henry appeared to be persuaded, but in effect humiliated his conservative councillors in the same way as the Canterbury plotters. Sending for Cranmer, as he had before, he warned him of what was afoot, and gave him his ring as a private token. When an attempt was made to arrest the Archbishop at the Council board the next day, he showed the token and exposed his enemies to a tongue-lashing from their irate master, from which the passage quoted at the head of this essay is an extract. The episode shows Henry in a curious light, but if his objective was to demonstrate to both sides their total dependence upon his own will, then he certainly succeeded. The King's personal religion may have been moving in an evangelical direction towards the end of his life. His will, with its massive provision for memorial Masses, suggests not; but the provision for Prince Edward's education, and the increasing dominance of the reforming faction in the Council after 1543 point in the opposite direction.[26] For reasons which are not entirely clear both Stephen Gardiner and his conservative allies, the Howards, completely lost Henry's confidence during the last few months of his life. The chief beneficiaries of this development were the Earl of Hertford and his political allies, but it was the faithful Cranmer who eased Henry's passage to eternity in January 1547, and was entrusted with the spiritual guidance of his son and heir.

Henry's death – the removal of his unique patron and protector – could have spelled disaster for Cranmer. Instead, he found his position strengthened and his authority enhanced because his interpretation of the Royal Supremacy was as convenient to Edward's minority government as it had been gratifying to the old King. Within a few weeks he petitioned for a new commission to exercise his archiepiscopal office, thus demonstrating that he considered it to be entirely dependent upon the Crown.[27] Gardiner was horrified. Although he owed his appointment to the King, and accepted the validity of the Royal Supremacy during a minority, in his eyes episcopal authority itself derived from consecration, and not simply from appointment.[28] A bishop did not cease to be a bishop because the King died. To Cranmer, however, the Church was a department of state for ecclesiastical affairs, and the proper institution to regulate its operation was the Parliament. He formed a close and sympathetic relationship with the Earl of Hertford, who became Duke of Somerset and Lord Protector in February 1547, and together they prepared a far-reaching programme of further reform. This commenced in the summer of the same year with a series of homilies, three of which were from Cranmer's own pen and dealt with the central and sensitive issue of Justification. From these writings it is clear that his position had changed slightly but significantly from that set out in the King's Book of 1543, which he had also had a hand in preparing. The latter had been strictly orthodox in insisting that both faith and good works were necessary to salvation, but by 1547 Cranmer was prepared to concede the primacy of faith, insisting at the same time that it could only be manifest in godly living.[29] This was still some way from the Protestant *sola fide,* but it was close enough to outrage religious conservatives and provoke a furious debate. By November the direction of

official policy was clear, and the Parliament which met in
that month repealed the Act of Six Articles and legalised
the marriage of clergy. For the first time in fifteen years
Margaret Cranmer had a lawful status, although it is not
apparent that she took much advantage of the fact. At
the end of 1547 the English Church was still orthodox
in doctrine, but its practices were becoming increasingly
deviant, and those who feared an imminent lapse into
heresy had ample justification for their opinion.

During the two years which followed Henry VIII's
death, Thomas Cranmer became a Protestant. Before
that he had been a schismatic Catholic of the new learning, or perhaps more accurately a true Henrician. No
married priest who rejected the Papal authority could
be described as orthodox, but he was not a heretic by
the criteria which the King applied, and that was all
that mattered. However, once his conscience was no
longer constrained by that of his idiosyncratic master
he began to develop his own distinctive theological
position. According to his own testimony he was converted from his earlier views on transubstantiation by
Nicholas Ridley in the course of 1548, and had already
moved to introduce communion under both kinds in
the Convocation of 1547. By 1548 also he had become
fully convinced that Justification was by faith alone,
and that the only true sacraments were Baptism and
the Eucharist. He had arrived at these views partly
by discussion, and partly by his own reading of Scripture, the Latin and Greek Fathers, and contemporary
continental theologians.[30] Consequently, it is a mistake
to attach European labels to him, as his enemies did
at the time. The Royal Supremacy remained central
to his thinking, and although he was instrumental in
inviting such foreign divines as Martin Bucer, Peter
Martyr and John ab Ulmis to England, the religious
settlement which he worked out with Edward's successive
Regents between 1548 and 1553 was *sui generis*. The Act
of Uniformity which Cranmer and Somerset between
them piloted through Parliament in January 1549 was
as revolutionary a measure as the Act in Restraint of

Appeals which had inaugurated the Royal Supremacy in 1533. In spite of retaining many conservative forms, the English Church became Protestant in doctrine and liturgy. Inevitably such dramatic change provoked resistance. There were risings in the Midlands and South West against the new Prayer Book, and in October Protector Somerset was overthrown, ostensibly by the religious conservatives. However, once established in power the leader of the coup, John Dudley, Earl of Warwick, decided for reasons which are not entirely clear, to jettison his conservative allies and throw in his lot with the Reformers.[31] Instead of being reversed, the Protestant policy was pushed ahead more energetically than before. Nevertheless, Cranmer's relations with Warwick (Duke of Northumberland from 1551) soon became extremely strained.

This was not on account of doctrinal disagreements, because the Archbishop was the main author and inspirer of the revised Prayer Book of 1552, and of the Forty Two Articles of 1553. The disagreement was political, and centred upon Northumberland's predatory attitude towards ecclesiastical property. Just as the Reformers of the day (including Cranmer) had reproached Henry VIII for not putting more of the monastic plunder to good use, so the Protestant bishops of 1551–2 criticised the Duke for his disposal of the confiscated goods of the chantries, and for his attempts to 'unlord' the bishops themselves by removing the endowments of their sees.[32] By 1553 Cranmer had become the victim of his own principles. Having committed his conscience to the Royal Supremacy, he was left with no ground upon which to resist the encroachment of a lawful authority intent upon reducing the Church to complete subservience. Whether Northumberland was actually as hostile to 'Godly' priorities as he was reputed to be may be doubted in the light of recent research, but leading Reformers such as Hooper and Knox denounced him as a 'carnal gospeller', and he effectively blocked Cranmer's attempt to give the English Church a reformed canon law.[33]

This estrangement deprived Northumberland of crucial Protestant support when the death of Edward VI in
July 1553 provoked a succession crisis. In the last weeks
of the King's life the Duke had conceived a scheme
to protect the Reformation, and his own position, by
advancing to the throne his young daughter-in-law Jane
Grey, in preference to the recognised heir, Edward's
conservative sister Mary.[34] Cranmer lent himself to this
scheme, along with other councillors, with many misgiv-
ings and because the dying King obviously desired it.
In doing so, he miscalculated disastrously. Mary tri-
umphed after an almost bloodless campaign lasting less
than two weeks, and immediately set about dismantling
her brother's religious establishment. The Archbishop
was impaled on the horns of a dilemma. Mary was
the Queen, and it was her will that the Mass should
be restored. On the other hand, Cranmer's conscience
had moved a long way since 1547, and by 1553 he
was as committed to Protestant doctrine and liturgy
as he was to the Royal Supremacy. Whichever way he
moved, he had to betray a principle. Towards the end of
August he prepared a declaration against the Mass, and
on 13 September the Council summoned him to explain
himself.[35] His reputation for compliance with royal commands may have caused them to hope for a dramatic
volte-face which could have been used to undermine the
whole Protestant position. If so, they were disappointed,
and the following day he was committed to the Tower.
From Mary's point of view, Cranmer was both a crimi-
nal and an enemy; a traitor for having supported the
pretensions of Jane Grey; a heretic for his theological
and liturgical writings; and the man who, more than
any other, was responsible for the humiliation of her
mother and herself. Treason was the easiest and most
obvious charge to bring home, and on 13 November
he was arraigned at the Guildhall, along with Jane,
her husband Guildford Dudley, and the latter's two
brothers Henry and Ambrose. The trial was a formality, but Cranmer's attempt to plead that it could not be
treason to obey the King's express command has some

significance.[36] He was probably right in claiming that his conscience would not have allowed him any other course, because in his eyes the King was above both statute and customary law. It would have been a confused argument if followed through, because Jane would have made a very poor candidate by Divine Right, but it was the constitution which Cranmer had offended rather than the Crown. At the same time the Parliament was invalidating the sentence of nullity which he had pronounced upon the marriage of Henry and Catherine in 1533. 'Thomas Cranmer, then newly made Archbishop of Canterbury, most ungodly and against all laws, equity and conscience prosecuting the said wicked device of divorce . . .' was now to be held primarily responsible for the actions of a master who could not be directly cited nor condemned.[37]

Over the next two years, while his work was systematically undone, Cranmer remained in prison. Mary regarded heresy as a more serious offence than treason, and intended to expose him to the jurisdiction which he had first and most deeply offended, that of the Pope. In April 1554 he was taken with Ridley and Latimer to Oxford in order that his academic and intellectual credentials should be discredited in disputation with the doctors of the University. It was not a trial, but neither was it the humiliation which was intended. Cranmer knew his regiment, but he was vulnerable on the question of authority, and had deferred to the vagaries of the royal will too often. This point was to be driven home with particular force when he was eventually tried by the Papal Commissary James Brooks in September 1555.[38] Mary had declined to use her own jurisdiction for heresy proceedings, but even the formal return of the realm to the Roman obedience in January 1555, which had launched the trials of lesser offenders, had been inadequate to touch a duly consecrated Archbishop. As *Legatus natus*, Cranmer was technically the equal of the Cardinal Legate, Reginald Pole, and therefore could not be tried by him. Consequently it was not until September that the slow moving judicature of the

Curia at last reached out to the city gaol in Oxford, and
Cranmer was brought to his answer. Again, the objective
was not merely to condemn, but to discredit. Even if he
recanted, there was no doubt that he was a Protestant,
but if he could also be made to appear an opportunist
and a hypocrite the cause which he represented might
be severely damaged. Cranmer's problem was that the
King and Queen had turned the only temporal authority
he acknowledged against religious truth as he now saw
it. In other words, they had set the Scripture against
itself. 'By the scripture the king is chief, and no foreign
person in his own realm above him. There is no subject
but to a king . . .' But the King was now saying 'celebrate
Mass, and obey the Pope'.[39] When faced with this stark
alternative, Cranmer at last abandoned his original principle, and declared that his conscience would not allow
him to return to idolatry, no matter what the King and
Queen might say. Brooks derived what satisfaction he
could from pointing out that he was now subjecting the
royal authority to his private conscience, but it was not
quite the public triumph he was looking for.

By Christmas the Archbishop's condemnation had
been confirmed in Rome, and preparations were put
in hand for his degradation and execution. At the same
time, doubts began to assail him, and were assiduously
encouraged by a group of Oxford friars who were
still hoping to bring off a spectacular recantation.[40] It
has sometimes been claimed that Cranmer's wavering
in the last few weeks of his life were the result of
fear, and reveal a lack of theological commitment. However, in view of his past history it is more likely that
the old conflict of priority was responsible. Could he
really be sure that God had not spoken once again
through his anointed? Under the pressure of his own
conscience rather than of imminent death, he recanted;
not once but five times with increasing explicitness and
self abasement. The friars were jubilant, but Mary and
Pole were alarmed and disconcerted. In normal circumstances such a penitent would have been reprieved,
but they had no intention of allowing the man whom

they both held to be primarily responsible for the woes
of England (and of themselves in particular) over the
last twenty years to escape with his life. Nor did Mary
wish to resort to the treason sentence of two years
before. The Council suppressed the published version
of his recantations, and the date for his burning was
fixed as 21 March.[41] Foxe was probably right when he
later claimed that the Queen was determined to burn
Cranmer whether he recanted or not, and he continued
in an agony of indecision right up to the last moment. He
had already seen his friends Nicholas Ridley and Hugh
Latimer perish in the flames, and had no illusions about
the physical reality of such a death; but he also knew, as
the day approached, that there was no way of avoiding
it. He prepared an orthodox statement of penitence and
submission to read at the stake, but when the moment
came, he jettisoned it and reaffirmed his Protestant
convictions. The Royal Supremacy, after all, was not
an end in itself but means to an end. The purpose
of temporal authority was to order a commonwealth in
accordance with the will of God, and that will had to be
truly identified. Three days later the Venetian ambassador, Giovanni Michieli, reported to his government

> On Saturday last, the 21, Cranmer, late Archbishop
> of Canterbury was burned, having fully verified the
> opinion formed of him by the Queen, that he had
> feigned recantation thinking to save his life, and not
> that he had received any good inspiration, so she
> considered him unworthy of pardon . . .'[42]

Thomas Cranmer was not made of the stuff of martyrs,
and he did not know that within five years he would be a
hero of the ascendency. On that damp and fatal morning
in Oxford he was answerable not to Mary, nor to Henry
VIII, but to his God.

Notes

Place of publication London, unless otherwise stated.
1. J.G. Nichols, *Narratives of the Days of the Reformation* (Camden
   Society, 1859), p. 258.

2. Servetus was a Spanish Unitarian, burned at the instigation of John Calvin in Geneva in 1555. Reginald Peacock, Bishop of Chichester, was tried and convicted of Lollard heresy in 1457. He recanted, and was imprisoned at Thorney Abbey until his death, probably in 1460.

3. He claimed descent from one of the companions of William the Conqueror, and his arms of the three cranes were also borne by a French family of the same name (Nichols, *Narratives*, p. 218). His mother was called Agnes, 'daughter of Laurence Hatfield of Willoughby, of like degree . . .'

4. Nichols, p. 219.

5. Jasper Ridley, *Thomas Cranmer* (1962), pp. 16–17; 'Processus contra Thomam Cranmer' in *The Works of Thomas Cranmer*, J.E. Cox (Parker Society, 1844–6), ii, pp. 545–57.

6. Cambridge University, Grace Book B (ii), p. 77; T. Fuller, *The University of Cambridge* (1840), p. 203; Ridley, *Cranmer*, p. 20.

7. J. Foxe, *Acts and Monuments of the English Martyrs*, ed. S.R. Cattley (1837–41), VIII, p. 5; G.W. Bromiley, *Thomas Cranmer, Theologian* (1956), pp. 12–27.

8. Ridley, pp. 26–7. Cranmer entertained a lifelong hostility to the canon law.

9. 'If a man takes his brother's wife, it is impurity; he has uncovered his brother's nakedness, they shall be childless' (Leviticus 20.21). Ralph Wakefield, the humanist scholar, also seems to have persuaded the King that, in the original Hebrew, the text read '. . . they shall be without sons'. *The Divorce Tracts of Henry VIII*, E. Surtz and V. Murphy (Angers, Moreanna, 1988), p. xiii.

10. Wolsey had begun to canvass opinion as early as 1527. *Divorce Tracts*, pp. ii–iii.

11. Richard Croke, Henry's agent in Bologna, seems to have antagonised the authorities, and to have been rescued by Cranmer from an embarrassing situation. Croke to Henry VIII, 17 September, 1530; *Letters and Papers of the Reign of Henry VIII*, ed. J. Gairdner et al.(1862–1910), IV, p. 6624.

12. Nichols, p. 238.

13. For Luther's views on the divorce issue, see *Letters and Papers*, X, p. 133; Ridley, p. 44–6.

14. P. Brooks, *Thomas Cranmer's doctrine of the Eucharist* (1965); C.W. Dugmore, *The Mass and the English Reformers;* Bromiley, *passim.*

15. Nichols, p. 243; Foxe, VIII, p. 34, p. 43; Cranmer, *Works*, ii, p. 550, p. 557.

16. *Divorce Tracts*, pp. xiii–xxiii.

17. Foxe, VIII, pp. 8–9; E.W. Ives, *Anne Boleyn* (Oxford, 1987), p. 303; J.J. Scarisbrick, *Henry VIII* (1968), p. 310.

18. Wolsey had repeatedly warned Campeggio that if Henry did not get his own way, he would take the law into his own hands, but Clement had treated such threats with scepticism.

19. For the Papal view of the English situation, see Carlo Capello to the Venetian Signory, 29 January, 1533; *Calendar of State Papers, Venetian*, IV, p. 847; also *Letters and Papers*, VI, p. 177.

20. *Calendar of State Papers, Spanish*, ed. Royall Tyler, et al. (1862–1954), XII, p. 4; D. Loades, *The Oxford Martyrs* (1970), p. 199.

21. Cranmer, *Works*, ii, pp. 237–9. The King amended Cranmer's draft in his own hand, increasing its humility of tone.

22. And also his usefulness. Ralph Morris, Cranmer's secretary, later wrote 'For at all times when the King's majesty would be resolved of any doubt or question he would but send to my lord overnight, and by the next day the King would have in writing brief notes of the doctors' minds, as well divines as lawyers, both ancient, old and new, with a conclusion of his own mind, which he could never get in such a readiness of none other . . .' Nichols, p. 249.

23. Nichols, p. 224.

24. Like other Reformers, Cranmer was certainly unhappy about the disposal of monastic property, but the main reason for the Act of Six Articles was probably the King's reaction to the Ten Articles of 1536, which represented the most 'advanced' position reached by the Henrician Church. Cranmer supported these articles, but they were probably drafted by Edward Fox. Ridley, p. 113; G.R. Elton, *Reform and Renewal* (Cambridge, 1973).

25. M. Zell, 'The Prebendaries plot of 1543: a reconsideration', *Journal of Ecclesiastical History*, XXVII, p. 241.

26. *Letters and Papers*, XXI, ii, p. 634; BL Stowe MS 576, f.10; J.G. Nichols, *Literary Remains of King Edward VI* (Roxburgh Club, 1857) I, xxix; D. Loades, *Tudor Court* (1986), p. 121.

27. Loades, *Oxford Martyrs*, pp. 60–5; Cranmer's view of the Supremacy was well summed up in his address at Edward's coronation. '. . . I openly declare before the living God and before the nobles of this land, that I have no commission to denounce your majesty deprived, if your highness miss in part, or in whole, of these performances [Godly government], much less to draw up indentures between God and your majesty, or to say that you forfeit your crown with a clause . . .' (*Works*, ii, p. 146). Obedience, he declared on another occasion, was due for conscience sake, because the King's laws were God's laws.

28. Gardiner to William Paget, 1 March, 1547; J.A. Muller, *The Letters of Stephen Gardiner* (Cambridge, 1933), p. 268; *Oxford Martyrs*, pp. 51–5.

29. *Certayne Sermons or Homelies* (31 July 1547); Ridley, p. 266; R.B. Bond, 'Cranmer and the controversy surrounding the publication of "Certayne Sermons or Homelies" (1547)', *Renaissance and Reformation*, XII, pp. 28–35.

30. Bromiley, *Thomas Cranmer, Theologian*; Brooks, *Thomas Cranmer's doctrine of the Eucharist*; K.J. Walsh, 'Cranmer and the Fathers, especially in the *Defence*', *Journal of Religious History*, XI, pp. 227–47.

31. W.K. Jordan, *Edward VI; the young king* (1968), pp. 28–36.

32. Hugh Latimer was most vocal in his denunciations of this
    behaviour '. . . thy princes are wicked [he quoted in 1549]
    and companions of thieves, they love rewards altogether . . .'
    (*Sermons and Remains of Bishop Latimer*, ed. G.E. Gorrie (Parker
    Society, 1845), p. 41.

33. W.K. Jordan, *Edward VI; the threshold of power* (1970), pp. 359–60;
    J. Strype, *Memorials of Thomas Cranmer* (1840), pp. 189–91; Ridley,
    pp. 330–4; D. Loades, 'The last years of Cuthbert Tunstall,
    1547–1559', *Durham University Journal*, LX, pp. 10–22.

34. Jane was the daughter of Henry Grey, Duke of Suffolk, and
    Frances, the daughter of Charles Brandon, Duke of Suffolk.
    Frances's mother, Mary, was Henry VIII's younger sister. Jor-
    dan, *Threshold of Power*, pp. 510–20.

35. Cranmer, *Works*, i, pp. 428–9; *Acts of the Privy Council*, IV, p. 346,
    p. 347; Foxe, VI, p. 394; VIII, p. 38; Peter Martyr to Heinrich
    Bullinger, 3 November 1553, *Original Letters relative to the English
    Reformation*, ed. H. Robinson (Parker Society, 1846–7), pp. 505–6.

36. PRO Baga de Secretis, KB8/23; *Fourth Report of the Deputy
    Keeper of the Public Records*, App. ii, pp. 237–8; *Oxford Martyrs*,
    pp. 119–20.

37. Statute 1 Mary, st.2 c.1; *Statutes of the Realm*, IV, i, pp. 200–1.

38. *Oxford Martyrs*, pp. 130–7; Foxe, VI, pp. 441 ff., VIII, pp. 45 ff.;
    Story and Martin also took part in the trial, and it was Story who
    put the point most clearly '. . . the same laws, being put away by
    a parliament, and now received again by a parliament, and have
    as full authority now as they had then; and they will now that ye
    answer to the Pope's holiness; therefore by the laws of this realm
    ye are bound to answer him . . .'

39. *Oxford Martyrs*, pp. 196–8.

40. *Bishop Cranmer's Recantacyons*, ed. J. Gairdner (Miscellanies of the
    Philobiblion Society) XV, pp. 51–65; Ridley, pp. 394–9; *Oxford
    Martyrs*, pp. 222–30.

41. *Acts of the Privy Council*, V, pp. 247–9; it was at this point that
    Cranmer allegedly had a dream in which he saw Christ contend-
    ing for his soul with Henry VIII. *Recantacyons*, pp. 79–82.

42. Foxe, VIII, p. 88; BL Cotton MS Titus A xxiv, f.87; *Calendar of
    State Papers, Venetian*, ed. Rawdon Brown et al. (1864–98), VI,
    p. 434.

II

After Cranmer
John R.H. Moorman

The 1662 Prayer Book is not used anywhere today. Who, for example, says the Ten Commandments at every celebration of the Eucharist? Or who says the Athanasian Creed thirteen times a year? It was said in my youth, when my mother always sat down for it as she did not believe in the condemnatory clauses. Bishop Hamilton of Salisbury said repeatedly that he would resign his bishopric if this Creed was in any way touched. Or again, who says the Commination Service on every Ash Wednesday, or even knows where to find it in the Prayer Book? Or, above all things, who informs the Vicar that he intends to come to Holy Communion on the following day?

Times change. After 325 years, a form of worship is bound to change to some extent. There have been attempts to bring out a new Prayer Book, first in 1928 when the proposed book was thrown out by the House of Commons, and again in 1980 when the *Alternative Service Book* was published. This is now very popular as it uses different language to make it more acceptable and more understandable. Fundamentally, however, Anglican worship is the work of Thomas Cranmer. Ought we to lose this?

Cranmer published the first English Prayer Book in 1549; but there had been one or two attempts to introduce English previous to this. In 1538 the English Bible was set up in the churches, although it was not used in the Mass until 1543. In 1544 an English Litany was introduced, followed in 1548 by an English Order of Communion. Although the Mass was said in Latin, the priest, after making his communion, said a penitential section in English, which was followed by the communion of the people. This was to be given to them in both kinds, as our Lord had said. *'Except ye eat the flesh of the Son of Man and drink his blood ye have no life in you.'* (Incidentally, this makes me feel that the Roman Mass, with communion in one kind only, is possibly invalid.)

Then in 1549, a fully English Prayer Book was ordered to be used. This was a noble piece of work, but not meant to be permanent. It was only a compromise, a step in the right direction. Bishop Gardiner approved of it, and said 'It is not far from the Catholic faith in regard to sacrifice and transubstantiation'; but Bishop Hooper called it 'defective and manifestly impious'. It was followed in 1552 by a much more Protestant book. For example the words of communion were changed from 'The Body of our Lord Jesus Christ', and 'The Blood of our Lord Jesus Christ', to simply 'Take and eat this', and 'Drink this', without telling the communicants what was being given to them. However, our book of 1662 is fundamentally that of 1552, not that of 1549.

The book of 1552 did not last long. In 1553 Edward VI died and Mary came to the throne. She, half Spanish, was a devout Roman Catholic who abolished all that her father, Henry VIII, had done and restored the medieval forms of service. When she died in 1558 she was succeeded by her sister, Queen Elizabeth, who brought back the Prayer Book of 1552, though with some changes. Vestments were reintroduced, the words of communion were given in both forms, and the obnoxious words in the Litany about 'the Bishop of Rome and all his detestable enormities' were omitted.

The Elizabethan Prayer Book was never fully accepted. During her reign, there was always a relentless conflict between Puritans and Churchmen with the Prayer Book as the battleground. The Puritans submitted to Convocation six articles: the abolition of all festivals except Sundays, apart from feasts of our Lord; the use of organs; the cross in Baptism; compulsory kneeling at the Communion; the Eastward position of the celebrant; and all vestments except the surplice. These six articles were rejected by only one vote at Convocation, which shows how strong the Puritans were.

They even, in 1584, published a *Booke of the Forme of Common Prayers*, which had been approved by Calvin.

Elizabeth died in 1603 and was succeeded by James VI of Scotland, a son of Mary, Queen of Scots, who became James I of England. Various attempts were made to get him to change the Prayer Book by getting rid of the surplice; by abolishing Confirmation; by changing the word 'priest' to 'minister'; omitting the sign of the cross in Baptism and removing the use of the ring in marriage. James rejected all these proposals and services continued to be conducted as laid down in the rubrics in the *Book of Common Prayer*.

In 1644 the Puritans won the day. They abolished the Prayer Book completely and brought out the *Directory*, a manual of directions on conducting services but containing no prayers, not even the Lord's Prayer. When Charles II was restored to the throne in 1660, a number of divines met at the Savoy Conference to consider forms of worship. The result was the *Book of Common Prayer* of 1662 which continues to be the authorised service book of the Church of England to the present day.

The Puritans were still active. In 1689 they proposed that alterations should be made: the word 'priest' was to be replaced by 'minister', 'Sunday' was to be called 'the Lord's Day', and the wearing of the surplice discontinued. Two good things were proposed. One was that the Beatitudes should be said instead of the Ten Commandments, the other that the words 'Because there is none other that fighteth for us, but only thou, O God' should be changed to: 'That we may serve thee without fear all the days of our life'. All these proposals were rejected by Convocation.

All through the eighteenth century there was agitation in favour of a fresh revision, but it had no effect. Gradually Morning and Evening Prayer, the two services most used on Sundays, were changed considerably by the addition of hymns and a sermon. Before this there were no hymns. People simply sang metrical versions of the Psalms. Sermons, which are mentioned only in the Communion Service, became very popular and were

used on every occasion. At this period they were at least
an hour in length.

The Tractarians were not as interested in worship as
in the doctrine of the Church. The post-Tractarians
brought in a number of changes. In 1889 the Bishop of
Lincoln (Edward King) was tried by the Archbishop of
Canterbury on six charges: mixing water with the wine
in Communion; using the Eastward position at the altar;
lighting candles on the altar; singing the *Agnus Dei*; taking the ablutions in public; and using the sign of the cross
in the Absolution and the Blessing. All these things are
common today. Indeed they were so common then that
in 1904 Parliament declared that 'the law of public worship in the Church of England is too narrow for the life
of the present generation'. Reform of the Prayer Book
was put in hand, and in 1927–8 a new Prayer Book was
introduced. It was thrown out by Parliament, but parts
of it were used by the clergy everywhere.

In the post-war years a number of experiments were
conducted, followed by issues, in booklet form, of separate alternative forms of Morning and Evening Prayer
and of Holy Communion. After long deliberation, a
Liturgical Commission produced the *Alternative Service Book*, published in 1980. Besides rites which use
the traditional language of worship (the 'thee and thou'
forms) the book contained a number of new services in
which every 'thou' and 'thine' was transformed into 'you'
and 'yours'. The *Venite* begins 'O come let us sing out to
the Lord: let us shout in triumph to the rock of our
salvation', using such words as 'sing out' and 'shout in
triumph' which are scarcely appropriate. The *Te Deum*
begins: 'You are God'. Prayers end with the words 'who
is alive and reigns' when 'who lives and reigns' would be
much better.

We may well ask if there is a special language of worship. After all, there is a language of the law-courts. Is
it something which we can learn? Is the language of
the *Alternative Service Book* the language which people
speak today? See, for example, on p.51 mention of 'the
old leaven of corruption', or on p.55, 'Father of majesty

unbounded', or on p.137 'we celebrate the memorial
of our redemption'. These are not expressions which
young people use today. They must learn the language
of worship. Why not learn 'thou' instead of 'you'?

I doubt whether the *Alternative Service Book* will last
very long. Shall we have a much more modern book? Or
shall we perhaps return to 1662?

III

Liturgical Language and Devotion
Gerald Bonner

Among the many possible definitions of the goal of the Christian life, I will propose one which, I trust, is not likely to arouse serious opposition: the eternal adoration of God by individual souls united in a fellowship of mutual love. I would emphasise both the individuality and the collectivity of this action. The identity of the individual soul is preserved. It is not swallowed up in the mass, but enjoys a relationship with God, through Christ, peculiar to itself. Nevertheless, individuation does not mean isolation. Individual souls are members of one Body, of which Christ is the Head, and while in this world there may be solitude, there can be no question of the servant of Christ being solitary, in this age or in the next. 'When I look at myself in particular,' said Dame Julian, 'I am obviously of no account. But by and large I am hopeful, for I am united in love with all my fellow Christians.'[1]

This conception of individuality being realised, and not annihilated, in community, is central to any discussion of the liturgical life of the Church Militant. From apostolic times to the present day it has been accepted that Christians will meet to worship as a group, but that this group-worship does not, and should not, constitute the sole prayer-life of the individual Christian. At an early date in the history of Christian devotion there developed the ideal of prayer without ceasing, an orientation of the mind and will which remains fixed, even when the Christian is engaged upon secular business or even asleep. One finds it in the spiritual teaching of the monks of the Egyptian desert in the fourth and fifth centuries. John Cassian, in the fifth century, speaks

of it in his *Conferences* and provides a formula: 'O God
make speed to save me: O Lord make haste to help me,'
to provide an increasing recollection of God in the mind
of the worshipper.[2] In the Christian East this form of
recollection developed into the famous devotion of the
Jesus Prayer: the continued recitation of the words 'Lord
Jesus Christ, Son of God, have mercy upon me, a sinner,'
a devotion which provides the theme for the nineteenth-
century Russian spiritual classic, *The Way of the Pilgrim*;[3]
and it is interesting in this context to remember that in
the Christian East the public worship of the church has
an enormous popular appeal and is conducted with a magnif-
icence and an elaboration which is rarely to be
found in the West.

Now it is apparent that, given individual variation of
taste and temperament, private devotion must vary from
person to person. Some worshippers will generally prefer to follow a set form of words, perhaps employing the
official service-books of their church. Others will adopt a
freer and more spontaneous language in talking to God,
which may amount to familiarity. There is a charming
story told by Martin Buber in his *Tales of the Hasidim*
about Rabbi Israel of Koznitz.

He liked to hum to himself proverbs and sayings current among the Polish peasants. After a Purim feast,
which he had presided over in great happiness, he
said: 'How right, what the people say:

> Doff your coat, dear soul, and prance
> Merrily at feast and dance

– but how curious a coat is the body!' Sometimes he
even spoke to God in Polish. When he was alone, they
would hear him say: '*Moj kochanku*,' which means: 'My
darling.'[4]

One can find parallels for this in Christian devotion.
Indeed, one would expect it of Christians, who have
received the spirit of adoption, whereby we cry, Abba,
Father (Romans 8.15), for the Aramaic word *'abbā*, originally used by small children, was not employed as a form of

address to God in ancient Judaism, and its use by Jesus expressed his consciousness of a unique relationship with God, a relationship now shared by his followers by grace of adoption.[5]

We cannot, then, lay down rules for individual devotion; the language which a Christian employs in private prayer is a matter which concerns him or her and God, and no one else. Furthermore, and beyond this, many of the masters of Christian spirituality have taught that the height of prayer is reached, not in words but in silence.

Sometimes [says John Cassian] the mind which is advancing to the true state of purity and has begun to be rooted in it, can conceive all these kinds of prayer [i.e. the supplications, prayers, intercessions and thanksgivings of I Tim. 2.1] in a single action; it cannot be understood, but may be compared to the leaping of a flame. It consists of a powerful and wordless pouring forth of prayer to God, which the spirit, with groanings that cannot be uttered, sends up though not conscious of its content. In that moment it conceives and puts forth what no one can describe, and which the mind apart from that moment cannot remember.[6]

And again:

The Lord's Prayer, given to us with his authority, seems to include the very pattern of a perfect prayer. Yet it carries those who use it to the higher state of prayer which I mentioned before, to that spark-like and ineffable prayer which very few men know by experience. It transcends the senses; is marked by no vocal expression, whether silent or aloud; but the mind, illuminated by an outflowing of light from heaven, does not define it in the narrow limit of human language. With the senses unified, it pours forth prayers, almost with violence, as a spring pours forth fresh water, and in a second's time darts up a prayer of such richness that afterwards the mind, returned to normality, cannot easily describe it.[7]

In a similar fashion St Augustine, the most spiritually-minded of the Latin Fathers, contrives to combine both the conception of continuous prayer and that of the prayer of silence by identifying the idea of longing – *desiderium* – with the action of prayer.

[The psalmist continues:] *And before thee is all my desire* (Ps 37.10 [38.9]) – not before men, who cannot see the heart, but *before thee is all my desire.* Let your desire be before him, and the Father, who sees in secret, will grant it to you, for your very desire is your prayer; and if the desire is continuous, so is the prayer. The apostle does not speak of *praying without ceasing* for nothing. Do we bend the knee without ceasing, do we prostrate our body or lift up our hands without ceasing that he should say: *Pray without ceasing?* If we call such things prayer, I do not think that we can do them without ceasing. There is another prayer, interior and unceasing, which is desire (*desiderium*). Whatever else you do, if you long for the eternal Sabbath you do not cease to pray. If you do not wish to cease to pray, do not cease to desire. If your longing continues, so will your voice continue likewise.[8]

The public prayer of the Church, however, although it grows out of private devotion, needs to be differentiated with some care. In her public prayers the Church is aware of herself as a collective and not simply as a group of individuals. Her petitions and praises cannot reflect the taste and temperament of any particular worshipper; there must be a common pattern and, to that extent, a certain constraint. It is a fact of human nature, at least in Western society and I suspect in most human societies, that when a group of individuals decides to act collectively, a degree of formality comes into its proceedings. The larger the group, the greater the formality is likely to be; but this is not always the case, and certainly not always the case in Christian worship. One can have a large and very informal prayer-group but two people saying the Office together in private are required in some degree to be formal, however much at ease they may be in one another's company and however simple the setting.[9] There will be an element of solemnity in their proceedings – understanding solemnity in the sense of the Middle English *solempne,* which does not exclude cheerfulness[10] – which will be lacking in the prayer-group and which proceeds from the fact that they are performing a rite which is governed by laid-down rules. One might say that the difference between the prayer-group and the recitation of the Divine Office resembles that between an informal party and a ball: both should be equally happy occasions for the participants but the dancing at the ball is governed by rules and if you ignore them you spoil the pleasure of the whole business, which lies precisely in trying to follow the rules.

I would suggest that many of our difficulties in liturgical matters today arise from an inability – or an unwillingness – to recognise this distinction between formality and informality in worship. There has been an attempt to replace what many would agree to have been the excessive formalism of the past – a congregation which sits, kneels or stands, always at the same time and a liturgy which follows a rigidly-determined course and is dominated by the minister – with something which is freer and more spontaneous. In principle there is much to be said for this approach. Anyone who has attended the worship of the Eastern Orthodox Church may well have felt that, notwithstanding the use of a liturgy of the utmost richness and elaboration, performed with a highly complex ceremonial, the Orthodox congregation which, of course, normally stands for most of the long service, often gives an impression of greater freedom and spontaneity in its worship than do Western Christians. Nevertheless, there is a major difference between Orthodox worship and that of Western liturgical reformers: the great majority of the Orthodox use the traditional liturgical languages of Eastern Christendom, Greek and Church Slavonic, neither of which is the everyday speech of the worshippers, and have resisted any attempt to modernise the language, being well aware that such a change would be more devastating than any change of church-furnishing or vestments. In the West, however, change of liturgical form involving change of language, to make the language of everyday life the language of public worship, has long been the desire of many liturgical experts, some of whom have gone very far indeed in their opposition to traditional forms of speech.

I think that most people will agree that the language of public worship should generally be that which commends itself to the majority of the worshippers. If people are made happy, if their sense of devotion is quickened by using the forms of everyday speech, however unpleasing and banal those forms may be, then I personally would not want to force them into using a traditional idiom which would be as unpleasing to them as modern liturgical diction is to me. What, however, needs to be considered is the common assumption of many modern liturgists that the only proper liturgical language is that of the man in the street, that any phrase, usage or word which is not immediately understandable by the ordinary man or woman must be excluded from the canon, even if its meaning becomes clear with a little reflection. I might cite as an example the substitution of 'nature' for 'property' in the Prayer of Humble Access. In order to spare your worshipper a moment's thought, you break up the rhythm of a fine sentence: 'But thou art the same Lord, whose property is always to have mercy.' One wonders how the modern reformers contrived to leave the infinitive 'always to have mercy' un-split. It must have been a great temptation, valiantly resisted.

There remains, however, a reasonable challenge: why should one not worship in the language of everyday life? Why should we employ a special, and to that extent, artificial, diction in addressing God, who is equally accessible in every language and in none?

To answer this, let us first remember the distinction already noted between individual and collective prayer, private and public devotion. The manner in which the individual worships and the language which he employs, if he does employ language, is between him and God. When, however, we come to the public worship of the church we cannot, as has already been said, satisfy the inclinations of every individual worshipper. A common form must be found, even if it leaves some unsatisfied. Moreover, there is an important difference between the atmosphere of private and public prayer conditioned by their environments. Prayer is indeed a talking with God, but the divine side of the conversation is rarely audible. In private devotion God's responses may consciously come in the mind of the worshipper, but in public prayer there will only be silences, which may not always be fruitful and may sometimes even be embarrassing.[11] In consequence public prayer, if it is to be dignified, must sacrifice some of the intimacy enjoyed in private devotion. Furthermore, the fact which we have already noted, that public prayer is by its very nature calculated to introduce an element of formality into worship, will have its effect on the language employed, and this will hold true of Christian bodies which do not employ set forms of prayer as well as of liturgical churches. As long as the Bible conditions Christian worship, so long will prayers be conditioned by the Bible. I cannot in this context resist a quotation from that classic of the kail-yard school of Scottish writing, *Beside the Bonnie Brier Bush* by Ian Maclaren, a collection of stories about the imaginary Scottish village of Drumtochty, Perthshire, in the sixties and seventies of the last century. The passage concerns the funeral prayer of Dr Davidson, the parish minister. The Church of Scotland does not use set forms of prayer, but,

> the Doctor's funeral prayer was one of the glories of the parish, compelling even the Free Kirk to reluctant admiration, although they hinted that its excellence was rather of the letter than the spirit, and regarded its indiscriminate charity with suspicion. It opened with a series of extracts from the Psalms, relieved by two excursions into the minor prophets, and led up to a sonorous recitation of the problem of immortality from Job, with its triumphant solution in the peroration of the fifteenth chapter of 1

Corinthians. Drumtochty men held their breath till the Doctor reached the crest of the hill ... and then we relaxed while the Doctor descended to local detail. It was understood that it took twenty years to bring the body of this prayer to perfection, and any change would have been detected and resented.[12]

It may well be that Dr Davidson's successor in Drumtochty is now delivering less elaborate prayers; but funerals, like weddings, are occasional services which, by their very nature, invite an elevation of style. Both are solemnities, which seem to demand something more than the everyday in language and rite. I have read that, in England, for both these services, the language of the *Book of Common Prayer* remains popular. One can understand why.

The great fallacy which has confused modern liturgists with regard to the language of public worship has been to regard language as no more than a means of communication and to ignore its emotional and affective role.[13] This is, no doubt, a reflection of a more general indifference to language in modern society, with a neglect of grammar and ordered thought in literary composition and of dignity and sonority in style, with the result that it has become very difficult for contemporary men and women to express emotion except in an incoherent and inarticulate form. This, in turn, places a heavy burden on the writer of prayers, because Christian prayers are governed by the logic of theology; one should not indulge in *battalogia* – incantations, the 'vain repetitions' of the heathen (Matt.6.7). Faced with the prospect of reconciling meaning with feeling in a concept of language which is dominated by the idea of communication, the liturgical composer is easily tempted to give up the struggle and to retreat into the safety of day-to-day language which fails utterly to rise to the context of his theme. Let me give one example, not from a prayer formula but from a translation of the Bible. In the Revised Standard Version, in the scene at the grave of Lazarus, in the eleventh chapter of the

Gospel of John, when Christ commands those present
to take away the stone, Martha is made to say: 'Lord, by
this time there will be an odor, for he has been dead four
days.' I believe that in American English the word odor
does not have the slightly affected tone which odour has
in English use, but I find it difficult to understand how
any translator, in the context in which the word was used
– the grave of a brother and the terrifying command of
the Lord – can have imagined that the euphemistically
genteel odor was the right word to render the sense of the
Greek *ozei*. The Authorised Version translates, brutally
but effectively: 'Lord, by this time he stinketh'; the New
English Bible: 'By now there will be a stench.' I suppose
that 'foul smell' would be acceptable; but to speak of an
odor suggests an amazing insensitivity to context, where
the horror of mortality encounters the power of the incar-
nate Word and Lazarus is raised from the dead.

Language, then, is not simply a means of communication; it has other uses. It is from language that organised
and reasoned thought arises – it may be possible, up
to a point, to think without words, but without words
thought will not get very far. Equally, one can have
emotion without words; but words make it possible, not
only to express but also to deepen emotion and, in the
case of a group, to focus emotion. Many people – I all
but wrote everyone, but in this age of prose it would be
well not to be too absolute – must have been on occasion
moved, even to tears, by a line of poetry, and found that
it expresses their own feelings with a precision which
they themselves could never have achieved. In the words
of Housman:

Experience has taught me, when I am shaving of a
morning, to keep watch over my thoughts, because,
if a line of poetry strays into my memory, my skin
bristles so that the razor ceases to act. This particular
symptom is accompanied by a shiver down the spine;
there is another which consists in a constriction of the
throat and a precipitation of water to the eyes; and
there is a third which I can only describe by borrowing

a phrase from one of Keats's last letters, where he says, speaking of Fanny Brawne, 'everything that reminds me of her goes through me like a spear.' The seat of this sensation is the pit of the stomach.[14]

If it should be argued that the effect of poetry is one thing, the effect of vocal prayer another, we may reasonably reply that it is perfectly proper for the worshipper to be emotionally stirred by the language of prayer. Worship is intended for the edification of the worshipper as well as for the adoration of God; we do not have to use words to communicate with God, still less to tell him anything. It is one of the misfortunes of modern English liturgical language that it sometimes gives the unhappy impression of telling God facts about his being and operations of which he appears to be ignorant ('Eternal God, the King of Glory, you have exalted your only son to your kingdom in heaven . . .') in a way which the older linguistic tradition, employing an archaic form, avoids. Descriptive and ascriptive language in prayer is for the glory of God and not for his instruction.

There is, then, a case for having a liturgical or sacral language for the edification of the worshipper. But there is another consideration: appropriate language may give a sense of historical continuity and remind the worshipper that when the Church prays she is praying, not only with angels and archangels but with the whole company of heaven, including the faithful departed, who now eternally pour out their adoration to God whom, being out of the flesh, they now behold with unveiled sight. We must of course keep a sense of proportion. It would be absurd to argue that we can only worship with the Church in heaven in the language of the past; but if we admit that our worship can be affected by the environment – and most Christian people will have experienced the peculiar effect upon one's feelings when worship is offered in a place which has for centuries been a house of prayer – then it would be unreasonable not to recognise a similar power of language to create that sense of historical continuity.

It has sometimes been argued by those who favour
contemporary language in the liturgy that this is, in fact,
the true historical tradition. Earlier ages, they assert,
used the language of the day and the bishop or presbyter celebrating the Eucharist did not employ set forms
of prayer but prayed extempore, according to his ability. This is, up to a point, true, but only up to a point.
It is true that Justin Martyr, describing the worship of
the Church of Rome about the middle of the second
century, says that the celebrant offers the eucharistic
prayer *hosē dunamis autō* – 'to the best of his ability' – and
it is clear that for many centuries afterwards the leading
theologians in the Church continued to compose their
own prayers. On the other hand, there exists a class of
literature called the Church Orders, manuals of Church
life and discipline, which do provide prayer-formulas.
The explanation seems to be that while the great theologians of the Church were perfectly capable of composing
prayers for themselves, less able bishops – and it should
be remembered that we are acquainted with only a tiny
number, and those the most distinguished of bishops of
the early Church – would be only too happy to have a
form of prayer provided, which they could use on Sunday without having the worry and effort of producing a
probably inferior version of their own. One may guess
that in the early Christian centuries received forms of
prayer and original compositions existed side by side.

This, however, still leaves open the questions: how
did the prayers of the Church during the first five or
so centuries sound in the ears of the congregation?
This, clearly, is a question which cannot be answered
decisively; but one can very reasonably suggest that they
would not have sounded like everyday speech. In the
Greek East they would, from earliest times, have been
affected by the language of the Septuagint, the Greek
version of the Old Testament adopted by the early
church, and the Septuagint would certainly not have
sounded like the Greek of everyday life. Indeed, it was
the impossibility of rendering certain Semitic words into
Greek which caused their introduction into the liturgy

untranslated – 'Amen' and 'Alleluia' are examples which have survived to the present day in almost all Christian languages. The Greek of the New Testament would have been closer to the vernacular, but even here one would find Semitic words like *marana tha,* while the epistles of St Paul, taken as a group, have a theological flavour and a highly personal style which would set them decisively apart from Greek secular literature. Altogether one may say that it is improbable that a pagan, attending a Christian church out of curiosity or interest (as he could have done, up to and including the sermon, before the dismissal of the catechumens), would have been unaware of any difference of language from the usages of ordinary conversation.

In post-Patristic times the Byzantine liturgy diverged even more markedly from colloquial Greek. Let me quote from the translators' preface to *The Festal Menaion* by Mother Mary and Archimandrite (now Bishop) Kallistos Ware, published in 1969.

So far as the general style of our translation is concerned, after much experimenting we decided to take as our model the language of the Authorised Version (the King James Bible). This, we realise, is a controversial decision. Many of our readers will probably feel that, if the liturgical texts are to come alive for people today, they must be rendered in a more contemporary idiom. To this it must be answered that the Greek used in the canons and hymns that are here translated was *never* a 'contemporary' or 'spoken' language. The Byzantine hymnographers wrote in a liturgical style that was consciously 'artificial', even though it was never intentionally obscure or unintelligible. As we see it, the language of the Authorised Version is best adapted to convey the spirit of the original liturgical Greek. We do not dispute the necessity for more modern translations of Scripture, and their great value – in certain contexts; but for our present purpose it was the Authorised Version that provided what we most required. For three centuries or more the

Authorised Version, and along with it the Anglican *Book of Common Prayer,* have provided the words with which English-speaking peoples throughout the world have addressed God; and these two books have become a part not only of our literacy but of our spiritual inheritance. So long as certain archaisms of language and constructions are avoided, the English of the King James Bible is still easily understood.[15]

In the Western, Latin part of the Roman Empire the situation was not quite the same as in the East. In the first place, in large areas of the Christian West, including Rome, the original liturgical language was not Latin, but Greek. The Roman Church worshipped in Greek, perhaps down to the fourth century. The home of Christian Latin is not Italy but North Africa. Here, although there may, initially, have been a period when the official liturgical language was Greek, the normal tongue of the educated was Latin and at an early stage, and certainly by AD 250, an officially recognised Latin translation of the Bible was available, which was to shape the character of Christian Latin. This translation may be said to have been marked by three characteristics: colloquialism; literalness; and ready borrowing from the Greek, e.g. words like *angelus, baptisma, diaconus* and *ecclesia.*[16] The result was a Christian technical language which was frankly despised by such pagan intellectuals as condescended to read it. It unblushingly used popular and ungrammatical forms, of which St Augustine has supplied as example:

> Again, that form (*floriet*) which we cannot now take out of the mouths of the congregation when it sings: *Super ipsum autem floriet sanctificatio mea* (Ps.132.18: *Upon himself shall my holiness flourish*) surely takes nothing away from the meaning; but the better-educated hearer would prefer a correction, and that we should say *florebit* rather than *floriet;* and there is no objection to such a correction being made other than customary usage.[17]

It was, however, precisely the use of such customary Latin in divine worship which 'gave a new dignity and sanctity to these humble forms of speech, and the language of the Bible and liturgy was destined to have a profound effect on the language of even the most highly educated and cultivated Roman Christians throughout the centuries.'[18] In effect, in its earlier days Christian Latin, although reflecting popular rather than literary use, would have sounded peculiar to the ordinary Latin-speaker because of the extensive importation of Greek words, and by the fourth century, by which time it seems to have replaced Greek as the liturgical language of Rome – it had taken over in Africa much earlier – it had become sanctified by use.

Accordingly, we may say that the existence of a specialised sacral language for divine worship seems to have been a feature of Christianity from the earliest times about which we have information and that whatever case exists for altering the language of the English liturgy from that of the Prayer Book of 1662, it does not rest upon the example of history. On the contrary, there is every reason to think that Christians, all down the ages, have employed specialised forms of language (*Sondersprache*) in public worship and have generally been reluctant to change them.

Such evidence clearly has a significance for the continued use of the *Book of Common Prayer* in the worship of the Church of England. In the course of my argument I have made a distinction between private devotion and public prayer and I think that this distinction is both valid and necessary; but of course we cannot, in practice, hold these two forms of prayer apart. Private devotion influences public prayer; public prayer affects private devotion. Here, I think, it is impossible to deny the influence which the *Book of Common Prayer*, together with the Authorised Version of the Bible, has exercised on the spirituality of the Church of England for more than three centuries. It has informed the language of devotion. It has affected literary use, and future generations which have lost touch with the Prayer Book will fail to recognise allusions in secular writers which would have been familiar to any instructed Anglican child in the

nineteenth century. This latter, though regrettable, is
not something which we can deplore theologically – we
do not compile our service books to provide material for
secular quotation. What is deplorable has been the attack
on a whole tradition of spirituality, despite the promises
which were made, when the *Alternative Service Book*
was introduced, that that tradition would continue to be
available for those who wanted it. As things are there is
a distinct possibility that within a generation the *Book
of Common Prayer* will have ceased to be used in the
Church of England.

Such a prospect is, in my view, both tragic and deplorable. It will mean that future generations will be cut off
from the tradition of spirituality which formed some of
the outstanding names in Anglican history. Furthermore,
the Prayer Book is not the heritage of any one particular party in the Church of England. If it has sometimes
been claimed by Evangelicals as 'their' book, it is worth
recalling that it was the book of John Keble, Edward
Bouverie Pusey and Charles Gore, and that in the
recent past even ritualistic Anglo-Catholics, while they
may have added to the text, normally made the Prayer
Book the foundation of their liturgy. The Prayer-Book
Catholic parish was, in the past, very much a
reality.

Let me say once more that I do not hold, and would
indeed strongly reject, the view that only one idiom is
appropriate for public worship. If we accept the propriety of using different liturgical languages, then we cannot reasonably insist that only one particular style of
language is appropriate for the liturgy. Nevertheless,
it remains true that for many people devotion is fos-
tered by a style which has historical associations and
which is in some degree different from that of daily
use. G.K. Chesterton observed that 'any man cut off
from the past . . . is a man most unjustly disinherited,'[19]
and it will be a tragedy if future generations of English
Christians should be robbed of their lawful heritage.
At the same time, it would be well for all those who
love and use the *Book of Common Prayer* to keep in

mind, with regard to its language, the words of Robert Meux Benson of Cowley, referring to ecclesiastical ritual in general:

> We should always remember that ritual is not for the purpose of pleasing ourselves. It is the offering of wealth, in form, art, and substance to God for his glory, since all creation belongs to him. If it is our fault that God is not glorified manifestly, we cannot look for the blessing of the worship. But if it is not our fault, the absence of outward beauty can make no sacramental difference in our service; and we ought not therefore to repine if we are called to worship where things are distasteful. Outward beauty should not be despised, but our Lord's words call us to regard it as of very little practical importance.[20]

There *is*, however, a practical concern in the matter of the language of liturgy when a substantial element among the worshippers of a particular church finds itself deprived of the forms to which it was accustomed, and which it was told would be preserved if there were a demand for them, and in consequence finds itself unable to worship with profit through the forms which have been substituted. No doubt this represents a deficiency on the part of the worshippers – those who were further gone on the way of perfection would be able to adapt themselves to any form of worship which was not heretical – but the fact remains that for many people, language has a positive effect in fostering or inhibiting devotion. In principle there is no difference between the Prayer Book formula: 'For thou only art holy, thou only art the Lord, thou only O Christ with the Holy Ghost art most high in the glory of God the Father' and that of Rite A of the *Alternative Services Book*: 'For you alone are the Holy One, you alone are the Lord, you alone are the Most High, Jesus Christ, with the Holy Spirit, in the glory of God the Father,' but I find the former infinitely more moving than the latter. Equally, I do not find in the Liturgical Psalter affixed to the *Alternative Services Book* that literary and affective quality which has made the Coverdale version dear to so many generations of users. The new translation may be a more accurate rendering of the Hebrew – a detail which in itself raises a question, since the standard version of the Psalms in the early church was in Greek and the decision to go back to the Hebrew was very much the idea of one man, St Jerome – but the effect upon me of this rendering of the collection of hymns which has formed the basis of the Divine Office ever since the fourth century, is less moving than that of the archaic diction of Coverdale.[21]

I realise that such a judgement is subjective. Indeed, I am forced to ask myself to what degree my personal predilection for the Prayer Book comes from antiquarianism and resistance to a change in my worshipping habits rather than from theology. One who is by trade a church historian must always have, at the back of his mind, the memory of the famous schism of the Old Believers in the Russian Church in the seventeenth century, when the Patriarch Nikon attempted to bring Russian liturgical practice into line with that of the Greeks, whom he supposed to provide the model of ancient practice, and aroused bitter opposition, led in particular by the Archpriest Avvakum. 'Wife,' he asked, 'what must I do? The winter of heresy is at the door. Am I to speak or to hold my peace?' 'Christ is strong', came the reply, 'and he will not abandon us. Get thee gone, get thee gone to church, Petrovich. Unmask the whore of Heresy.'[22] Nikon ruthlessly suppressed opposition to his reforms. The Old Believers were exiled to Siberia, were mutilated, and put to death, sometimes by being burnt alive, over issues which included making the sign of the cross with two fingers rather than with three and consecrating the sacrament on a linen cloth rather than a proper antimensium (consecrated altar-cloth). How far were the Old Believers justified? 'Even the smallest neglect of the traditions leads to the complete contempt of dogma'[23] – but can Anglicans, who have always made a distinction between things which are the essence of the faith and things which are *adiaphora*, indifferent, regard the wording of public prayer as pertaining to the essence of faith? The Russian Old Believers formed a sect which, despite savage repression, has persisted in Russia to this day. I take it that none of us would feel that the Prayer Book was an issue which justified schism. Are we then merely being obstructionist and reactionary over an issue which does not justify intransigence?

My answer would be as follows. In itself the language of liturgy is not a matter of faith and could certainly not justify a schism; but the continued use of the *Book of Common Prayer* is a serious matter for two reasons. The first is specific and immediate, namely, the manner in which its demise is being accomplished, in parishes and theological colleges alike, in spite of the assurances which were given when the *Alternative Services Book* was brought in that the *Book of Common Prayer* would continue to be available for those who desired it. It is in the interest of the Church, no less than ourselves, to make a protest. The second reason is more general and, in the long term, more important, and turns on the fact that any liturgy which has been in use over centuries and supplies a spiritual tradition ought not to be abandoned to satisfy the demands of those who, although they use historical arguments (not always convincingly) for its disuse, are really non-historical in their outlook and concerned to bring the Church into conformity with the present, transient age, rather than to keep her in contact with her roots. That word *aggiornamento* – 'up to date' – so much in use during the Second Vatican Council, while no doubt appropriate in its day, has become for some people a sort of principle, and a dangerous principle for an institution which, by its very nature, is bound so to pass through things temporal as not finally to lose the things eternal. It is certainly wrong for the Church to try to live in the past; but the present is not only determined by the past, both genetically and historically, but has also much to learn from the past. That phrase of the Apostles' Creed, *the communion of Saints*,[24] should serve to remind us of the bond that unites living and departed Christians, and the retention of liturgical forms which the departed held dear, in the language which they employed, will help us, if we are sensitive to such things, to understand the spiritual inheritance which we have received from them, and to turn our hearts and minds to the worship and adoration of that God whom we and they alike confess.

This paper was not originally composed with any commemoration of Thomas Cranmer in mind; yet it is impossible not to feel gratitude to the man who provided the materials of what was, for three centuries, the liturgy which both distinguished and held together the different churches which make up the Anglican communion.[25]

Notes

1. *Revelations of Divine Love*, 9, tr. Clifton Wolters (Penguin Classics, 1966), p.75.
2. Cassian, *Conl.* 10, 10, tr. Owen Chadwick, *Western Asceticism*, Library of Christian Classics, Vol. XII (London, 1958), pp.239–43.
3. *The Way of the Pilgrim and the Pilgrim continues on his Way*, tr. R. M. French (London, repr. 1950).
4. Buber, *Tales of the Hasidim: The Early Masters*, tr. Olga Marx (London, 1956), p.289.
5. C. E. B. Cranfield, *A Critical and exegetical commentary on the Epistle to the Romans*, Vol. I (Edinburgh, 1975), p.400: 'In origin an exclamatory form used by small children, it had by the time of Jesus come to be used more extensively, being no longer confined to the speech of children ... [It] was not used as a form of address to God in ancient Judaism ... Its use by Jesus expressed His consciousness of a unique relationship to God, and His authorizing them [His followers] to address God in this way is to be understood as His giving them a share in His relationship to God.'
6. Cassian, *Conl.* 9, 15, tr. Chadwick, p.221.
7. Ibid., 9, 25, Chadwick, pp.226–7.
8. Augustine, *Ennar. Ps.* 37, 14: 'Subiecit: *Et ante te est omne desiderium meum.* Non enim ante homines, qui cor videre non possunt, sed *ante te est omne desiderium meum.* Sit desiderium tuum ante illum; et Pater qui vidit in occulto, reddet tibi. Ipsum enim desiderium tuum, oratio tua est; et si continuum desiderium, continua oratio. Non enim frustra dixit apostolus: *Sine intermissione orantes.* Numquid sine intermissione genu flectimus, corpus prosternimus, aut manus levamus, ut dicat: *Sine intermissione orate?* Aut si sic

dicimus nos orare, hoc puto sine intermissione non possumus fa-
cere. Est aliqua interior sine intermissione oratio, quae est desiderium. Quidquid aliud agas, si desideras illud sabbatum, non
intermittis orare. Si non vis intermittere orare, non intermittere
desiderare. Continuum desiderium tuum, continua vox tua est.'
CCL xxxviii, 392.

9. Clearly, there can be no absolute separation of the two forms.
One has only to note their relation in, for example, the Rule of
St Benedict, to realise that they are interconnected.

10. See C. S. Lewis, *A Preface to Paradise Lost* (London, 1942),
pp.15–16.

11. This is not to deny the value of periods of silence in communal
public worship, which are of great antiquity and are specifically
provided for in the Office services of the *Alternative Services
Book*.

12. It should be added that on the particular occasion with regard to
which the doctor's prayer is mentioned – the funeral of a brilliant
son of the parish, who had died of consumption after gaining the
highest academic honours – Dr Davidson, when he 'had already
sighted Job, was carried off his course by a sudden current, and
began to speak to God about Margret and her son, after a very
simple fashion that brought a lump to the throat: ... "Lord,
have peety upon us, for we a' luved him, and we were a' prood
of him."' But who will blame the doctor, in such circumstances,
for breaking down and abandoning formality?

13. For what follows, see Christine Mohrmann, *Ecclesiastical Latin. Its
origins and character* (London, 1959).

14. Housman, 'The name and nature of poetry' in *Selected Prose*, ed.
John Carter (Cambridge, 1961), p.193.

15. *The Festal Menaion* (London, 1969), pp.13–14.

16. L. R. Palmer, *The Latin Language* (London, 1964), pp.180ff. esp.
p.186; Mohrmann, *Ecclesiastical Latin*, pp.30ff.

17. Augustine, *De Doctrina Christiana* 2, 13, 20: 'Illud etiam, quod
iam auferre non possumus de ore cantantium populorum:
Super ipsum autem floriet sanctificatio mea (Ps.131.18,LXX), nihil
profecto sententiae detrahit, auditor tamen peritior mallet hoc
corrigi, ut non *floriet* sed *florebit* diceretur; nec quicquam impedit
correctionem, nisi consuetudo cantantium.' *CCL*, xxxii, 45–6.

18. Palmer, *Latin Language*, p.189.

19. Chesterton, 'Avowals and Denials' in *On Man: Heir to all the Ages*,
quoted by Lewis, *A Preface to Paradise Lost*, p.63.

20. M. V. Woodgate, *Father Benson: Founder of the Cowley Fathers* (London, 1953), p.97.

21. Cf. the remarks of Ernest Clapton, *Our Prayer Book Psalter:
containing Coverdale's version from his 1535 Bible and the Prayer Book
version by Coverdale from the Great Bible 1539–41* (London, 1934),
p.xxvi: 'And for the Psalter as a whole, take the AV, the RV.,
versions such as Perowne's or Driver's, and after reading any or

all of them, read once more the Psalter in the Prayer Book and
we feel at once the genius, the tenderness, the soothing touch, the
dignity and the majesty of Coverdale's version.'
22. Meyendorf and Baynes, 'The Byzantine Inheritance in Russia' in
Byzantium. An Introduction to East Roman Civilisation, ed. Norman
H. Baynes and H. St L. B. Moss (Oxford, 1949), p.387.
23. Ibid., p.388.
24. The precise meaning of the phrase has been much discussed. I
assume that it refers to fellowship with holy persons rather than
to the Eucharist. See J.N.D. Kelly, *Early Christian Creeds*, 3rd edn
(London, 1972), pp.388–97.
25. Recognising this debt does not necessarily imply acceptance of
Cranmer's final eucharistic theology, on which see E. C. Ratcliff,
'The English Usage of Eucharistic Consecration 1548–1662' in
Liturgical Studies, ed. A. H. Couratin and D. H. Tripp (London,
1976), pp.203–21.

IV

Cranmer and the Daily Services
Anthony Gelston

One of the distinctive features of the English Reformation is the dominant role played in it by liturgical change. It is well known that the first English *Book of Common Prayer* of 1549 was very largely the work of Thomas Cranmer, and it seems[1] that he had been working on the revision of the daily services for at least ten years previously. His English Litany had already been issued as a separate service in 1544. It is in his work on the daily services and the Litany that Cranmer's liturgical genius found its highest expression, and it is significant that these are the services which were felt to require the least radical, and particularly the least structural, modification in the liturgical revision of the 1960s and 1970s. The Roman Catholic Oratorian Louis Bouyer could describe it in 1956 as 'a Divine Office which is not a devotion of specialists but a truly public Office of the whole Christian people', and recorded his admission 'that the Offices of Morning Prayer and of Evensong, as they are performed even today in St Paul's, Westminster Abbey, York Minster, or Canterbury Cathedral, are not only one of the most impressive, but also one of the purest forms of Christian common prayer to be found anywhere in the world'.[2]

It is not intended in the following pages to offer a detailed analysis of the way in which Cranmer produced these masterpieces or of the various sources on which he drew.[3] We shall be content rather to take note of the broad principles on which he worked, and to evaluate his achievement both retrospectively by relating it to the background of medieval usage and contemporary reform movements and prospectively by observing how

it has fared in the Church of England in the present
century. Since most readers will be familiar with the
Book of Common Prayer of 1662 rather than with its
predecessors, we shall use the text of the 1662 book
as a basis for study, and begin by drawing attention to
the more important ways in which the earlier books of
1549 and 1552 differ from it.

The prefatory matter of the 1662 book includes a
section entitled 'Concerning the Service of the Church',
which is with only slight modifications the Preface of the
1549 book. From this we learn what Cranmer's guiding
principles were. They may conveniently be tabulated
under five headings.

(a) The whole, or at least the greater part, of the Bible
should be read over in the course of the year, and in
particular the whole of the Psalter should be used. This
was seen as the restoration of primitive practice and the
correction of medieval abuse, by which a small number
of psalms were used frequently and the rest omitted,
and the reading of the books of the Bible was begun
but never completed. The restoration of the use of the
whole Psalter and most of the Bible would profit clergy
and laity alike in living a godly life, and would also in
particular equip the clergy for both their pastoral teaching ministry and their confuting of heretical doctrine.

(b) The services were to be held in the vernacular so that
the laity in particular might understand what was being
said and thus participate intelligently in the worship
offered and profit from the instruction to be derived
from the public reading of the Scriptures.

(c) The rules ordering the content of the services in relation to the calendar had become so complex that 'many
times there was more business to find out what should
be read, than to read it when it was found out'. In the
interests of simplicity and practicality a straightforward
Calendar and Lectionary was produced, and the orders
of service were simplified at the expense of the loss of

invitatories, responds, etc. The services would be briefer and more straightforward, and only a Bible and Prayer Book would be required for their performance.

(d) Only material which was actually scriptural or consonant with Scripture was to be used. Such non-biblical material as readings from the Fathers or from the lives of the saints was to be omitted. Here we find the Reformation principle of purity of doctrinal content, tested by conformity with Holy Scripture.

(e) The varying local 'uses' of Sarum, Lincoln, York, etc., were to be abolished, and a single 'use', that of the *Book of Common Prayer*, was to be observed throughout the Church of England. Any differences of opinion as to how the provisions of the Prayer Book were to be put into practice were to be resolved by the diocesan bishop, and in 1552 provision was made for the diocesan to refer any dubious questions to the archbishop.

Three major emphases emerge as we review these principles. The first is that these are services of Common Prayer, intended for the laity as well as the clergy. Although the notes appended to the Preface make provision for the clergy to say Matins and Evensong privately in any language, it is clearly intended that public recitation with a congregation was to be the normal practice. This emphasis was strengthened in the 1552 book with the addition of the provision for the parish priest to toll the bell a convenient time before the services so that the laity may 'come to hear God's word, and to pray with him'. One celebrated instance of this in the following century is recorded in Izaak Walton's *Life of Mr George Herbert*: 'Some of the meaner sort of his Parish, did so love and reverence Mr *Herbert*, that they would let their Plow rest when Mr *Herberts Saints-Bell* rung to Prayers, that they might also offer their devotions to God with him: and would then return back to their Plow'.[4]

The second main emphasis that emerges is on the need for intelligent participation in the services. This comes

out particularly in the substitution of the use of the
vernacular for that of the Latin of the medieval services.
It also inspired the abbreviation and simplification of the
services, and in particular the provision for the regular
reading of the Scriptures for the doctrinal, practical and
devotional edification of clergy and laity alike.

The third main emphasis was on doctrinal purity.
Conformity with Holy Scripture was to be the criterion
by which material was retained or rejected. Almost the
only new material contributed by Cranmer was some
of the collects, but those newly composed by him (e.g.
those for the first two Sundays in Advent) are marked
by their scriptural content.

The prefatory material was followed by directions for
the reading of the Psalter and of the rest of the Bible.
The Psalter is divided into sixty portions of psalmody,
to be used consecutively over the two daily services
of a secular month. The February cycle began on 31
January and ended on 1 March; in later months with
thirty-one days the psalms for the thirtieth day were to
be repeated on the thirty-first, and in leap years both
psalms and lessons for 25 February were repeated on the
following day. The lessons similarly followed the secular
year, the Old Testament being read continuously over
the two daily services, but the New Testament being
read in separate morning and evening cycles. Generally
a whole chapter was read at a time. The Old Testament
followed the order of the books in the Bible except for
Isaiah, which was reserved for Advent. From 5 October
to 27 November the first lessons were from the Apocrypha: Tobit, Judith, Wisdom, Ecclesiasticus and Baruch.
The Gospels and Acts were read in sequence three times
a year at Matins and the Epistles similarly three times
a year at Evensong. The Revelation, however, was not
read at all, except on occasions when a proper lesson
was taken from it on one of the feasts for which such
provision was made (e.g. All Saints on 1 November).
Proper psalms for certain days and proper lessons for
these and certain other days which did not fall on calendar dates were first provided in the 1552 book.

We turn now to the actual content of the daily services. Both begin with the Lord's Prayer, though without the doxology, which was not added until the 1662 book. The opening versicles and responses follow. The first pair were to be used at Matins only in the 1549 book, as in the medieval services, but they were added at Evensong in 1552. The *Gloria Patri* was separated into a third versicle and response only in the 1662 book; in the earlier books it was treated as an entity, together with 'Praise ye the Lord' which replaced the medieval *Hallelujah* (which it translates) except from Easter to Trinity Sunday. The revival of the use of Tudor settings of the responses in choral services has familiarised modern worshippers with the 1549 format. The addition of the response 'The Lord's Name be praised' from the Scottish 1637 book was first made in England in the 1662 book, thus completing the ordering of this material into four exchanges between priest and people.

The *Venite*, Psalm 95, was retained from the medieval services as an introduction to the psalmody for the day, and accordingly used at Matins only. The 1549 rubric specified that it was to be used 'without any Invitatory', and this is an instance of the pruning of the medieval services in the interests of simplicity. The invitatories were refrains varying with the season, sung before the *Venite* and repeated in part or in whole after each verse. Together with the antiphons used in connection with the psalms and canticles they offered on occasion suggestive hints for the interpretation of fixed texts in the spirit of the season, but they undoubtedly added to the complexity of the services, and Cranmer's pruning enabled the basic structure to stand out far more clearly. The use of the Easter Anthems in place of the *Venite* was introduced in the 1552 book; in the 1549 book they formed part of a special devotion before the beginning of Matins on Easter Day.

The central part of both offices consists of psalms and canticles interspersed with lessons. Here Cranmer introduced a substantial change from the medieval services, giving equal weight to the reading of the Scriptures in course as to the offering of psalmody in course. The use of *Gloria Patri* at the end of each psalm and of *Benedicite* and the Gospel canticles was retained, as was the climactic use of the Christian canticles, two of which were now used at each office. This facilitated not only a practical alternation between the offering of praise and the reception of God's Word in the Scriptures, but also a progress within each service from Old Testament to New Testament, which was at most adumbrated in the medieval services by the use of a Christian canticle to conclude the series of psalms. In Cranmer's services the psalms and the Old Testament lesson are linked to the New Testament lesson by a canticle, and the appropriateness of the *Magnificat* in this position at Evensong has always been recognised as one of Cranmer's master-strokes. The second canticles (*Benedictus* at Matins and *Nunc Dimittis* at Evensong) are equally appropriate as offerings of thanks for the New Testament revelation. The first canticle at Matins in the 1549 book was to be the post-biblical *Te Deum Laudamus* (including the secondary final eight verses) except in Lent when the apocryphal canticle *Benedicite* was to be used; in the 1552 book the two were allowed as alternatives. In 1552 the use of specific psalms (respectively 100, 98 and 67) as alternatives to the three Gospel canticles was also introduced, probably in deference to the more extreme reformers' dislike of the latter. This, however, obscures the movement from Old Testament to New, and cannot be judged one of Cranmer's better second thoughts.

The order of the prayers which follow was also modified in the 1552 book, and here Cranmer's second thoughts may well be regarded as an improvement. In the 1549 book the prayers began with the *Kyries,* the Apostles' Creed and the Lord's Prayer. Then followed the six pairs of versicles and responses as in the 1662 book. The salutation 'The Lord be with you' and its response together with the invitation 'Let us pray' followed, leading directly into the Collect for the Day and the two fixed collects. In the 1552 book the Creed was brought forward to follow the second canticle immediately and thus serve as a bridge between the central part of the service which is almost entirely biblical in content and the prayers which follow. The Creed in this position may be felt to be a further response to the Scripture readings, in which the outline of the faith as a whole is celebrated and reaffirmed as the context within which the particular readings of the day are to be understood. The salutation and its response together with the invitation to prayer were brought forward to follow the Creed immediately, and now form a natural introduction to the prayers. The remainder of the material at this point in the 1549 book now followed without interruption in the same sequence as in the 1662 book.

Two points in this section require further comment. Immediately after Evensong the text of *Quicunque vult*, the so-called Athanasian Creed, is printed in the 1549 book with a rubric directing its use immediately after the *Benedictus* at Matins on six festivals: Christmas, Epiphany, Easter, Ascension, Pentecost and Trinity Sunday. In the 1552 book a selection of seven saints' days was added (as in the 1662 book), presumably in an attempt to secure an approximately monthly use of this Creed. Nothing is said to indicate that it was to be a substitute for the Apostles' Creed, a direction which first appeared in the 1662 book. It was in fact used in the medieval services as a canticle at Prime, and it was probably as a canticle that Cranmer sought its continued occasional use. Its position however must have suggested its use in place of the Apostles' Creed.[5]

The Collect for the Day was followed in the medieval offices by memorials. These consisted of an antiphon, a versicle and response and a collect. They either commemorated a saint or expressed some particular intention. Cranmer simplified this procedure by appointing two fixed collects to follow that for the day. The second collect at each service was a (different) prayer for peace, while the third collect related respectively to morning or evening. These two collects were the only point at which the two services differed after the second canticle.

The daily services in the 1549 book were thus somewhat shorter than those of the 1662 book. The essential
content has remained with remarkably little change,
and extends in the 1662 book from the first Lord's
Prayer to the third collect. The penitential introduction in the 1662 book, consisting of Scripture Sentence,
Exhortation, General Confession and Absolution, was
prefixed to Morning Prayer in the 1552 book, the rubric
suggesting that it should also be used at Evening Prayer,
but this was not specifically indicated by being printed as
part of the evening office until the 1662 book. The style
and content of this penitential introduction show the
strong influence of the Reformation, but a confession
and absolution were to be found among the prayers at
Prime and Compline in the Sarum offices, and it was
probably felt desirable to include this element in the
daily services, particularly as the decreasing frequency
with which Holy Communion was celebrated meant that
the confession and absolution in that service would not
necessarily follow even on Sundays.

The other element which is very sparsely represented
in the offices of the 1549 book is that of intercession,
which appears only in a very succinct form in the
second set of versicles and responses. At the end of
the Communion Service, however, a rubric directed the
use of the Litany and at least the first part of the
Communion Service on Wednesdays and Fridays and
'other days, whensoever the people be customably assembled to pray in the church, and none disposed to
communicate with the Priest'. The 1552 book made
it clear that the Litany was to be used on Sundays,
Wednesdays and Fridays, 'and at other times, when it
shall be commanded by the Ordinary'. In the 1552 book
the Ante-Communion included the 'general prayer for
the whole state of Christ's church militant here in earth'.
It is clear therefore that adequate provision was made
for intercession on at least three days in the week.
The prayers following the third collect at Morning
and Evening Prayer in the 1662 book and the set
of occasional prayers and thanksgivings (of which the

prayer for Parliament and that for all conditions of men and the general thanksgiving were for general use) came gradually into use between 1559 and 1662, so that the rubrics and provision in the 1662 book represented essentially the codification of long custom (including also the provision for the anthem). Of this intercessory material little besides the Litany derives from Cranmer himself.

The Litany, issued in 1544, is the earliest composition of Cranmer to find a place in the Prayer Book. It suffered little modification in the 1549 book; indeed it was not even printed out in the original edition of that book. It was originally intended as a procession introducing the Communion Service rather than as an appendage to Matins, although the decrease in frequency of celebrations of Holy Communion had the effect of making it appear part of the Office. Cranmer's sources included the Sarum Litany for Rogation and Lent, the Litany used at the commendation of the soul in the Visitation of the Sick and Luther's Litany, while the closing prayer and probably some other details are derived from the Greek Liturgy of St John Chrysostom.

The last of the suffrages seems to be largely Cranmer's own work, and reflects alike his liturgical sense and his devotional temper. The material beginning with the antiphon 'O Lord, arise' as far as the response 'Graciously hear us' was derived from an additional section of the Sarum Litany for use in time of war. As such it was appropriate enough in 1544 when the King was about to invade France, but it was retained in the Prayer Books so that it became a permanent part of the text. The second collect, immediately before the closing prayer from the Liturgy of Chrysostom, represents a conflation in 1549 of two distinct prayers in the 1544 text, between which came three other prayers, two of which appear in the 1662 book in different places. One is the prayer for the clergy and people in the prayers appended to Morning and Evening Prayer, and the other is the prayer beginning 'O God, whose nature and property' in the Prayers and Thanksgivings upon several occasions which follow the Litany in that book. The Grace was added in the 1559 book.

Two passages in the 1544 text are of particular interest. The Sarum Litany contained a long series of invocations of the saints, and this element was preserved in a very reduced form in 1544 in the following three petitions, which came immediately after the four opening invocations of the Trinity:

> Holy Virgin Mary, mother of God our Saviour Jesus Christ, pray for us.
> All holy angels and archangels, and all holy orders of blessed spirits, pray for us.
> All holy patriarchs, and prophets, apostles, martyrs, confessors, and virgins, and all the blessed company of heaven, pray for us.

These invocations were removed when the Litany was first printed in the later editions of the 1549 book. The other passage consists of an extra clause in the last of the deprecations, immediately after the words 'privy conspiracy':

> from the tyranny of the bishop of Rome, and all his detestable enormities.

This clause was omitted in the 1559 book, and replaced by 'and rebellion' in the 1662 book, when the words 'and schism' were also introduced later in the same deprecation.

Cuming aptly summarises the main characteristics of Cranmer's working methods as illustrated in the Litany:

> Many of the chief features of Cranmer's liturgical work are already discernible in his version of the Litany: bold handling of traditional forms, notably by abbreviation and conflation; borrowing from different portions of the Sarum rite; insertion of Reformed elements into the traditional framework; and occasional recourse to a totally unexpected source.[6]

Our account of Cranmer's work on the daily services as it resulted in the provisions of the 1549 and 1552 books is now complete. In passing we have noticed a number of changes he made in the material which he took over from the medieval services. What is most impressive when we review his work as a whole is the manner in which he has succeeded in pruning the intricate mass of medieval material to produce the essentially simple services of the Prayer Book. In the first place he reduced a scheme of eight daily services to two. This he did by fusing elements of Matins, Lauds and Prime to produce the morning office, and elements of Vespers and Compline to produce the evening office, leaving altogether out of account the short offices of Terce, Sext and None used during the day. Of the canticles, for instance, the *Venite* and *Te Deum Laudamus* are derived from Matins, the *Benedicite* and *Benedictus* from Lauds, the *Quicunque vult* from Prime, the *Magnificat* from Vespers and the *Nunc Dimittis* from Compline. In the second place the practice of reading both psalms and the rest of the Bible in course is found in the medieval offices only at Matins, although the course of psalms is continued and completed at Vespers. Yet this combination of psalmody and the reading of Scripture forms the basis of Cranmer's offices, and as we have seen he reordered the structure of their central part creatively so as to underline the importance of these primary elements. In the third place, as we have also seen, there was a great deal of pruning, partly for doctrinal reasons but much more in the interests of simplicity, brevity and practicality.

One major omission from the medieval services however has not yet been mentioned. Each office contained a metrical hymn. This preceded the psalms at Matins, Prime and the lesser hours and the Gospel canticle at Lauds, Vespers and Compline. Cranmer had in fact taken considerable trouble over the Latin hymns in his earlier work on the offices, but he confesses that 'mine English verses want the grace and facility that I could wish they had'[7]. This is probably the reason for the absence of hymns from the 1549 book. The original (longer) rendering of *Veni Creator Spiritus* in the Ordering of Priests was the only version in the first English Ordinal of 1549–1550, and is sufficient indication of the undesirability of the wholesale introduction of English metrical hymns of this quality. The plain truth is that the time was not yet ripe for the blossoming of English hymnody, and England had to wait until the time of Isaac Watts and Charles Wesley for the emergence of reformed hymns of high poetic quality and rich biblical content.

It is undeniable that the English offices were the poorer for the total loss of this element. Only gradually were hymns permitted as a supplement to the services, and no official direction of suitable hymns has ever been made. Some of the medieval office hymns, even if they contained elements that were unsuitable for use in reformed worship, were packed with scriptural allusions which the Reformers would presumably have found very much to their taste. One thinks immediately of such hymns as the Passiontide *Vexilla Regis prodeunt* and the Eastertide *Ad cenam Agni providi*. The loss of these hymns to the English offices is the more regrettable since Luther was in a position to produce German versions of some of these hymns, e.g. Ambrose's Advent hymn *Veni, Redemptor Gentium (Nun komm, der Heiden Heiland)*, the Pentecost hymn *Veni Creator Spiritus (Komm, Gott Schöpfer, Heiliger Geist)* and Ambrose's Trinity hymn *O Lux beata Trinitas (Der du bist drei in Einigkeit)*. Luther also contributed to the German services a number of original hymns with similar biblical content, such as his two Christmas hymns *Vom Himmel hoch da komm ich her* and *Vom Himmel kam der Engel Schar*.

Ironically Luther's success as a hymn writer is not matched by his liturgical sense. In his *Deutsche Messe* of 1526 Luther retained the daily services for use in schools, but they consisted of a loose string of items including psalms, hymns, Scripture readings, an exposition (in the morning) and one canticle, the *Magnificat* (in the evening). The concluding prayers comprised simply the Lord's Prayer, Collect and concluding *Benedicamus Domino* with the response *Deo gratias*. Antiphons were retained, but not responses, and there was little shape or structure to the services.[8] On Sundays the services were slightly fuller, and included *Te Deum Laudamus* or *Benedictus* in the morning.

The comparison with Luther reminds us that Cranmer was not working in a vacuum. He was aware of much that was going on in the Continental Reformation. A more direct influence on his early work on the daily services however was that of Cardinal Quiñones, who produced a first revision of the Roman Breviary in 1535 and a more conservative second recension in 1536. Cranmer's Preface to the 1549 book, itself a modification of that to his earlier drafts, is indebted in turn to that of Quiñones. One of Quiñones' principal aims was a more continuous reading of Holy Scripture and the use of longer readings on any one occasion. Many antiphons, responds, hymns, etc. were omitted to make room for this greater provision for the reading of Scripture. Quiñones retained the scheme of eight daily services, and accordingly arranged for the Psalter to be recited once a week, three psalms being assigned to each office. Three lessons were provided at Matins: one from the Old Testament, one from the New Testament and the third a patristic or hagiographical reading. The whole of the New Testament and a good deal of the Old Testament was covered in the course of the year. On the other hand Quiñones' conception of the office was essentially in terms of private recitation by individual clergy, and the aspect of participation in the common prayer of the church was largely lost. One detail in Quiñones' work which may have influenced the daily services in the 1552 book was the placing of the confession and absolution near the beginning of Matins (although after the Lord's Prayer). Once again we may feel that for all his indebtedness to Quiñones at a seminal stage of his thinking Cranmer's work on the daily services stands out as by far the greater liturgical achievement. Anglicans indeed have reason to be grateful for a form of daily service which is truly communal, profoundly scriptural, and retentive of much of the most valuable of the contents of the medieval offices.

In the second half of this paper we turn to consider how Cranmer's work on the daily services has fared within the Church of England during the present century. The story must begin with the Shortened Services Act of 1872, which permitted the abbreviation of Morning and Evening Prayer on weekdays by the omission of the Exhortation, the *Venite*, all but one of the appointed psalms, one lesson and one canticle, the *Kyries* and the second Lord's Prayer, and the three prayers following the Third Collect. The reduction of the scriptural content and the abandonment of the structure of the central part of the offices were extremely unfortunate, and the omission of the second Lord's Prayer (which stands at the head of the section of the service devoted to prayer) in favour of the first (which was a survival of medieval private preparation for taking part in the office) showed little liturgical sensitivity. This was the first legal variation in the text of the Prayer Book services since 1662, but since it consisted simply of permission to omit specified portions it did not result in a new edition of the Prayer Book.

A new lectionary, still based on the secular calendar, but making greater provision for proper lessons, had been legally enacted in 1871, and this was now printed in the Prayer Book in place of the old lectionary. In 1922 a further new lectionary was produced, breaking new ground in that it followed not the secular calendar but the ecclesiastical year. An attempt was made to match particular books of the Bible to the seasons of the liturgical year, the only instance of which in Cranmer's lectionary was the retention of the practice of reading Isaiah in Advent. The 1922 lectionary revived the medieval practice of beginning Genesis in Septuagesima, and varied readings from the gospels and epistles between morning and evening.

The abortive Prayer Book as proposed in 1928 was in practice widely used in churches, particularly in those parts where its changes were of practical rather than doctrinal significance, but less use of some of its provisions was made than might have been because copies of the 1928 book were not generally provided for the laity in the pews. The main changes in the daily services were as follows. The offices themselves began at 'O Lord, open thou our lips' and ended with the Third Collect. A series of seasonal invitatories was provided for optional use with the *Venite*, but they were to be used only twice, once before the *Venite* and a second time after its concluding *Gloria Patri*. The *Venite* itself was shortened to the first seven verses, and might be omitted altogether on weekdays that were not holy days. The *Benedicite* might be shortened, and Psalm 51 (or Psalm 40 if Psalm 51 had already been used) was allowed as a further alternative to the *Te Deum Laudamus*. In place of 'fighteth for us' in the fifth of the second set of versicles and responses was substituted 'ruleth the world'. This last detail was the only change in the office of Evensong. *Quicunque vult* might be used at either service but was entirely optional. Suggested occasions for its use were Trinity Sunday, the First Sunday after Christmas and the Feast of the Annunciation, but its use was allowed also on the remaining traditional days.

A new introduction to Morning or Evening Prayer was provided, and its use was required on all Sundays except principal feasts, unless another service was to follow immediately. This introduction contained an extended selection of opening Scripture sentences, not all of them penitential but many of them having seasonal relevance, and briefer alternative forms of exhortation, confession and absolution. The first Lord's Prayer was omitted. The Litany contained one or two additions and modifications, mainly to bring it into line with modern life (such as the inclusion of travellers by air), and might end with the *Kyries* if Holy Communion were to follow immediately, or with the Lord's Prayer, one or more of the Occasional Prayers and Thanksgivings, the Prayer of St Chrysostom and the Grace. The traditional material after the Lord's Prayer was retained for optional use, or could be used independently of the Litany on Rogation

Days, at penitential seasons and in times of trouble. The
Occasional Prayers and Thanksgivings were considerably extended and covered many topics to which no
reference had been made in earlier Prayer Books (e.g.
prayers for schools, for the peace of the world and
for industrial peace). The provision of a versicle and
response (but not an antiphon) before most of these
prayers was reminiscent of the medieval memorials, but
little use was made of them because the laity rarely had
copies of the book in the pews to enable them to make
the responses. This section ended with three alternative
conclusions to the Prayer of St Chrysostom and the
Grace, any of which might also be used directly after
the Third Collect at Evensong. A rubric at the end of this
section permitted prayer to be offered in the minister's
own words after the conclusion of any service, subject to
any direction which the bishop might give.

Three significant developments are to be noted in
these provisions. The first and most striking is the evidence of a return to Cranmer's provisions in the 1549
book as the essential content of the Anglican offices,
particularly on weekdays. Not only do the alternative
orders explicitly begin with 'O Lord, open thou our
lips' and end with the Third Collect, but the changes
proposed within this core of the service are minimal and have in fact had little following. The second
development reflects a growing awareness that when
an introduction and additional prayers are required, as
for instance when one of these offices is a main Sunday
service, there is need and scope for considerably greater
freedom. Not only is much more discretion allowed in
the question of how much additional material is to be
used on any particular occasion, but there has also been
much greater change in the introduction of alternative
and additional forms to those of the 1662 book. The
third development was a happy improvement on one of
Cranmer's basic reforms without sacrificing the essential
simplicity and comprehensiveness which he sought to
achieve. This was the adoption, as in the medieval services, of the liturgical year as the framework for the daily

lectionary. The comprehensive and orderly reading of the Bible during the year, which Cranmer achieved by adopting the secular calendar as the framework for his lectionary, was maintained in a different form in the 1922 lectionary with the added advantages of seasonal relevance and a less mechanical adherence to the order of the books as they appear in the Bible.

The *Alternative Service Book* of 1980, as is well known, was the product of an intensive period of liturgical revision during the previous fifteen years, experienced at parochial level in three series of alternative services authorised for experimental use for limited periods. In the case of the daily services there was in effect a fourth series, for *Series 2 Revised* introduced the most radical changes, derived in the main from the seminal work of the Joint Liturgical Group, who in 1968 published the first edition of their proposals in *The Daily Office*.[9] This is not the place to review the various proposals as they were made and modified in the light of experience. We are concerned here merely with the new forms of the daily services as they actually appear in the *Alternative Service Book*.

The first fact that requires attention is that there are alternative forms of both Morning and Evening Prayer. The full forms are recommended for use on Sundays, and since the shorter forms do not contain any material that is not present in the full forms we shall confine our attention mostly to the latter. The short form of Matins is roughly similar to that of the 1549 book in scope and structure, but it omits the canticle between the Scripture readings, and the prayers after the Creed are limited to the Lord's Prayer, the Collect of the Day and one of two morning collects. The short form of Evensong contains an optional penitential introduction, but only one Scripture reading (from the New Testament) and one canticle, after which follow only the Lord's Prayer, the Collect of the Day (optional) and the collect 'Lighten our darkness'. These reductions from the scope and modifications to the structure of the offices in the 1549 book may be felt to have conceded too much to modern

demands for brevity and for the avoidance of very much
unvarying material. The evening office in particular has
lost the shape and structure which Cranmer gave it and
the deliberate gradual movement from Old Testament
to New Testament through the *Magnificat* which was
one of his most brilliant creative touches. Both the
shorter offices may be felt to be seriously defective in
the section devoted to prayer, although it is no doubt
intended that full advantage is to be taken of the rubric
at the end which allows a variety of additional prayers
after the concluding collect. But when so much scope is
allowed to local choice is there not a loss of the sense of
participation in the common prayer of the whole church,
which was one of Cranmer's principal aims?

The other marked innovation of a general kind in the
daily services in the *Alternative Service Book* is the fact that
they are written in modern language idiom. This was
adopted for all services in the *Alternative Service Book*
except Rite B for the Eucharist, and must therefore
be regarded as part of the general ethos of worship in
the new services in the Church of England since it was
first introduced experimentally in the Series 3 services in
1973. It is hardly possible to offer an objective evaluation
of this change, which has generated emotive responses
both in its favour and in opposition to it. Inevitably much
of the literary beauty of Cranmer's English has been lost
in the modernised forms, but it is worth remembering
both that certain words like 'conversation' have changed
their meaning since his day, and that some, even of his
prayers, were not without obscurity (the sequence 'that
both . . . and also that . . .' in the second collect at Evensong being somewhat infelicitous). Some of the most radical changes in the modern forms derive from the work of
the International Consultation on English Texts which
was not unnaturally adopted by the Church of England's
Liturgical Commission with only minor modifications.
The *Gloria Patri*, Apostles' Creed, Lord's Prayer, Gospel
Canticles, *Te Deum Laudamus* and *Gloria in excelsis* are all
derived from this source. The text of the *Liturgical Psalter*
generally bound with the *Alternative Service Book* is also

the result of an ecumenical project, and first appeared in 1977 as *The Psalms: A New Translation for Worship*[10]. This text was naturally used for the invitatory psalms in the new services (95–96,100 and 134). It is perhaps worth making a plea that the evaluation of the order and content of the new services be kept separate from that of the use of modern language and that of specific judgements of text and interpretation which underlie the ICET texts.

As we turn to the full forms of the new services we notice that the general structure is hardly changed from that of the offices in the 1662 book. The only substantial structural innovation in the core of the services is the provision of an optional invitatory psalm or its equivalent before the psalms at Evensong, parallel to the *Venite* at Matins. A rubric after the Third Collect directs that any of the following items may then be used: prayers, one of the endings, a sermon, hymns and a blessing. The omission of any mention of an anthem is presumably not intended to imply that this is no longer permitted! A rubric also permits the sermon to be preached immediately after the second (New Testament) reading, while further rubrics suggest a hymn at the beginning of the service and allow the use of hymns at other points.

The new forms in the introductory material are a natural development from those in the 1928 book. An even wider selection of Scripture sentences is provided, mostly of a seasonal character. These are, however, preceded by the exhortation setting out the purposes of the act of worship. This is done more succinctly and comprehensively than in the form provided in the 1928 book, although the absence of the latter's reference to the 'whole company of heaven' may be regretted. The confession and absolution are those of the Rite A Eucharist, and the use of the alternative confessions in that rite is also allowed by rubric. The confession may be introduced by a specifically penitential Scripture sentence or a simple bidding or both. The whole penitential section is serious and objective, without being unrealistic in expression, and may be felt to be the appropriate late twentieth century counterpart of the forms introduced in the 1552 book. As in the 1928 book the Lord's Prayer is not used in the introduction, but reserved for use in the section of the service devoted to prayer.

The opening versicles and responses are modified in several respects. The first exchange is recast to conform essentially to the wording of the Liturgical Psalter, and most of those of the second set of versicles and responses which are derived from the Psalter are similarly recast. The second exchange is replaced altogether by a new one, which to some extent anticipates and itself replaces the *Hallelujah* of the medieval services and its adaptation by Cranmer. The loss of the opening verse of Psalm 70 is a departure from an unbroken tradition from the medieval offices, in which it was found in each of the eight daily services, and may for that reason be regretted, although the new sequence of responses does maintain the note of praise throughout. The *Gloria Patri* is said or sung in unison, a return to the usage of the medieval services and Cranmer's forms, and this now forms the climax of this section.

There has been some very constructive development of the invitatory psalm. The attempt in the 1928 book to reintroduce invitatories in the strict sense with Psalm 95 has been abandoned, but the total loss of the note of judgement entailed by the restriction of the *Venite* to the first seven verses Psalm 95 in that book has been repaired ingeniously by the appendage of the last verse of Psalm 96 to the first part of verse 8 of Psalm 95. An even more creative stroke, worthy of Cranmer himself, was the placing of the *Jubilate Deo* (Psalm 100) at this point as an alternative to Psalm 95. Its position in the 1552 book as an alternative to the *Benedictus*, as we have seen, destroyed the movement from Old to New Testament, but it came to be widely used (perhaps because of its brevity) and popular. The third verse however is much more appropriate at the beginning of the offering of praise, and this reordering of familiar material is to be warmly welcomed. The Easter Anthems are conveniently printed at this point in the service where they are actually used and this too is a practical improvement.

The one major structural innovation in the offices of the *Alternative Service Book,* as already noted, is the introduction of a corresponding invitatory psalm or its equivalent before the psalms at Evensong. Three forms are provided. The first, Psalm 134, is familiar to many worshippers from its use as an evening psalm at Compline, and its form and content make it eminently suitable for use as an invitatory psalm. The second is the ancient hymn 'O gladsome light', which may also be sung in other translations, of which Keble's 'Hail, gladdening Light' comes immediately to mind. It is very satisfactory that this early Christian text should be given a place in Anglican liturgy, and this particular place for it is felicitous. This too may be felt to be an enrichment in the spirit of Cranmer himself. The third form provided consists of the Easter Anthems. There seems no good reason why their use should be restricted to Matins, particularly in an age when in a number of churches Sunday Evensong remains a congregational service but Sunday Matins is so no longer.

The provisions of the *Alternative Service Book* for the use of the Psalter represent considerable development from those of earlier Prayer Books. As in the 1928 book proper psalms are provided for Sundays and Holy Days, including now the individual Greater Holy Days (such as the New Testament Saints' Days). The weekday psalms are now ordered, as an alternative to Cranmer's monthly scheme, in conjunction with the Scripture readings within the framework of the liturgical calendar. They are still used in numerical order, with no concessions to such features as duplications, and the average content of psalmody prescribed for each service is considerably less than in Cranmer's scheme. The psalms are spread over a period of just under ten weeks, but are so arranged that the same psalms are not appointed always for either morning or evening use. A worshipper regularly attending only one of the offices will now be familiar with all the psalms, in a way which has not hitherto been possible. The 1928 book bracketed certain verses and one whole psalm (58) for optional omission; the same practice has been followed in the Liturgical Psalter with some variation in the passages suggested for omission. *Gloria Patri* may be used at the end of each psalm or once only at the end of the group of psalms, and the Jewish doxologies at the end of the Psalms 41, 72, 89 and 106 may be omitted when a Christian doxology is used.

The lectionary follows broadly the lines of the 1922 lectionary, with one important exception. The fact that there is no Old Testament reading in the shorter form of Evensong in the *Alternative Service Book* has necessitated the division of the Old Testament readings into two distinct cycles, of which one is followed at Matins and the other at Evensong (if required). In alternate years, with very few exceptions, the weekday lessons for morning and evening interchange. A worshipper regularly attending Matins only will thus hear the whole cycle of biblical readings over a period of two years, and the worshipper regularly attending the shorter Evensong only will hear the whole New Testament cycle over the same period. Where both daily services are attended, and the full form of Evensong is used, the whole biblical cycle will be read in the course of each year. Readings from the gospels and from the rest of the New Testament alternate within each cycle, and only rarely is a book begun in the morning and completed in the evening or vice versa. One further innovation in the lectionaries of the *Alternative Service Book* is that wherever apocryphal readings are appointed alternative readings from the canonical Old Testament are provided. This meets the scruples of those who object to apocryphal readings, but raises the difficulty that those who do wish to use them have to do so at the cost of omitting part of the Old Testament cycle.

There have also been creative developments in the use of the canticles in the *Alternative Service Book*. Another quasi-Cranmerian stroke is the use of the *Benedictus* between the Scripture readings at Matins instead of after the New Testament reading, following the analogy of the *Magnificat* at Evensong. These two Gospel canticles are uniquely fitted to mark the transition from Old to New Testament in this way. This particular change in the position of the *Benedictus* was made in the original form of the *Series 2* services, which also has the distinction of having restored the used of *Gloria in excelsis* as a canticle at Matins (in which role it has a longer history than in its use in the Eucharist where alone it found a place in earlier Anglican Prayer Books), and of being the last revision of the offices to include the *Quicunque vult* even for optional use. The complete loss of the latter is a matter for regret. Its appropriateness on Trinity Sunday and on certain feasts of our Lord which emphasise the Incarnation (such as the First Sunday after Christmas, the Epiphany, the Transfiguration and perhaps the Ascension) cannot be denied, and it ought to be possible to produce a version for use in worship in which the damnatory clauses are omitted.

By the time the *Alternative Service Book* appeared the number of canticles available had grown considerably. In addition to the three Gospel canticles, the *Benedicite* and the *Te Deum Laudamus* of the Prayer Book offices and the *Gloria in excelsis* restored in *Series 2* there are three further canticles from the New Testament: the *Song of Christ's Glory* (Philippians 2. 6–11), *Great and Wonderful* and *Glory and Honour* (both catenas of passages from the Revelation). There is a further selection of verses from the same apocryphal passage as the *Benedicite* forming the canticle *Bless the Lord* (traditionally *Benedictus es*); this has long been used as a canticle in East and West, and entered Anglican Liturgy in the American and Scottish Prayer Books of the 1920s. The remaining canticle, recommended specially for use in Lent, is *Saviour of the World*, which first appeared in the *Congregational Hymnal* of 1860. It is inspired by the antiphon *Salvator Mundi*, which was used by Cranmer in the Visitation of the Sick and has remained there in subsequent Prayer Books.

This means that no less than eleven canticles are available, and in the shorter forms of the offices these are arranged so that each is used on a particular weekday, the twelfth place on Saturday evening being filled by the Easter Anthems or in Lent a repetition of *Saviour of the World*. At the end of the full forms of the services rubrics permit two alternative schemes, one with two varying canticles at each weekday office and the other retaining *Benedictus* and *Magnificat* as the invariable canticles between the Scripture readings but using the remainder as varying second canticles after the New Testament reading. Yet another possibility is to follow the rubrics as printed in the full form of the services, according to which there is a choice of three canticles (two only between the readings at Evensong) at each position. Further permitted modifications are the use of *Te Deum Laudamus* without the closing suffrages, or the latter by themselves, and a substantial shortening of the *Benedicite*.

It is interesting to speculate whether Cranmer would have approved this increase in the diversity of the canticles. The use of *Gloria in excelsis* and *Benedictus es* at least seems to be in keeping with the spirit of Cranmer's work on these services, and the greater flexibility and variety do not seriously conflict with the essential simplicity of his arrangement, although they do reflect in common with many other features of both the 1928 book and the *Alternative Service Book* a much greater freedom of choice which inevitably weakens the sense of participation in a form of worship which is being used throughout the Church of England. The day for such uniformity has however passed beyond recall, and it may still be claimed that these are relatively minor variations within an order which is recognisably the same, and which has not lost the essential character which Cranmer imposed on the Anglican offices. They have also reduced the proportion of the service which remains unvarying from day to day with the consequent danger of inattention.

There have been a few changes in the section of the services following the Creed. The salutation with its response and the bidding to prayer have disappeared, and this is a little surprising in view of the occurrence of the salutation at two points in the Eucharist in addition to the Peace. Perhaps its retention here, with a rubric directing its omission when the offices are said privately, would have been more in keeping with the spirit of Cranmer. The full form of the Lord's Prayer with doxology is natural when the prayer is used only once in the service. In the versicles and responses which follow, in addition to accommodating the wording partly to that of the appropriate passages in the *Liturgical Psalter*, new responses have been provided to the second, fifth and sixth versicles, and the fourth exchange has been replaced by a completely new one based on Psalm 67. 2. Something certainly needed to be done about the fifth response, as was already recognised in the preparation of the 1928 book. Opinions will vary how necessary the other changes were. New translations of the Second and Third Collects are provided, and an alternative modern Third Collect for Matins is less unsuitable than the traditional form when Matins is a congregational service in the middle or late morning.

Under a section headed 'Prayers for Various Occasions' are to be found first a modern version of the Litany, which requires separate consideration below, and then a selection of prayers corresponding broadly in scope to the provisions of the 1662 book. Under the heading 'State Prayers' are to be found a prayer for the Queen and all in authority under her, and only slightly modified versions of the prayers for the Royal Family and for the Clergy and People. No separate prayer for Parliament is provided. The prayer for all conditions of men appears as a General Intercession, and is subdivided into three sections with an opportunity for the insertion of material of current or local concern and a response. The General Thanksgiving is only very slightly different from the 1662 form. A new prayer of dedication is provided, suitable for use at the end of the service. This in turn is followed by modern forms of the Prayer of St Chrysostom (including a second much freer

version) and of five of the collects provided by Cranmer
for use at the end of Ante-Communion Three endings
are provided: the Grace, a form based on Ephesians 3.
20–1, and the salutation and *Benedicamus Domino* with
their traditional responses (as already in the 1928 book).
Finally there are two blessings. One is based on Numbers
6. 24–6 and appeared in the 1662 book, while the other
is a modern form.

Rubrics permit the use of the Litany after the collects at
Matins or Evensong, or in place of the prayers at either
service, i.e. immediately after the Creed. In the latter
case the Lord's Prayer, the Collect for the day and the
Grace are added at the end. On other occasions one of
the concluding prayers is said and the Lord's Prayer may
be added. The scope of the Litany itself extends only
as far as the end of the suffrages in Cranmer's form,
although the use of the *Trisagion* as the final response
may be seen as a replacement for the material between
the suffrages and the Lord's Prayer in Cranmer's text.
The opening invocations (which are much briefer) and
the closing suffrage must always be used, but a selection
of appropriate material from the intervening deprecations, obsecrations and suffrages is permitted. The only
occasion when the Litany is prescribed is at ordinations,
and the absence of any suggestion of its traditional
use on Sundays, Wednesdays and Fridays, not to mention Ember and Rogation Days, may be regretted. This
degree of freedom of usage (and non-usage) is however
characteristic of the *Alternative Service Book* as a whole.

The actual recasting of the Litany has for the most
part been sensitively done. The clause 'Remember not'
is omitted, and in general the penitential tone is considerably lightened. The clause 'In all time' is logically brought
forward to follow the last of the deprecations and precede the obsecrations, and the latter are extended with
a new clause referring to the earthly ministry of Christ.
The suffrages are arranged distinctly into three sections
dealing respectively with the Church, the world and areas
of human need, and the last section includes a petition
for the departed. Other new emphases are on the unity

and mission of the church, the need for peace and justice in the world and the needs of the homeless and hungry. Intercession must relate to the needs of the contemporary situation, and it is hardly surprising that this is a part of the new services where innovations have been felt necessary. The new Litany remains a comprehensive intercession on Cranmer's lines, and it is to be desired that greater use will be made of it in this modern form.

An evaluation of the daily services of the *Alternative Service Book* in relation to Cranmer's work must begin with the recognition of linear development. Cranmer's five basic principles remain the basis of the modern services. The chief difference emerges over the principle of uniformity of 'use'. There has been no reversion to the following of varying local 'uses', but the degree of permitted variation and scope for insertion of material of local or temporal concern (e.g. in the General Intercession) undoubtedly undermine the sense of participation in an act of worship which is essentially identical throughout the Church of England on any particular day. Such uniformity would not be welcomed by most English Anglicans today, and would certainly prove impossible to enforce. It may however be questioned whether the pendulum has not swung too far in the opposite direction. Some criticisms have been made above of the shorter forms (particularly of Evensong), and it might have been conducive to a wider use of the full forms had the permitted abbreviations been indicated merely by the printing of the numbers of optional sections in a different colour (as is in fact done to some extent already) in the full forms. The increased variety of practice permitted by the rubrics also militates against Cranmer's principle of simplicity, but it does not take long to familiarize oneself with the permitted variations, and there is no practical difficulty in conducting the office with only the Service Book and the Bible. It is difficult to conclude that Cranmer's basic principles have not been maintained in the new services.

If the main departures from Cranmer's work are in the direction of increased freedom of variation, which sometimes results in what is effectively a loss of the structure of the service as conceived by Cranmer (as in the shorter Evensong), it is good to be able to discern some traces of a return to Cranmer's forms. The fact that there has been little change to the structure of the core of the services from that of those in the 1549 book is testimony to the enduring value of Cranmer's work. It is in the penitential introduction and the intercessory prayers after the Third Collect that the most substantial revision of detailed content has been made. In one detail there is a happy return to the actual form of Cranmer – in the unison saying or singing of the *Gloria Patri* in the opening responses. A few of the detailed changes are of such a happy nature that one could imagine Cranmer himself making them had he lived to refine his work further after the forms of the 1552 book. The change in the position of Psalm 100 to its new role as an alternative invitatory psalm, the interchange of the positions of the *Benedictus* and the *Te Deum Laudamus* so that the former forms a bridge between the Old and New Testament readings analogous to that formed by the *Magnificat* at Evensong, and the reintroduction of the *Gloria in excelsis* as a canticle at Matins all seem to be developments in the spirit of Cranmer's own work. They show that the guiding principles by which he did his detailed work are still alive in the minds of the liturgical revisers who produced the *Alternative Service Book*.

Are there any further developments which might be desirable? Any positive answer to such a question must be tentative and can hardly be more than an expression of personal opinion. Three very different suggestions may perhaps be mentioned. One of the changes in the provisions of the *Alternative Service Book* is that of an alternative scheme for the use of the Psalter at the daily services. This scheme has a number of merits, but it may also be criticised at a number of points. Two in particular may be mentioned. The average amount of psalmody used at any one service is considerably less than the average amount in Cranmer's monthly scheme, and it is interesting that most cathedrals have adhered to Cranmer's scheme for the Psalter even when following the lectionary of the *Alternative Service Book*. The other point is that, like Cranmer's scheme, it follows the numerical order of the Psalms exactly. Lectionaries since 1922 have claimed freedom from the order of the biblical books. Is it not time to ask whether for liturgical purposes an order of the Psalms different from the numerical order might be preferable?[11]

A second suggestion will appear even more radical, and to some readers may appear to conflict with one of Cranmer's five basic principles. There is however something to be said for a rubric allowing the reading of a non-biblical lection at the point where the preaching of a sermon is permitted. One thinks particularly of the anthology *From the Fathers to the Churches*, edited by Brother Kenneth CGA,[12] which is essentially an adaptation for Anglican purposes of the non-biblical lection from the modern Roman Catholic Office of Readings. The Anglican adaptation secures Cranmer's principle of conformity with scriptural doctrine. Even if this practice were adopted mainly by clergy saying the office privately it could be an enrichment, and its ecumenical significance is obvious.

A third suggestion is much more modest, and consists simply of the possibility of including some of the other ancient morning and evening collects as alternatives to the Third Collects. This would be an extension of the scope of variable forms analogous to that now provided for the canticles. These suggestions, however, must await the time when further revision of the *Alternative Service Book* services is felt to be desirable. Most English Anglicans at present feel the need for a period of stability and the opportunity to become familiar with the new forms before embarking on further changes.

The noted liturgist E. C. Ratcliff, in a lecture delivered in connection with the fourth centenary of Cranmer's death in 1956, had this to say of his liturgical work:

Whatever the defects of his two Prayer Books, Cranmer's liturgical achievement, considered against the limitations which beset him, is nothing short of the prodigious ... In his liturgy he bequeathed to the newly reformed English Church an instrument of worship which was to ensure to it a principle of life, and which also, in its remarkable combination of the traditional with the contemporary, of the old with the new, was to be not the least important factor in imparting to Anglican Christianity its distinctive stamp.[13]

The extent to which his forms of the daily services remain the basis of those of the *Alternative Service Book* and the fact that a weekday Evensong at many English cathedrals today is minimally different from the order of the 1549 book (particularly if a Tudor setting of the responses is used) are the best testimonies to the creative nature and lasting value of his work.

Bibliography

J. H. Blunt, *The Annotated Book of Common Prayer* (London, 1884).

F. E. Brightman, *The English Rite*, I (London, 1915).

E. Cardwell, *The Two Books of Common Prayer, set forth by authority of Parliament in the reign of King Edward the Sixth*, second edition (Oxford, 1841).

G. J. Cuming, *The Durham Book* (London, 1961, repr. 1975); *A History of Anglican Liturgy* (London, 1969); *The Godly Order*, Alcuin Club Collections 65 (London, 1983).

J. Dowden, *The Workmanship of the Prayer Book* (London, 1899); *Further Studies in the Prayer Book* (London, 1908).

J. E. Hunt, *Cranmer's First Litany, 1544 and Merbecke's Book of Common Prayer Noted, 1550* (London, 1939).

R. C. D. Jasper and P. F. Bradshaw, *A Companion to the Alternative Service Book* (London, 1986).

J. W. Legg, *Cranmer's Liturgical Projects*, Henry Bradshaw Society, Vol. L (London, 1915).

F. Procter and W. H. Frere, *A New History of the Book of Common Prayer*, (London, repr. 1949).

E. C. Ratcliff, 'The Choir Offices', in *Liturgy and Worship*, edited by W. K. Lowther Clarke and C. Harris (London,

1932, repr. 1964), pp. 257–95; 'The Liturgical Work of Archbishop Cranmer', *Journal of Ecclesiastical History*, 7 (1956), pp. 189–203, reprinted in E. C. Ratcliff, *Liturgical Studies* (London, 1976), pp. 184–202.

Notes

1. See e.g. Cuming, *Godly Order*, chapter 1.
2. *Life and Liturgy* (London, 1956, repr. 1978), p. 47. I owe this reference to A Religious of C.S.M.V., *The Work of God*, Studies in Christian Worship III (London, 1964), p. 48.
3. Such analyses may be found in several of the works mentioned above, to which my indebtedness will be apparent.
4. Cited from *The World's Classics 303* (London, 1927, repr. 1956), p. 302.
5. Compare Cosin's Note S III cited in Cuming, *Durham Book*, p. 83.
6. *History*, p. 55.
7. Cited in Procter and Frere, *History*, p. 42.
8. Some details are given in Cuming, *Godly Order*, pp. 23–5.
9. Ed. R. C. D. Jasper (London, 1968).
10. London, 1977.
11. See further my article 'The Psalms at the Daily Services', *The Churchman*, 89 (1975), pp. 267–75.
12. London, 1983.
13. *Liturgical Studies*, pp. 198–9 (=JEH 7, pp. 202–3).

V

Cranmer's Pastoral Offices: Origin and Development
Kenneth W. Stevenson

It is a well known fact of life, when liturgy is under consideration, that people tend to be at their most conservative when the church touches them at critical points in the life-cycle. Thus, we must not be too surprised if, when looking at Cranmer's Pastoral Offices, we find a discreet blend of ancient and modern (at least as far as Cranmer perceived both those qualities). The *Book of Common Prayer* (1549) contains both a 'Forme of Solemnization of Matrymonie', 'The Order for the Visitation of the Sicke, and the Communion of the Same', together with 'The Ordre for the Buriall of the Dead'.[1] It is significant that the far left wing of the Reformation came to regard marriage as a purely civil ordinance (as it came to be in the time of the Long Parliament); visiting the sick at best a marginal exercise, requiring no proper liturgical provision; and burying the dead as no more and certainly no less than putting the body underground, without so much as a liturgical farewell. In this little foray into liturgical history, we shall outline Cranmer's 1549 rites, in their origins and intentions; we shall then go on to discuss what happened to them, up to and including 1662; finally, we shall attempt to take a wider view and see them in the perspective afforded by the gap between our time and his, and, of course, take into account some of the thinking behind contemporary liturgical reforms. Whatever Cranmer might or might not have thought of the *Alternative Service Book* (1980), we may be sure of one thing: he would without doubt have been on the side of change.

The Prayer Book of 1549

Geoffrey Cuming once observed that 'The Form of Solemnisation of Matrimony follows the Sarum service with only minor rearrangements and alternations.'[2] It is certainly true that the 1549 marriage rite expresses many of the insights of medieval English nuptial liturgy. In our own study, we took care to note that, for Cranmer, the role of the priest is all-important.[3] In the Sarum rite the priest is, in all essentials, the president of the rite, standing by while the couple make their vows to each other,[4] in the presence of the Church, and then proceeding to celebrate the Eucharist, with the customary ceremonial associated with the nuptial blessing. What Cranmer does is to adapt many of the Latin prayers so that they speak of marriage in relational terms, and that means (among other things) having marriage prayers that bless the bride *and* the groom throughout (the Latin nuptial blessing had for centuries blessed only the bride, an inequality recently wrestled with by the Roman revisers after the Second Vatican Council).[5] Significantly, the first part of the Sarum rite was conducted in the vernacular, so that Cranmer's work was done for him. A few changes are made to the vows, for example, 'to love and to cherish' is added, perhaps suggesting the insights of a now married Archbishop; and the clause 'if holy church it will ordain' is replaced by 'according to God's holy ordinance', thus downgrading the sacramental status of marriage, though keeping it at the level of an important feature of the Church's life. At the end of the service comes the ominous direction that 'the new married persons (the same day of their marriage) must receive the holy communion', but there is no provision of Propers for a nuptial Eucharist. None the less, the sources Cranmer uses are predominantly medieval. After the couple have made their vows, the priest quotes Matthew 19.6 ('Those whom God hath joined together. . .') as a comment on what has taken place. Unlike many continental Catholic rites, the medieval Sarum rite

gives the priest no special formula to bind the couple
together. Here, Cranmer judiciously supplies Scripture,
inspired by Hermann Von Wied's *Consultation*. At root,
the conservatism shows through. The priest, instead of
meeting the couple at the door, meets them at the head
of the nave; part two of the service still takes place
before the altar; but the new service involves no prayers
at home.

The Visitation and Communion of the Sick results in a
similar compression.[6] The medieval services for visiting
the sick led *via* the Penitential Psalms into the private
confession and absolution, followed by extreme unction, communion from the reserved sacrament, and the
commendation of the dying. Originally, these rites were
separate, since their purposes were distinct. Cranmer
begins with Psalms 143 (i.e. the *last* of the Seven Penitential Psalms) after the greeting of Peace. Instead of nine
collects, there are two, adapted from two of the medieval Latin ones. The priest then exhorts the sick person
towards faith, in a lengthy mini-homily, which naturally
leads into the affirmation of baptismal vows. (Cranmer
expects the sick person to make more responses – the
medieval formula has merely '*credo firmiter in omnibus*'!)*
Everything is geared towards building up the faith of the
believer. Confession may now be heard privately (it is
optional), and the form of absolution unequivocally for-
gives the penitent with an 'I absolve thee' text, as found
in medieval Sarum. Why did Cranmer use such a priestly
convention? The question has become controversial in
England in recent years, because even though such a
text is to be found in the Prayer Book, it is not able
to commend itself to modern Protestant liturgists.[7] Perhaps Cranmer deliberately inserted it here because of
the intimacy of the pastoral context: an individual penitent opening his/her heart out. I doubt if there is a
self-conscious residual Catholicism about it. The rite
leads into Psalm 71, which began the office of Extreme
Unction; but before anointing the person (which is

---

*I firmly believe in it all.

optional, like private confession earlier), the priest says a quasi-blessing, based on scriptural texts, to confirm once more the faith of the believer. The anointing (of forehead or breast, not of seven different parts) is accompanied by a somewhat self-conscious formula, as if Cranmer were a little nervous about keeping it.[8] Psalm 13, a psalm of trust, follows appropriately. For the Communion, reservation is permitted, if from a Eucharist on the same day (this would count as 'extended Communion' in modern parlance[9]), but if there is to be a celebration, Propers are provided, as well as a way of abbreviating the rite. In some respects, celebrating the Eucharist in someone's home would have marked the most radical departure from tradition in this package of rites for the sick. There is no concession to those who would like prayers for the dying.

The Funeral rite once more compresses into a short space what would have been phased through Vespers of the Dead (in the house of the deceased), procession to church, Matins and Mass in church, procession to the grave, the committal, and procession back to the church.[10] Realising some flexibility is in order, Cranmer begins at the 'church stile', and his rite consists only of three sections, procession, committal, and service in church (the service in church may precede committal). Drastic simplification is the order of the day, and this is hardly surprising in view of the Reformation's general protest against late medieval liturgies of death.[11]

The procession moves to the strains of the now well known 'Sentences', so familiar to its contemporary hearers today that the theological impact Cranmer perhaps intended may be somewhat muted. God is a God of the living, and of faith, and while sadness is the mood of the occasion, the backdrop must be the Resurrection of Christ. The committal begins with some adapted material from medieval sources, but the formula recited by the priest takes as its inspiration the Sarum *'commendo animam'* (uttered also by the priest); however, it speaks directly about the hope of the resurrection of the body. Curiously, another commendation follows, as if repeating the act, and a collect concludes this part of the series. Psalm 116 leads the procession into church, where I Corinthians 15 is the lesson, and the office ends with some *preces* and another collect, again on the theme of thanksgiving and resurrection. A Proper for Holy Communion follows, the epistle taken from the Requiem Mass formula (I Thess. 4), but the Gospel is new (John 6, 37–40). Theologically, the main themes absent from this scheme are praying for the departed, so that their sins may be forgiven. Instead, the congregation gives thanks for the Easter faith. Once again, Cranmer's theological rationale is visible beneath the traditional literary dressing and liturgical conventions that have survived.[12]

Reactions to 1549

Whether 1549 was intended as a *ballon d'essai*, to lead deliberately into an intended more radical revision in 1552, the fact remains that some of the traditional features retained in 1549 disappear in the intervening years. The marriage rite retains the ring (even though some Protestants, notably Calvinists dislike it as popish), though provision for the giving of other tokens (allowed in 1549) is deleted. Mention of Tobias and Sarah (from Tobit, in the Apocrypha) also disappears from prayer. Otherwise there is little change at all. Martin Bucer liked the idea of Communion at marriage.[13]

In the Office for the Sick, however, there are some drastic alterations. The Psalm disappears at the beginning. Anointing is omitted (Bucer did not approve, even though he knew its Scriptural warrant[14]); and Communion can only be administered at a full celebration – no reservation from the sacrament in church. For the Funeral rite,[15] everything takes place at the graveside, and the Proper for Holy Communion goes, because Bucer (and others) disliked the principle of celebrating the Eucharist 'for' the deceased, or at least in a way that would allow folk who wanted requiem masses to have a service that could be understood as such.

The Prayer Book of 1662

The intervening century saw considerable liturgical restlessness, not only with the Commonwealth and outlawing of the Prayer Book, but also in the acceptance of the new rites among ordinary people. For example, John Cosin observed that the custom of giving coins at marriage, along with a ring, survived in the (conservative) North East.[16] (The writer experienced it in twentieth-century rural Lincolnshire.) It would be interesting to know how the detailed alterations between 1549 and 1552 to the Office for the Sick were actually digested by parishioners in different parts of the country. Eucharists were celebrated in commemoration of departed notables in the time of Elizabeth I.[17]

What did 1662 do to Cranmer's pastoral offices? For Matrimony, the alterations were few and far between. The rubrics are tightened up; the couple must kneel down for the prayer after they are declared man and wife; and the concluding direction about Communion at marriage is softened, so that the couple are recommended to receive 'at the time of their marriage, or at the first opportunity after their marriage'. The weak ending to Cranmer's marriage rite (it only really works if it leads straight into a Eucharist) is only resolved with the 1689 *Book of Comprehension*'s suggestion of a collect and blessing.[18]

For the Offices of the Sick,[19] minor adjustments are made to the substance of the rite. The most important, however, come at the end, for the series ends with the Aaronic blessing, and the addition of four prayers, for a sick child, for a sick person when there is no hope of recovery, the commendation of a departing soul, and a prayer for a person troubled in mind or conscience. It is significant that these are the four concerns that are noticeably lacking in Cranmer's own rites, in 1549 and

1552, and their inclusion in the Restoration Book betrays no mainstream Protestant sensitivities. The Funeral service was restructured,[20] so that the church service preceded the graveside rite, as (apparently) had often been the case. Here, perhaps, was an example of Cranmer's ideals not meeting popular usage. As with the Offices for the Sick, which lacked a liturgical full-stop in 1552 and got one in 1662, so with the Funeral rite; 1662 gives it the Grace at the end.

Reappraisal

It is hard to comment adequately upon a set of services that are so much bound up with the culture that produced them – thoroughly post-medieval in their style and theology. Marriage, sickness and death are all handled with extreme care. Even after the alterations of the Restoration, Cranmer's rationale, use of sources, and theological convictions shine through. As Geoffrey Cuming once wrote: 'Cranmer's service [i.e. the Burial Office] shows again his extraordinary skill in picking out small portions of a lengthy whole and welding them into a convincing unity.'[21]

That 'unity' is not without bathos and paradox. The priest is still the focal point in acting out a kind of drama. He leads bride and groom to the altar – but there is probably seldom a Communion. Cranmer has the option of taking a sick person through an elaborate set of minor offices that now really do feel like different courses that are part of a main meal – yet anointing is deleted in 1552, and Communion was probably only celebrated for the dying who were both devout and confirmed (not always the same thing!). He could see beneath the multiplicity of medieval offices for the dead a keen and acute awareness of the need to cope with the tragedy of death by going through different phases – yet the phases *he* worked out in 1549 required the deletion of eucharistic worship and a wholesale reshaping in 1662. On that score, one is left with the impression that great liturgical revisers may never see their most cherished assumptions working out in practice as long as there is room for improvements, afterthoughts, and the general quest for that bugbear of all good liturgy – 'relevance'.

We may note that some of the 1549 material which disappeared in 1552 reappeared in later centuries. The Non-Jurors were not averse to anointing,[22] the Tractarians liked nuptial Eucharists,[23] and many a twentieth century Prayer Book from other Provinces of the Anglican Communion found it needful to supplement Cranmer's rich prose, resorting to a stronger theology of commending the departed to God's mercy, rather than the somewhat bald statement of resurrection hope.[24] Martin Luther's conviction that the departed 'sleep' until the day of the resurrection (a theme found in some medieval Offices of the Dead)[25] showed a fruitful back door into some of the pastoral concerns of the medievals, while avoiding the overtly judgemental aspects of the theology which undergirded their pastoral practice. Liturgical history, as always, is full of ironies.

Did Cranmer know what he was doing? The answer must be 'Yes'. At no point are Reformation theological principles of the 'Centre-Left' betrayed, and we may hazard a guess that the 'Centre-Right' were happy with what they got, too. One only has to look at the lists of sources compiled by generations of Prayer Book commentators to see that those sources, whether real or imagined, at no point dictate the 'tunes' to be sung by the rite in question.[26] If one is to award marks in some sort of assessment, the writer has to admit that, for him, the order of merit is the same as the order in which the services appear. Marriage must come first – a veritable masterpiece, which has so much of creative continuity about it, yet which sorts out some of the medieval muddle. The Offices for the Sick come second, even though they sadly lose the anointing of the sick (what would have happened had Bucer *liked* anointing, but *condemned* nuptial Eucharists?). And for all his stress on the resurrection hope at funerals, Cranmer cannot quite cope with the transition from this life to the next; there is too much

of a dichotomy between those who mourn and the one
who has gone before in faith. On the other hand, many
a contemporary twentieth-century 'Paschal' funeral is so
jolly in its assertion of Jesus Christ's conquest of sin and
death that there is no room for plain, human mourning.

That brings in another factor – comparison between
Cranmer's work and that of twentieth-century revision.
Such comparisons are inevitably unfair because of the
very different worlds in which the respective rites were
written. Who would dare to compare the Gregorian
Sacramentary's eucharistic rite as it was actually used in
the seventh century at Rome, with the Tridentine Mass
of 1570 as celebrated in a side chapel of a French cathedral (perhaps by an unwilling priest who would rather
be saying his own, local rite anyway)? None the less, the
comparison must be made, if only to make the point that
the liturgy, unlike the Bible, does not have canonical status, and therefore one must expect it to change, preferably more than once in every 400 years. The fact remains that, at the Restoration, Cranmer's rites, in adapted
form, assumed an importance, a definitive form, of such
a kind as to remove the possibility of any other edition
being promulgated within the Church of England again.
(Until the accession of Charles II, every Protestant
monarch had brought in a new Prayer Book, although
the alterations were minimal.)

The basic comparison must be based on the changed
sociological condition of both pastor and people in the
ensuing centuries. Anthony Russell[27] has shown how
the professionalism of the clergy suddenly became more
marked in the course of the nineteenth century and then
has declined in the course of the present one. Today's
priest is sometimes to be found surrounded by talented
and trained lay assistants, eager to help with marriage
preparation, bereavement counselling and the like; and
the visitation of the sick, in whatever form, is frequently
the privilege of such lay ministers, whether in praying
with the sick, giving them Communion (albeit from the
reserved sacrament) or in assisting with the laying on of
hands and anointing.

With the sociological changes have also come developments in theology. Not that today's revised rites invari-
ably or successfully express these theological changes,
nor is it suggested that all the changes are for the good.
It is a fact that we need a new marriage rite that better
expresses the *passage* from betrothal to marriage (and
thus holds together both the darkness and the light
of that way of living), instead of cramming twenty-five
minutes of false happiness into a Saturday afternoon.
We also need new rites for visiting the sick that speak
more of healing and less of illness as a thunderbolt from
heaven. (One of the additions to the second prayer near
the start of the Visitation rite in 1662 is the petition,
'Sanctify, we beseech thee, this thy fatherly correction
to *him*; that the sense of *his* weakness may add strength
to *his* faith, and seriousness to *his* repentance. . . .'[28])
We also need new rites for funerals that somehow
grip the people of God as they mourn their loss, give
thanks for a life that has not ended, commend a loved
one to the arms of a merciful Redeemer, and somehow do all of that with tears of sadness and smiles of
hope.[29]

Cranmer's genius lay as much in handling sources and
language as in his understanding of people's needs and
the processes through which they must pass at crucial
stages in their development as human beings in the sight
of God.[30] Anglicans have a great deal for which to be
thankful in an Archbishop who knew from first-hand
experience each one of these pastoral offices. In today's
much changed world, the key to how we use him aright
in our generation may well lie in those very needs and
processes. Whatever may have been the liturgical *praxis*
up and down the country of Cranmer's liturgical *theoria,*
whether in solemnising marital unions, ministering to
the sick, or celebrating Christian death, his pastoral
offices certainly stand in sharp contrast to the clinical,
privatised and attenuated 'occasional offices' that have
evolved in religious consumerism today, against which
our (not entirely satisfactory) revised liturgies, with their
corporatist focus, are an eloquent protest, following as

they do in their own way in the master-liturgist's footsteps.

Notes

1. Comparative texts and sources listed in F.E.Brightman, *The English Rite*, II (London, 1915), pp. 800–79.
2. G.J.Cuming, *A History of Anglican Liturgy* (London, 1982), p. 63.
3. K.W.Stevenson, *Nuptial Blessing; A Study of Christian Marriage Rites*, Alcuin Club Collections 64 (London, 1982), pp. 134ff.; and Stevenson, *To Join Together; The Rite of Marriage*, Studies in the Reformed Rites of the Catholic Church V (New York, 1987), pp. 91ff.
4. K.W.Stevenson, 'The Marriage Rites of Mediaeval Scandinavia – a Fresh Look', *Ephemerides Liturgicae* 97 (1983), pp. 550–7; and Stevenson, 'Marriage Liturgy: Lessons from History', *Anglican Theological Review* 68 (1986), pp. 225–240.
5. K.W.Stevenson, '"Benedictio nuptialis": Reflections on the Blessing of The Bride and Groom in Some Western Mediaeval Marriage Rites', *Ephemerides Liturgicae* 93 (1979), pp. 457–78.
6. See text in Brightman, op. cit., pp. 818–47. See also Cuming, op. cit., pp. 63f.
7. See Colin Buchanan, *Latest Liturgical Revision in the Church of England: 1978–1984*, Grove Liturgical Study 39 (Bramcote, 1984), pp. 29–33.
8. C.W.Gusmer, *The Ministry of Healing in the Church of England: An Ecumenical-Liturgical Study*, Alcuin Club Collections 56 (Great Wakering, 1974) pp. 70ff.
9. D.Smethurst, *Extended Communion: An Experiment in Cumbria*, Grove Worship Series 96 (Bramcote, 1986).
10. Cuming, op. cit., pp. 64ff. See text in Brightman, op. cit., pp. 848–79.
11. G.Rowell, *The Liturgy of Christian Burial*, Alcuin Club Collections 59 (London, 1977), pp. 74ff.
12. See Stevenson, *Nuptial Blessing*, p. 140.
13. E.C.Whitaker, *Martin Bucer and the Book of Common Prayer*, Alcuin Club Collections 55 (Great Wakering, 1974), p. 124. He also thought that Cranmer's 'three reasons' for marriage ought to be reversed so that the order is companionship, sexual union, children, instead of the other way round. Many a pastor talking over marriage with a couple has had reason to side with Bucer.
14. Whitaker, op. cit., pp. 124ff.
15. Whitaker, op. cit., pp. 126f.
16. G.J.Cuming, *The Durham Book* (London, 1961), p. 237, 'And some marvel it is, that those Words, *and other Gifts of Gold and Silver*, should be taken out of the book in the fifth of K. Edward, whereas

Bucer liked them so well: but it is a general Custom still to observe this Order in the North part of the Kingdom.'

17. See Rowell, op. cit., pp. 87ff.
18. See Stevenson, *Nuptial Blessing*, p. 146.
19. See text in Brightman, op. cit., pp. 818ff. The Aaronic blessing, beloved by the other Reformers, was not used by Cranmer, and only appeared in 1662 in the Visitation of the Sick, and also, in a shortened form, in the Commination Service.
20. See text in Brightman, op. cit., pp. 848ff., and also Cuming, *A History of Anglican Liturgy*, pp. 111f. See also G.J. Cuming, *A Godly Order*, Alcuin Club Collections 65 (London, 1983), pp. 153f.; restructuring appears to have been at Sanderson's instigation.
21. Cuming, *Godly Order*, p. 65.
22. See Gusmer, op. cit., pp. 75ff.
23. See Stevenson, *Nuptial Blessing*, p. 236, n. 38, for details.
24. See Rowell, op. cit., pp. 93ff.
25. Correspondence with Knud Ottosen, Department of Church History, Århus University, Denmark (part of forthcoming major study).
26. For example, in the marriage rite, the priest asks 'Who giveth this woman to be married to this man?' immediately prior to the vows; no such corresponding formula occurs in the medieval English rites, except the *York Manual*, where the priest asks, 'Who gives me this wife?' It would seem that Cranmer wanted to make a point of the giving of the bride, but wished to avoid upgrading the role of the priest. See Stevenson, *Nuptial Blessing*, p. 135.
27. A.Russell, *The Clerical Profession* (London, 1980), esp. pp. 76ff.
28. See Brightman, op. cit., p. 823.
29. See Rowell, op. cit., p. 114.
30. To reshape marriage rites around betrothal and celebration of marriage is argued in my article, 'Van Gennep and Marriage – Strange Bedfellows? A Fresh Look at the Rites of Marriage', *Ephemerides Lithurgicae 100* (1986), pp. 138–51; and, at greater length, in my *To Join Together* (see note 3 above).

VI

'And with thy Holy Spirite and Worde': Further Thoughts on the Source of Cranmer's Petition for Sanctification in the 1549 Communion Service
Bryan D. Spinks

In the reformulation of the Roman *canon missae* in the 1549 Communion Service, before the institution narrative, and corresponding to the *Quam oblationem*, Cranmer gave the following petition:

> Heare us (O merciful Father) we beseech thee: and with thy holy spirite and worde, vouchsafe to bl+esse and sanc+tifie these thy gyftes, and creatures of bread and wyne, that they maie be vnto vs the body and bloude of thy moste derely beloved sonne Jesus Christe.

On account of the reference here to the Holy Spirit it was commonly assumed by earlier commentators that this petition was inspired by the epiklesis found in the Eastern anaphoras, and in many of the Mozarabic and Gallican anaphoras. Wheatley, for example, commenting on the petition, wrote that it is a particular petition for the descent of the Holy Ghost upon the sacramental elements such as 'was always inserted in the Primitive Forms'.[1] John Johnson, noting the invocation of the Holy Spirit in primitive liturgies, asserted:

> Our first Reformers here in *England* restored this most pious and Apostolical Prayer (tho' they placed it before the Words of Institution, contrary to the ancient Method) but in the Review of our *Liturgy*, two or three Years after, it was wholly omitted.[2]

A similar judgement was made by Brett,[3] and, for example, by Scudamore[4] and Gasquet and Bishop.[5] In the *English Rite* F.E. Brightman gave as parallels (and possible sources) the epiklesis from Byzantine Basil and the *Quam oblationem,* and described the 1549 petition as 'combining the Eastern with the Western conception of the "form" of consecration by the addition of the Invocation of the Holy Ghost, while avoiding the difficulties this might involve for a Western by placing the Invocation before, instead of after, the recital of the Institution.'[6] After Brightman a host of commentators have, with or without qualification, echoed this view, including Clarke and Harris,[7] Frere,[8] Bard Thompson,[9] and at one time, apparently, Geoffrey Cuming,[10] and most recently Marion J. Hatchett.[11]

Although Cranmer does seem to have been acquainted with the liturgies of Byzantine Basil and St Chrysostom, and just possibly St James,[12] the actual use he made of these seems to have been minimal. As regards the anaphoral epiklesis, Cranmer's petition is markedly different from the alleged sources. It comes before the narrative of institution (as in Egypt, but unknown to Cranmer) and not after; it links word and Spirit; and the Father, not the Spirit as in Basil, is the author of the sanctification. Furthermore many commentators relying on the authority of *The English Rite* have failed to notice that in an article in 1927 Brightman retracted his earlier confidence expressed in 1915.[13] In that article Brightman listed a series of Western comments on the Eucharist where the Holy Spirit is linked with the consecration of the elements. Amongst the more notable examples is a passage from Florus of Lyons[14]; a passage from Gratian (attributed to St Augustine) – '*quia non in merito consecrantis sed in verbo efficatur Creatoris et in virtute Spiritus Sancti*'* – which found its way into the Sarum, Hereford and York Breviaries for Corpus Christi;[15] and Durandus of Mende in his *Rationale* where in discussing the *Quam oblationem* he refers to the agency of the Holy Spirit[16]. All of these were probably known to Cranmer.

---

*because it is not effected by the merit of the one consecrating, but by the word of the Creator and by virtue of the Holy Spirit.

Frere also mentioned some of these earlier Western writers,[17] but expressed the view that at the time of the Reformation, they were dead voices. Against this Ratcliff pointed to the popular collection of sermons by John Mirk, *Festyuall*, which between 1483 and 1532 went through some nineteen editions. The book was rather like a medieval forerunner to the sermon service of John Paul the Preachers Press, either to give the priest some ideas, or to provide a ready made sermon. The number of editions suggest that it was a widely used book. In the sermon on Corpus Christi, Mirk described the sacrament as 'goddes owne body in fourme of breed made by the uertue of crystes wordes that the preste sayth & by werkynge of ye holy gooste'.[18] Such an association of Spirit and word was therefore commonplace in Tudor England, and thus there is no necessity at all to look East for the source of the petition. However, Brightman was still of the opinion that the words 'bless and sanctify' were derived from the anaphora of Byzantine Basil. In an unpublished paper, Ratcliff observed that the words seem to be merely the English rendering of a common formulary found in the *Benedictiones diversae* of the Medieval Manuals and Pontificals, where *bene+dicere et sancti+ficare* or *bene+dic et sancti+fica* are found. In fact, some forms give an almost exact parallel to the opening words of the 1549 petition:

> Exaudi, Domine, preces nostras, clementissime Pater, et haec purificanda vasa . . . bene+dicere et sancti+ficare digneris . . .

Ratcliff concluded that for the whole petition Cranmer 'looked no further than the familiar tradition of the West'.[19]

The cumulative evidence presented by Brightman (1927) and Ratcliff makes it almost impossible to make any convincing appeal to the Eastern anaphoras as the source and inspiration of this petition in the 1549 Communion Service. No word, phrase or idea in the passage lacks a convincing parallel in the familiar Western sources. Furthermore – as for example in the exhortation to the marriage service – Cranmer was quite content to draw upon popular traditional medieval theology. Nevertheless, it must be asked why, in their concern to find verbal parallels, both Brightman and Ratcliff omitted to investigate whether or not the Reformation itself provided possible sources of inspiration. In the unpublished paper already referred to, Ratcliff at one point stated: 'It was Cranmer's aim not merely to provide an English Communion Service, but to provide an English Communion Service embodying sound doctrine as judged by reformed standards.'[20] Were there, therefore, any Reformation precedents of linking Spirit and word in a petition for consecration?

Cranmer was well acquainted with the writings of both Luther and Zwingli.[21] In his Sermon against the Fanatics of 1526 Luther does draw a comparison between the annunciation and incarnation in St Luke's Gospel and the divine action in the Eucharist: 'For as soon as Christ says "This is my body", it is his body through the word and power of the Holy Spirit.'[22] But this is not typical of Luther. His theology is Christocentric, and he is very much a word-man. If Christ said it, that is sufficient. This is reflected in his own Formula Missae and Deutsche Messe, where the words of institution are not accompanied by any petition whatsoever. Zwingli is at first sight more promising. He wrote: 'Before I say anything or listen to the teaching of man, I will first consult the mind of the Spirit of God (Psalm 85): I will hear what God the Lord will speak.'[23] Commenting on this, W.P. Stephens notes that the combination of Spirit and word in Zwingli expresses the fact that it is God who makes the word effective.[24] Thus in expounding Isaiah 59.21 with its reference to the Spirit and word, Zwingli stresses that the Spirit is placed first, for without the Spirit the flesh misunderstands the word. Yet for Zwingli, although the Spirit is operative in the sacraments,[25] his main concern is to stress that the Holy Spirit is necessary for a true understanding of Scripture. The petition to bless and sanctify the elements by Spirit and word is one which would not have suggested itself to him readily. In his Epicheiresis of 1523, in the second prayer of his revised canon, Zwingli's theology gives rise to a very different petition:

Quicken us, therefore, by your Spirit and never deprive us of your word; for your word is the vehicle of your Spirit, and assuredly it will never return to you empty.[26]

Certainly Zwingli's concern for the Spirit and word could have inspired Cranmer, but not obviously so.

Cranmer seems to have been less well acquainted with, or less sympathetic to Calvin's writings on the Eucharist than with either Luther or Zwingli. Nevertheless, he could not have missed Calvin's stress on the importance of the Spirit for understanding the word, and the role of the Spirit in the Eucharist. In the *Institutes* Calvin argues that the word is the promise or seal, but sacraments do not avail one iota without the energy of the Holy Spirit.[27] The words of Christ, 'This is my body', etc., need to be embraced by the meaning which the Spirit of God suggests.[28]

There were, however, two other Reformation theologians of the Reformed school who wrote on the Eucharist, whose views were well known to Cranmer, and who actually assisted with the English reforms: Martin Bucer and Peter Martyr Vermigli.

Bucer arrived in England in 1549, and became Regius Professor of Divinity at Cambridge. Like Calvin, he stressed the importance of the Spirit, and in the *Gospels* (1536) argued that the confirmation of faith rests not on the power of the symbols themselves, but on Christ's power which is dispensed 'by his Spirit through word and sacred symbols'.[29] The sacrament is effective where the Spirit of Christ is at work and the words and visible signs of the sacraments are grasped with faith.[30] In his *Censura* (comments on the 1549 Prayer Book) he criticised the petition since it asked God to bless and sanctify the elements (suggesting transubstantiation) instead of the communicants. He suggested that it should be recast as follows:

Hear us, O merciful Father, bless us and sanctify us by thy Word and Holy Spirit, that with true faith we may receive in these mysteries the body and blood of thy Son to be the food and drink of eternal life.[31]

It is noteworthy that Bucer was content to retain the reference to word and Spirit.

Much more suggestive are the views of the Italian Reformed theologian, Peter Martyr Vermigli. He arrived in England in 1547 and lodged with Cranmer before being appointed Regius Professor of Divinity at Oxford. As a direct result of his lectures on 1 Corithians and the Eucharist, a disputation was held at Oxford in 1549. In the tract and disputation, as in subsequent writings, Martyr stressed the link between consecration of the elements, word and Holy Spirit.[32] In *Disputatio* IV.Q2 he wrote:

> He is able to make common bread and wine a most effectual sacrament . . . such a change in it, in which bread and wine are translated from the natural order, and profane degree in which they were, to a sacramental state and order, both by the work of the Holy Spirit and by the institution of the Lord.

It is interesting to compare this with Cranmer's view of consecration: 'the separation of any thing from a profane and worldly use unto a spiritual and godly use'.[33] Martyr, however, is quite explicit that this is achieved by the work of the Holy Spirit and the words of institution. Cranmer's petition of 1549 could hardly have expressed his view better. Thus in Tract 80 Martyr could say of the efficacy of the sacrament:

> these things are not attributed unto the elements for their own sake, but because of the institution of the Lord, the power of the Holy Spirit, and the plain sense of the words . . .

And in a letter to Bucer (15 June, 1549):

> I acknowledge that we truly receive the thing of the sacrament, that is the body and blood of Christ; but I say thus, as this is done by soul and faith, meanwhile I grant that the Holy Spirit is effectual in the sacraments, by the power of the Spirit and institution of the Lord.[34]

Martyr was still of this view in his work of 1561, *Dialogus de Utraque in Christo natura*.

Martyr was invited to submit notes on the 1549 Prayer Book, but these are no longer extant. One may conjecture

from his writings that he would have been much happier
with the petition than was Bucer. We know that on at least
two points he influenced the 1552 Prayer Book.[35] Did he
influence Cranmer's thoughts for 1549? Is it possible that
his conversations with Cranmer in 1547 and 1548 inspired
Cranmer to include this petition in 1549? Defending Martyr's views against Dr Richard Smith, Cranmer wrote:

> Of Peter Martyr's opinion and judgment in this matter
> [i.e. eucharistic doctrine], no man can better testify than
> I; forasmuch as he lodged within my house long before he
> came to Oxford, and I had with him many conferences in
> that matter, and know that he was then of the same mind
> that he is now, and as he defended after openly in Oxford,
> and hath written in his book.[36]

What can be said with certainty, however, is that in
addition to older Western theologians, and a popular pre-
Reformation sermon, the link between word, Holy Spirit and
sanctification in the Eucharist is also found in the writings
of the Reformation. Since the 1549 Communion Service was
designed to express 'sound doctrine as judged by reformed
standards', these latter may well have been Cranmer's
immediate inspiration. However, although its intended
reformed theology could be expressed and expounded by
someone of the calibre of Peter Martyr, Bishop Gardiner
drew attention to the fact that the doctrine of transubstantiation could also be expressed in similar phraseology. Thus
the reference to sanctification by word and Spirit did not
survive the 1552 revision.

Notes

1. C. Wheatley, *A Rationale Illustration of the Book of Common Prayer of the Church of England* (3rd edition, 1720), p. 289.
2. John Johnson, *The Unbloody Sacrifice* (London, 1714, 1718), Part II, Chap. III, pp. 175–81.
3. Thomas Brett, *A Collection of the Principle Liturgies . . . With a Dissertation . . .* (London, 1720), pp. 126–8.
4. W.E.Scudamore, *Notitia Eucharistica* (London, 1876), pp. 588–9.
5. F.A.Gasquet and E. Bishop, *Edward VI and the Book of Common Prayer* (rev. edn, London, 1928), p. 169.

6. Op. cit. (London, 1915) Vol. 1, p.cvi; cf. Vol. 2, p. 692.
7. 'The Holy Communion Service' in W.K. Lowther Clarke and C. Harris, *Liturgy and Worship* (London, 1932), p. 342.
8. W.H.Frere, *The Anaphora* (London, 1938), p. 196.
9. Bard Thompson, *Liturgies of the Western Church* (New York, 1962), p. 233.
10. G.J. Cuming, *A History of Anglican Liturgy* (1st edn, London, 1969), p. 79. A rather different view is given in *The Godly Order*, Alcuin Club Collection 65 (London, 1983), p. 96.
11. Surprisingly without any qualification, in *The Study of Anglicanism*, edited by Stephen Sykes and John Booty (London and Philadelphia, 1988), p.124.
12. A copy of St James was apparently written for Henry VIII. F. E. Brightman, *Liturgies Eastern and Western* (Oxford, 1896), p. li.
13. F.E.Brightman, 'The New Prayer Book Examined', *Church Quarterly Review* 104(1927), 219–52.
14. *Expositio Missae* 81,84.
15. *Decretum III* de consecr.ii.72.
16. *Rationale* IV. X 1. 10.
17. Frere, op. cit., p. 177.
18. E. C. Ratcliff, 'The English Usage of Eucharistic Consecration 1548–1662' in ed. A. H. Couratin and D.H. Tripp, *Liturgical Studies* (London, 1976), p. 206; *Festyuall* 1508 edition, fol. xlix verso.
19. The paper, which was in the possession of the late A. H. Couratin, has no title, and is hand-written. Abbreviated pieces appear in one or two of Ratcliff's published papers on the Prayer Book, but the paper itself does not seem to have been published.
20. Ibid., p. 9.
21. See Peter Brooks, *Thomas Cranmer's Doctrine of the Eucharist* (London, 1964).
22. WA 19:491; ET in LW 36:341.
23. Z1 377.7–21. Quoted in W.P. Stephens, *The Theology of Huldrych Zwingli* (Oxford, 1986), p. 59.
24. Ibid., p. 135.
25. Ibid., p. 191.
26. R.C.D. Jasper and G. J. Cuming, *Prayers of the Eucharist: Early and Reformed* (3rd edn, New York, 1987), p. 185.
27. *Institutes* 4.14.5,8,9.
28. Ibid., 4.17.25.
29. W.P. Stephens, *The Holy Spirit in the Theology of Martin Bucer* (Cambridge, 1970), p. 255.
30. Ibid.
31. E.C. Whitaker, *Martin Bucer and the Book of Common Prayer*, Alcuin Club Collection 55 (Great Wakering, 1974), pp. 52–4.
32. See Joseph C. McLelland, *The Visible Words of God* (Edinburgh and London, 1957); Salvatore Corda, *Veritas Sacramenti*. A Study in Vermigli's Doctrine of the Lord's Supper (Zurich, 1975). Corda writes: 'Three essential factors, says Vermigli, concur in bringing a

sacrament into existence: Christ's Institution, God's Word, and the power of the Holy Spirit. Should any of these elements be missing, one cannot properly speak of a sacrament any longer' (pp. 107–8).

33. *On the Lord's Supper* (Parker Society, 1844), p. 177.
34. McLelland, op. cit., p. 274.
35. A. Beesley, 'An Unpublished Source of the Book of Common Prayer: Peter Martyr Vermigli's *Adhortatio ad Coenam Domini Mysticam*' in *Journal of Ecclesiastical History* 19(1963), pp. 83–8. See also C. H. Smyth, *Cranmer and the Reformation under Edward VI* (Cambridge, 1926).
36. *On the Lord's Supper* (The Answer to Smith's Preface), p. 374.

VII

The Worthy Communicant
Hugh Bates

Within a year of the death of King Henry VIII, in December 1547, an Act of Parliament[1] was passed enacting that after the first day of May in the following year, no one shall 'by words or otherwise, deprave, contemn, despise or revile the Sacrament'. The Act then goes on to require that the Sacrament 'should be ministered to all Christian people under both kinds, than under the form of bread only'. The connection between these two parts of the Act is not immediately obvious. It was certainly not the intention that there should be a 'free for all' and a general licence for unlimited blasphemy for the next six months! A separate Royal Proclamation had closed that loophole. Rather, it was confidently anticipated that, by May 1548, the form of the administration of the Sacrament would have been publicly and officially established. After this there would be no place for dissent or contradiction as, indeed, there was no place for it now. The sequel suggests that both the theology of the Sacrament as well as the manner of its administration had already been decided. Henceforth, the Sacrament of the Altar was to be, theologically and liturgically, a 'no-go' area. There was to be no more discussion, pamphleteering or controversial preaching. The administration of the Sacrament under both kinds and to all Christian people, and the consequences of this decision which had been made, are now no longer negotiable. This Act may be taken to mark the beginning of the process which culminated in the passing of the Act of Uniformity in January 1549 and the publication of the First Prayer Book of King Edward VI some six months later. The re-formation of the Eucharist was the priority within the larger scheme of the total re-formation of the worship of the English Church, which is arguably

Thomas Cranmer's greatest achievement, and indisputably his most influential.

   The practical problems, alone, that were created by the overturning of the custom of time immemorial would have been enormous: the rearrangement of church space to accommodate the new requirements; perhaps the provision of new communion plate to accommodate the influx of new communicants. If there was nobody to communicate, could there be no celebration? Practically speaking, how was the Communion of the People actually to be administered? The existing Order of the Mass made no provision for it. This problem, at least, was anticipated and answered in *The Order of the Communion*, prefaced by a Royal Proclamation and distributed to schools, colleges and parish churches for use after 1 March, 1548. Before considering the contents of the Order, it is worth noticing the deliberate rapidity with which the reform gathered momentum. It is remarkable by the standards of modern liturgical revision, the more so when we remember the very rudimentary means of production and distribution of material in the sixteenth century, quite apart from the work of preparing what was to be produced. This is especially true of the 1549 Prayer Book, a detailed and complicated piece of work by any standards, but one which does not bear the marks of hasty composition. To a lesser degree the same is also true of the 1548 Order. Rather less than four months between the passing of the Act of Parliament and its delivery, hot from the press, to the altars of parish churches, is altogether too unrealistic a time scale for both composition and production. The implication is that both the policy of the reform of worship and also the programme of its execution had already been decided by the end of 1547, and much of the material of the projected prayer book was, at the very least, in an advanced stage of preparation. Cranmer himself is known to have been interested in the revision of the Daily Office as early as 1543/4.[2] The Reformers had the advantage over liturgical revisers of later generations in that their proposals were introduced and carried not synodically, but by King in Parliament. While the Convocations appear to have been consulted on questions of practical detail and to sound out opinion, the main proposals were not themselves open for discussion or amendment. This procedure leaves much less to chance, and is far less open to the tactics of delay or obstruction. *The Order of the Communion* of 1548 is not, therefore, to be seen as an emergency or stop-gap response by the Church to the requirement of the Act of Parliament. It is the liturgical expression of the intention of the Act, and furnishes the rationale of it in such a way that the communicant who uses the Order attentively will be left in no doubt about what he is doing and what is happening to him when he receives the Sacrament faithfully and devoutly.

In the brief months between its publication and the introduction of the 1549 Prayer Book, the Order was used for the administration of the Communion of the People after the Communion of the Priest at the end of the Latin Mass. Part of its contents are so familiar as to be known by heart by all practising Anglicans of mature years: the Invitation – 'ye that do truly and earnestly . . .' – the Confession, Absolution, Comfortable Words, Prayer of Humble Access, and Words of Administration, 'The Body (or Blood) of our Lord Jesus Christ which was given (or shed) for thee preserve thy body and soul unto everlasting life'. After Communion the people depart with the familiar blessing of the Prayer Book. Much less familiar, though, even to the most regular worshippers, are the preceding Exhortations, which have long been quietly neglected. The first is the notice to be given on the Sunday or Holy Day beforehand of the intention to celebrate:

Upon daye   next I do entēd by Goddes grace to offer to all such as shalbe godly disposed, the most cōfortable Sacramēt of the body and the bloud of Christ, to be taken in remembraunce of his most fruictful and glorious passion.

The intending communicants are then reminded of the benefits of the Passion, our sins are forgiven and we are

made partakers of the Kingdom of Heaven. Of these benefits

> we be assured ... if we come to the said Sacrament,
> with hartie repentaunce of our offences ... and most
> harty thākes to be geuen to Almightye God, for his
> infinite mercy and benefites, geuen and bestowed
> upon us his unworthye servauntes ... for whome he
> hathe not only geuen his body to death and shed his
> bloud, but also doth vouchesaufe in a Sacrament and
> misterye to geue us his body and bloud spiritually to
> fede and drynke upon.

The Exhortation then goes on to stress the crucial importance of worthy receiving,

> ... the Sacrament, being so divine and holy a thyng to
> them which receaue it worthely, & so daungerous to
> them that will presume to take the same unworthely. ·

The communicant is therefore bidden to prepare himself by examination of conscience, repentance and
amendment of life, and above all to ensure that he
is reconciled in love and charity with his neighbours.
For those unable to quieten their consciences, either
the counsel of the priest, and possibly also the ministry
of absolution through auricular confession, is strongly
recommended. But those who are not so troubled are
assured that the General Confession provided by the
Order will be perfectly adequate. The one is not to judge
the other.
    On the day of Communion the second Exhortation
repeats the same theme, warning the people against
coming to the altar casually or unprepared,

> for as the benefite is great, if with a penitent harte,
> and liuely faith we receue this holi Sacrament (for
> then we spiritually eate the flesh of Christe and drinke
> his bloud: Then we dwell in Christ and Christ in us
> ...) so is the daunger greate, if we receiue the same

> unworthely, for then we become guilty of the body
> and bloud of Christ our sauior, we eate & drinke our
> awne dampnacion (because we make no difference of
> the Lordes body . . .).

The Exhortation then returns to the subject of the benefits of the Passion and the reason for the institution of
the Sacrament:

> and to thende that we shoulde alwaye remember
> the excedyng loue of our Master and only sauiour
> Jesus Christ thus doīg for us, and the innumerable
> benefites which by his precious bloudsheddyng, he
> hath obteyned for us, he hath left us ī these holy
> misteries as a pledge of his loue, and a contynuall
> remembraunce of thesame, his awne blessed body
> and precious bloud, for us spiritually to fede upon
> . . .

Finally, all obvious and notorious sinners and all who
are not in love and charity, who have still managed to
survive this prolonged assault upon their consciences,
are warned to withdraw. The priest pauses to allow them
to do so, being admonished to take note of any who do,
for future reference. Then turning to those who remain,
he addresses them in the familiar words, 'Ye that do truly
and earnestly repent you of your sins'.

What follows is too well known, as has been said, to
need a detailed description. But a point of interest is the
question of in what sense the absolution is an absolution?
There is a significant difference between the words of
1548 and 1549:

1548 Our blessed Lorde, who hath left power to his Church, to absolve all penitēt synners from their synnes, and to restore to the grace of the heueñly father such as trulie beleue in Christ, haue mercy upon you, pardon and deleuer you from all synnes . . .	1549 Almightie God our heavenly father, who of his great mercie hath promysed forgeuenesse of synnes to all them whiche with hartye repentaunce and true fayth turne unto him: haue mercy upon you, pardon and deleuer you from all youre synnes . . .

The form of 1548 is, superficially at least, more akin
to that of the traditional declaratory absolution. That

of 1549 is far less ambiguous. Here forgiveness is
conditional on the penitent turning to Almighty God
with hearty repentance and true faith. The force of the
Comfortable Words is now fully apparent, assuring the
penitent, by these incontrovertible texts of Scripture, of
God's mercy beyond all shadow of doubt. But these are
already present in 1548, which would indicate that the
same interpretation is to be placed on the Absolution
here as well. Possibly this is only a difficulty for those
who have become accustomed to hearing the Invitation, Confession and Absolution outside the context of
the foregoing Exhortations. At this point the intending
communicant will have known what is expected of him
or her. They will have considered the saving Passion of
Christ, and the nature and purpose of the Sacrament
which they are to receive. In one form or another they
will have made an act of penitence for their past sins.
They will be reconciled to their neighbours in love and
charity. So now they approach the Sacrament, certainly
in no spirit of presumption, but trusting in God's promised mercy. If they can affirm all this of themselves, with
their hands on their hearts as it were, then they are
indeed making a difference of the Lord's body, and they
will truly and spiritually eat the body of Christ and drink
his blood in the Sacrament which he instituted in his holy
Gospel, and commanded us to continue as a perpetual
memory of his precious death until his coming again.

On the surface, and in broad outline, *The Order of
Communion* of 1548 may not be altogether untypical of
what would have happened in the medieval Church
when Communion was administered to the people. This
may have been very much the exception rather than
the rule, but it did happen on occasion and needed to
be accommodated when it did. How this was actually
done was left in large measure to the discretion of
the celebrant. An example of this is to be found in
the Harleian MS 2383.[3] This comprises a vernacular
exhortation, preceded by a form of private confession,
and followed by a long absolution. Here also the stated
requirement for receiving the Sacrament is a proper

faith and hearty penitence leading up to rudimentary general confession. Maskell comments, 'The reader will observe the remarkable similarity of several of the sentences in this exhortation with [sic] that ordered in our present liturgy.' Granted the parliamentary will that the Sacrament should now be administered to all Christian people under both kinds, 1548 or something very like it would have been the natural and obvious way of doing so. What, if anything, has changed? Though the approach to absolution may differ in 1548 and the later Prayer Books, the emphasis on the need for repentance is common to both. Where the Harleian MS and 1548 differ is in their understanding of 'proper faith'. In the former, faith consists in the belief that 'yt ys Godds body, flesche and blode, yn the forme of bred' that is received. In the latter, however, 'liuely faith' is understood in terms of 'the remembraunce of his most fruictful and glorious passion', and of 'the innumerable benefites which by his precious bloudsheddyng he hath obteyned for us'. Moreover, the Sacrament is now carefully and deliberately distinguished from the Passion. It is the remembrance of the Passion but not the Passion itself. Christ has not only given his body to death on the cross and shed his blood for us, *but also* 'doth vouchesaufe in a Sacrament and misterye to geue us his body and bloud spiritually to fede and drynke upon'. The operative word is now 'spiritually', and the spiritual eating and drinking of the body and blood of Christ takes place when the Sacrament is received with a penitent heart and lively faith.

All of this is to be understood in the light of what Cranmer himself says in his *Defence of the true and Catholic Doctrine of the Body and Blood of our Saviour Christ*, published in 1550, and written to confute the four great errors of the papists: Transubstantiation, the Real Presence of Christ in the consecrated elements, that wicked men may eat the Body and Blood of Christ, and the Propitiatory Sacrifice of the Mass. Cranmer sets out to show how Christ is both truly present and received in the Sacrament. First of all he insists that the language

of John chapter 6, for example, about eating the flesh
of the Son of Man and drinking his blood, is not to be
taken literally as physical eating, but figuratively and
sacramentally – nowadays we would say 'parabolically'.

> Christ teacheth us that we receive very bread and wine
> . . . as sacraments to admonish us that as we be fed with
> bread and wine bodily, so we be fed with the very body
> and blood of our Saviour Christ spiritually.[4]

> . . . these speeches 'to eat Christ's body and drink his
> blood', 'to call bread his body and wine his blood', be
> speeches not taken in the proper signification of every
> word, but by translation of these words '*eating*' and
> '*drinking*' from the signification of a corporal thing to
> signify a spiritual thing; and by calling a thing that
> signifieth by the name of the thing that is signified
> thereby.[5]

One cannot help feeling that the thinking and writing of
some contemporary Roman Catholic theologians must
be giving the reforming Archbishop a certain amount
of wry satisfaction![6] It follows that the bread and wine
are 'significant' not for what they are in themselves but as
they are 'consecrated' by their separation from a worldly
use to a spiritual and godly one. The use to which the
bread and wine are to be put will be all important. They
become holy 'when they are separated to that holy use
by Christ's own words, which he spake for that purpose,
saying of the bread, *This is my body*; and of the wine, *This
is my blood*.' This purpose is realised when the bread
and wine are eaten and drunk 'in remembrance of
him', so that 'whosoever with a lively faith doth eat
that bread and drink that wine, doth spiritually eat,
drink, and feed upon Christ sitting in heaven with
his Father.'[7] From this it can be seen how 1548 gives
an altogether different and deeper dimension to the
traditional requirements of faith and repentance before
receiving the Sacrament. It is no longer the implicit
threat that something very unpleasant will happen to

anyone who receives the Sacrament unworthily, a peril which in one way or another had already deterred people from approaching the altar too frequently for over a thousand years.[8] Cranmer is much more precise. Christ is truly and spiritually present where the Sacrament is received worthily. Where it is not so received Christ is not present in any sense whatsoever.

True to Article XXIX Cranmer insists on the impossibility of an evil person being able to receive the body of Christ, directly contradicting St Thomas Aquinas:

> Good and evil men are sharing
> one repast, a doom preparing
> varied as the heart of man.[9]

By contrast, to cite a representative passage,

> all men, good and evil, may with their mouths visibly and sensibly eat the Sacrament of Christ's body and blood; but the very body and blood themselves may not be eaten but spiritually, and that of the spiritual members of Christ, which dwell in Christ and have Christ dwelling in them, by whom they be refreshed and have everlasting life.[10]

The worthy communicant, who 'feeds on him by faith with thanksgiving', is united to Christ and is made 'a very member incorporate' of his mystical body. The unworthy communicant does not and cannot receive the body and blood of Christ. But this is not to say that the act of eating and drinking was simply null and void for him. If he does not 'discern' or 'make a difference of' the body then he is surely eating and drinking damnation to himself. He has not the least understanding of the meaning of 'the body'. His lack of faith and hardness of heart effectively exclude him from having any part in Christ. So, for a wicked man to receive the body of Christ is both a logical and a theological impossibility. If Christ is not truly and spiritually present it must follow that he is truly and spiritually absent. This absence of Christ is nothing more or less than damnation.

Far from being a temporary expedient, *The Order of the Communion* of 1548 became more and more deeply embedded in the Communion services of the two later Prayer Books. In 1549 the Exhortations are placed after the Creed and have been parted from the Invitation, Confession and Absolution which precede the Communion. Now, in the new English Rite, priest and people communicate together. But in the second Prayer Book of 1552 the two parts of the Order are once more reunited. Throughout this process the substance of the hortatory material is largely retained, but adapted and rearranged to match the situation as it developed. For example, the procedure for announcing the intention to celebrate and for repelling notorious sinners has become properly established. Significantly also it has become necessary for the Curate to rebuke the congregation for persistent non-attendance. As ever, devotional habit lags far behind theological progress. By 1552 the private Mass was a thing of the past. Curate and people communicated together or not at all. If at the end of the liturgical marathon of Matins, Litany and Ante-Communion, the parson invited all who truly and earnestly repented to draw near and join him at the Lord's table and nobody approached, that was the end of the business.

What used to be the Canon of the Mass has, in 1552, now been fully incorporated into the 1548 Order which is now the heart and core of the rite, and has been neatly tailored to correspond with and express its theology:

> graunt that wee, receyuing these thy creatures of bread
>   and wyne,
>   accordinge to thy sonne our Sauioure Jesus Christ's
>   holy institucion,
>   in remembraunce of his death and passion,
> maye be partakers of his most blessed body and bloud.

'Who in the same night that he was betrayed . . .' is necessary to pick up and make fully explicit the 'holy institucion'. The Saviour had instituted a 'perpetuall memorye of his precious death' and commanded that it be continued until his coming again, and this is the way that he did it. The Lord's words and actions at the Last Supper determine the form and character of the Sacrament and the promised blessings that are to be received through it. It would be most untrue to say that the 1552 prayer is no longer 'a prayer of consecration', but it is not consecration as traditionally understood as bringing about some kind of change in the elements. Rather, the bread and wine are consecrated as the Sacrament of Christ's true and spiritual presence when they serve the purpose for which they have been set apart in accordance with the Saviour's intention and express command. If there is 'a moment of consecration' in any sense of the words, it is when the communicant receives the bread and wine with the words, 'Take and eate this in remembraunce that Christ dyed for thee, and feede on him in thy hearte by faythe, with thankesgeuing.' After this moment he is able to address God as Father in the Lord's Prayer; to offer himself, soul and body, as a reasonable, holy and lively sacrifice (where previously the sacrifice of Christ had been offered in the Mass); or, alternatively, to give thanks that he has been made a very member incorporate in the mystical body, which is the blessed company of all faithful people, and also an heir, through hope, of the everlasting kingdom. The worthy communicant may now indeed be said to dwell truly and spiritually in Christ, and Christ in him.

It is not the purpose of this essay to discuss the sources of the material used by Cranmer in the composition of the Order of 1548 or the First and Second Prayer Books. Even less is it to enter into the controversy about which, if any, of the competing doctrinal party lines of the Reformation might be found to dominate his finished work. Cranmer was very much his own man, and does not appear to have been over concerned to become type-cast as a Zwinglian, Lutheran or Calvinist, much, as it turned out, to the disappointment of the more extreme partisans of the Reformation. But this is not to be taken as meaning that his approach is merely eclectic or compromising – the first in a long line of the instances of Anglican 'comprehensiveness'. On the contrary, his approach is severely practical and pastoral. It is to make sense of, and reinterpret, the confused shambles (as he saw it) of the late medieval rite, in such a way that people will be able to participate in worship intelligently, so that when they come to church on this or that occasion they will know precisely what they are supposed to be doing and why.

A parallel example of this approach is his treatment of the Rite of Confirmation. By the end of the medieval period this had become a meaningless survival in the Pontifical, imperfectly understood and haphazardly administered.[11] It must have been tempting to discard it altogether, but instead, by a neat semantic shift, Confirmation is reinterpreted as the candidates' 'ratifying and confirming' the vows and promises made by parents and godparents at Baptism. The Prayer Book Catechism is now provided as the means by which the candidates are to be instructed as to the nature and meaning of these promises, and it is to be taught diligently, after the second lesson at Evening Prayer, by the curate of every parish, on Sundays and Holy Days. Fathers, mothers, masters and dames are required to ensure that their children, servants and prentices attend. Their eventual public profession of a mature faith now becomes the precondition of their admission to Communion. This begs a whole host of questions, liturgical and theological, about what Confirmation was or ought to be. But within the *Book of Common Prayer* its place and purpose is clear and unambiguous. So by this means Cranmer succeeded, for better or worse, in laying down the major guidelines of the Church of England's strategy for the pastoral care and spiritual nurture of its young people, which has been followed, largely without question or deviation, over the succeeding centuries.

The Eucharist presented a far more complex and intractable situation, but the method of treatment and reconstruction is not dissimilar. In common with a modern student of liturgy and doctrine, Cranmer would have found much to criticise in the late medieval rite. The basic shape and action were obscured beneath a massive accumulation of ceremonies and devotions, meaningful once, perhaps, but now meaningless. Cranmer's particular, and very proper, concerns were the language barrier which excluded the great majority from effective participation in what was supposed to be the central act of the church's worship, and also the replacement, by various forms of extra-liturgical devotion, of the Communion itself, contrary to scriptural intention and the Lord's explicit command. Here, if nowhere else, people needed to be absolutely clear about what they were supposed to be doing in church and why.

No doubt it was easy enough for Cranmer to exercise his sarcasm at the expense of simple un-reformed souls:

for what else made the people run from their seats to the altar, and from altar to altar, and from sacring, as they called it, to sacring peeping, tooting and gazing at the thing which the priest held up in his hands, if they thought not to honour the thing which they saw? What moved the priests to lift the Sacrament so high above their heads, or the people to cry to the priest, 'Hold up, hold up'; and one man to say to another, 'Stoop down before'; or to say, 'This day I have seen my Maker', and, 'I cannot be quiet unless I see my Maker once a day'?[12]

But perhaps he does them less than justice. Even Cranmer himself concedes that the people thought, however misguidedly, 'to honour the thing which they saw'. This represented a well established tradition of devotion. By way of example, Dom Gregory Dix cites Langforde's *Meditatyons for goostly exercyse. In tyme of the masse.*[13] This is a vernacular manual to guide the devotions of the faithful who are present at Mass, on the principle that the least ceremonies are not without profound meaning. For example, the right hand of the altar represents the life of innocency which man lost by sin, and the left hand the miserable life the which we

now be in. The maniple, worn by the priest, recalls
'the roips with the whiche the knyghtes dyd bynd our
Sauyor's hands', and the stole the rope with which his
tormentors drew his body to the cross, and so on and
so on. The symbolism is disconnected, arbitrary and, to
our way of thinking, quite inconsequential. The modern
worshipper would find it impossible to use. But its value
may readily be appreciated for someone who had been
brought up on the code. The general theme of the tract
is set by the opening words,

> The preste going to masse signifyeth and representyd
> the Sauyor off the worlde our most swett Redeemer
> Cryst Iesu whyche cam from hewyn to the vaile of
> myserie this wrechyd world to suffer Passyon for
> mans Redemptyon. And therfor the processe of the
> masse representyd the verey processe of the Passyon
> of Cryst.

The recurring notes are, 'Remember', 'Haue medi-
tatyon', 'Consyder', 'Let us haue afore the eyes of
oure Soule'. The worshipper who is able to participate in the Mass by way of this series of acts of faith
and recollection will not have spent his time in vain. Dix
asks, very pertinently,[14] whether there is so much difference between the faith and devotion of Langforde's worshippers and those whom Cranmer exhorted in 1548

> aboue all thynges to geue most humble and hartie
> thankes . . . for the redemptiō of the world, by the
> death and passion of our saviour Christ both God &
> man who did humble himselfe euen to death upon the
> crosse for us miserable sinners liying in darknes and
> the shadow of death that he might make us children
> of God and exalte us to euerlasting life.

If we concede Dix's point, there was no radical difference between the devotional ethos of the worshippers at
the old Latin Mass and those who gathered round the
Lord's Table in 1552. Cranmer, moreover, demanded

no such change, and probably it never occurred to him that he might do so. His main concern was the restoration of communicating attendance which was intended, at a stroke, to purge the rite of its errors and disorder, and to unite its disconnected ceremonies and symbols within the single focus of the Passion of Christ. This was no longer to be recalled, one way or another, in its various aspects at this or that point of the rite, but concentrated on the moment when, by faith with thanksgiving, the communicant received the Sacrament of the bread and wine, which Christ himself had instituted as a perpetual memory of his most precious death and Passion. It is, of course, a spiritual eating and drinking, but might not the non-communicating attender at the Mass, who was following Langforde's direction, also claim, with some justice, that he too had made a truly spiritual communion?

Cranmer makes his great, positive and personal contribution in three ways. First, in his simplicity and directness. 'The incomparable language of the *Book of Common Prayer*' has come to acquire the cracked ring of a well worn cliché. But one has only to read 1548 alongside either Langforde or the Harleian MS to appreciate the truth of it. The presence of a trained mind and a master of the language is very apparent. Second, by the theological consistency in the way in which his object of the restoration of communicating attendance is achieved. For any tradition, it is absolutely essential to insist that incorporation into Christ, the ultimate fruit of the Sacrament, cannot happen apart from the faith of the one who comes to it. Just as Cranmer's exposition of the New Testament material has more than stood the test of time, so all that is said in the Exhortations about a proper preparation for Communion still needs to be taken very seriously by minister and people alike. Third, in the way that his theological insights and understanding have been superbly crafted into liturgical expression. In this respect he had a distinct advantage. Probably no other theologian and pastor, either before or since, has had the genius, the scope, or the opportunity to create his own liturgical forms. By 1552 his work had crystallised into a fully self-consistent rite, so that anyone who participates in it attentively, whether by listening or following the book, is left in no doubt about what is happening and why it is. It has the added merit that, within its limits, the end result does not do violence to previous devotional practices, but, if anything, purifies and enhances them.

Cranmer's achievement needs to be fully appreciated before one ventures to criticise. One criticism, adumbrated by Dix [15] and echoed by Parish Communion zealots, is that Cranmer's service encourages an individualist and isolationist devotion. It is hard for us, after four and a half centuries, to envisage the original intended setting of the service. It is not the 'early service' in a parish church which has undergone a Victorian gothic restoration, some time after the Public Worship Regulation Acts of the last century, pretending to be a Low Mass with only a modicum of success. We would see it rather differently if we could imagine the group of those who had earnestly repented of their sins and were in love and charity with their neighbours, gathering elbow to elbow and cheek by jowl around the Lord's Table. Cranmer himself was well aware of the need not to draw too hard and fast a line between the faith of the individual and the faith of the Church.

The more serious criticisms spring rather from the very success of the enterprise, and began early with the Prayer Book of the first Elizabeth. At a theological level, one surfaced in the controversy in the 1560s between Jewel on the one side and Harding and Scot on the other, who accused the English Church of 'abrogating consecration'. Jewel was able to show, at least to the satisfaction of most of his contemporaries, that the English Church was guiltless on this charge, though those who interpreted the Prayer Book *ad litteram* were not so easily convinced[16]. But the stubborn question still remains: can the Eucharist really be reduced without remainder to man's response to God's once for all action in Christ, as Cranmer attempts to do? Is Christ only present in the response of the faithful communicant, to put it crudely? The weakness of Cranmer's achievement is that it is too neat and successful. He has said all that he thinks needs to be said, so clearly and definitively, that he has left no room for anyone to say anything more. But, as is shown by the long history of Prayer Book Revision, whether conservative or radical, it has always been felt that there is more to be said.

Arising from this there is the question of whether and in what sense, if at all, the Sacrament can still be understood as a means of Grace. Cranmer may have given the game away when, towards the end of the *Defence*, he asserts, 'and the sacrifices of the old law were prognostications and figures of the same then to come, as our sacraments be figures and demonstrations of the same now passed'[17]. A few pages later, he adds, 'but he ordained them for this intent, that every man should receive them for himself, to ratify, confirm and establish his own faith, and everlasting salvation'[18]. This appears as an acute practical problem in the rubrics of 1552 about giving the Sacrament to a dying man. If there has been no time to alert the curate, if there is lack of company to receive with him, then let him be advised that if he repents and believes 'he doeth eate and drinke the body and bloude of our Sauoiur Christ, profytably to his soules healthe, althoughe he doe not receyue the Sacrament with his mouth'. Granted that this may be standard teaching for someone dying alone, it seems hard all the same that the Prayer Book could not find room for accommodation when the church's ministry was available. The suggestion seems to be that the receiving of the Sacrament is a badge of righteousness, the expression of the Grace in which one stands, rather than a means of growth. The danger here is the encouragement, not so much of individualism, but of a spiritual élitism. An example of this might be the words of the old man in 1904, who had been brought up in Thomas Keble's parish: 'I have often heard Sir John Keble preach . . . I was confirmed as a boy, but of course I never took Communion. That was for the quality.'[19]

The 'quality' need not be confined to the inhabitants of the 'big houses', but may include their various clients and dependants. A similar attitude may still be detected among octogenarian and nonogenarian faithful Anglicans in the present writer's own experience. Whether or not he intended it, Cranmer has something to answer for, for all that there is much for which he is rightly and properly to be honoured.

Bibliography

F.E. Brightman, *The English Rite* (London, 1915).

Everyman's Library, *The First and Second Prayer Books of Edward VI* (London, 1910, repr. 1957).

H. A. Wilson, ed., *The Order of Communion, 1548*, Henry Bradshaw Society, no. 34 (London, 1907).

J. Wickham Legg, ed., *Tracts on the Mass*, Henry Bradshaw Society, no. 32 (London, 1904).

Thomas Cranmer, *A Defence of the True and Catholic Doctrine of the Sacrament of the Body and Blood of our Saviour Christ*, ed. Henry Wace (London, 2nd impr., 1928); abbreviated *Defence*.

Notes

1. H. A. Wilson, *Order of Communion, 1548*, pp. vii–xiii.
2. J. Wickham Legg, ed., *Cranmer's Liturgical Projects*, Henry Bradshaw Society, no. 50 (London, 1915).
3. W. Maskell, *Monumenta Ritualia Ecclesiae Anglicanae* (London, 1846–7) III, pp. 348–9.
4. *Defence*, I. p. xvi.
5. *Defence*, III. p. x.
6. e.g., Hans Küng, *On being a Christian* (London, 1977), p. 325 and footnotes.
7. *Defence*, III. p. xv.
8. Edmund Bishop, 'Fear and awe attaching to the Eucharistic Service,' in *The Liturgical Homilies of Narsai*, R.H. Conolly, Texts and Studies, VIII.1 (Cambridge, 1909), Appendix 2, pp. 92ff.
9. *English Hymnal*, no. 317, verse 9.
10. *Defence*, IV.p. iv.
11. J. D. C. Fisher, *Christian Initiation, Baptism in the Medieval West: a*

study in the disintegration of the primitive rite of initiation, Alcuin Club Collections 47 (London, 1965), chap. 8.

12. *Defence*, V. p. ix.
13. G. Dix, *The Shape of the Liturgy* (London, 2nd edn, 1945, repr. 1954), p. 605.
14. Dix, p. 607.
15. Dix, p. 608.
16. E. C. Ratcliff, 'The English Usage of Eucharistic Consecration 1548–1662', *Theology* 60, no. 444 (June, 1957), pp. 229–36; no. 445 (July, 1957), pp. 273–80; repr. *E. C. Ratcliff Liturgical Studies*, ed. A. H. Couratin and D.H. Tripp, pp. 203–21 (London, 1976).
17. *Defence*, V. p. v.
18. *Defence*, V. p. x.
19. S. C. Carpenter, *Church and People 1789–1889* (London, 1959), part 2, p. 255.

VIII

'Baptisme doth represente unto us oure profession'
Stephen W. Sykes

Modern hermeneutical theory should alert us to the fact there is a diversity of ways in which a liturgical text can be 'read' and that the 'reader' should himself or herself become the subject of careful reflection. This is especially the case when one considers that a significant number of those who 'read', for example a baptismal liturgy, have themselves been performers of the ritual drama to which it points. It alters one's relation to a text when one has been involved to that degree; and the liturgy of baptism is, or should be, nothing if not self-involving for all participants, as we shall see.

It is, perhaps, a difficulty with this line of argument that the text which we shall consider, that of the 1552 *Book of Common Prayer*, is liturgically obsolete, having been replaced first by the lightly revised but standard text of 1662, and secondly by the widely used revision of 1928 (An Alternative Order of the Ministration of Publick Baptism of Infants). None the less we shall assume first that, because Cranmer's 1552 text was substantially retained in later revisions, it can be read from the standpoint of a participant; and, secondly, that such a reading should focus on structures, dramatic actions, rhythms and repetitions, as well as upon overt doctrinal content.

Anglicans, of course, have a further motive for taking seriously the text of 1662. The Church of England declares in its canon law that its doctrines may be found in particular in its Articles, Prayer Book and Ordinal.[1] It is true that a later Canon qualifies this by speaking of those sixteenth- and seventeenth-century documents in the past tense as 'this inheritance of faith'; but even here it demands, from those who make the Declaration of Assent, loyalty to that inheritance, as an example of how God has guided the Church in the past.[2] This is to speak only of the Church of England, and by no means all the Provinces of the Anglican Communion treat the Articles, Prayer Book and Ordinal of the Church of England as the chief examplar of their own doctrinal stance.[3] Even so, the Archbishop of Canterbury is bound by the Canon Law of the Church of England and, as the personal focus of communion in the Anglican Communion, supplies an authoritative norm for the belief of the whole. Attention to the 'inheritance' of the *Book of Common Prayer* is, therefore, an integral element (to put it no higher) in the theological formation of all Anglicans.

We have spoken of the doctrine contained in the *Book of Common Prayer*. But is this not in tension with our earlier emphasis on structures, dramatic actions, rhythms and repetitions? It has to be admitted that Anglican history has been scarred by an exclusive emphasis on the doctrinal use of the Prayer Book. In the specific case of Baptism, for example, one need only recall the bitter controversies of the later nineteenth century relating to baptismal regeneration, or those of the twentieth century concerning the gift of the Holy Spirit in Baptism and in Confirmation. Christian liturgical texts have doctrinal content and can be studied as repositories of doctrine. It is also correct to regard them as of outstanding importance in the discharge of the teaching office of the church, in the sense that if they inculcate false doctrine the damage they can inflict is exceptionally serious. But it is a failure of some consequence when liturgical texts are examined as though they were simply a collection of dogmatic declarations or confessional statements put into the mouths, alternately, of priest and people. Of course it is true that liturgies have often been made the vehicles of theological instruction, especially in the Reformation and Counter-Reformation, and it is a matter of delicate judgment to perceive when the boundary between appropriate doctrinal content and intrusive theological propaganda has been crossed. For all that, it remains the case that 'reading' the text of the ministration of Baptism involves being responsive to what is conveyed to the participant by its structure, dramatic actions, rhythms and repetitions as well

726   PUBLIC BAPTISM

PUBLIKE BAPTISME

S Non plures quam vnus vir & vna mulier debent accedere ad suscipiendum paruulum de sacro fonte . . . nisi alia fuerit consuetudo approbata: tunc tamen vltra tres amplius ad hoc nullatenus recipiantur.

H parentes infantium Pastoribus Ecclesiarum id maturius significare, & ab iis Baptismum . . . infantibus suis petere humiliter debent. . .

When there are children to be Baptised vpon the Sonday, or holy daye, the parentes shall geue knowledge   ouer nyght or in the mornyng, afore the beginning of Mattyns   to the curate. And then the Godfathers,   Godmothers, and people, with the children, muste be ready at the church-doore,either immediatly afore the last Canticle at Mattens,   or els immediatly afore the last Canticle at Euensong,   as the Curate by his discrecion shal appoynte.   And then

S In primis deferatur infans ad valuas ecclesie:

& inquirat sacerdos ab obstetrice vtrum sit infans masculus an femina. Deinde si infans fuerit baptizatus domi:

standing there, the pryeste shall aske whether the chyldren bee   Baptysed or no. If they aunswere .No. Then shall the prieste saye thus.

H Lieben freunde in Christo, wir hören alle tag auss Gottes wort . . . Das wir von Adam her alle sampt in sünden empfangen vund geboren werden . . .

S. Jo. iii 5

DEare   beloued, forasmuche as al men be conceyued and borne in sinne, and that
no man borne in synne, can enter into the kingdom of God (except he be regenerate, and borne a newe of water, and   the holy gost) I beseche you to cal vpon God the father through our Lord Iesus Christ, that of his bounteouse mercy he wil graūt to these childrē that thing whiche by nature they cannot haue, that is to saye,   they maye be Baptised with   the holy ghost, and receyued into Christes holy churche, and bee made   lyuely membres of the same.

Necessary doctrine f. Q iv. : made againe the liuely membres of Christis mysticall body.

Then the priest shall saye.

L   Last vns beten.

Let vs praye.

Almechtiger Ewiger Gott der du hast durch die sindflutt, nach deynem gestrengen gericht, die vngleubige welt verdampt, vnd den gleubigen Noe selb acht, nach deyner grosssen barmhertzigkeyt, erhalten. Vnnd den verstockten Pharao mit allen seynen ym rotten mer ersewfft, vnd deyn volck Israel trockenn durch hin gefuret, damit dis bad deyner heyligen tauffe zukunfftig bezeychnet, vnd durch die tauffe deyns liebes kindes vnsers herren Ihesu Christi den Iordan vnd alle wasser zur seyligen sindfluth vnd reychlicher abwasschung der sun-

ALmyghtie and euerlasting God, whiche of thy iustice didest destroy by floudes of water the whole worlde for sinne, excepte .viii. persons, whome of thy   mercye (the same tyme) thou dydest saue
in the Arke: And when thou dydest drowne in the reade sea wicked King Pharao with all his armie, yet (at the same time) thou didest lead thy people the children of Israel safely through the middes therof: whereby thou diddest figure the washing of thy holy baptisme: & by the baptisme of thy welbeloued sōne Iesus Christ, thou

From: F.E. Brightman, *The English Rite* (London, 1915) II, pp. 726f.

PUBLIC BAPTISM

1552	1661

Publique Baptisme.

¶ ᵃAnd note, that there shall be for every male child to be baptized, two Godfathers, and one Godmother: and for every female, one Godfather and two Godmothers.

¶ When there are chyldren to be Baptysed vpon the Sonday, or holy day, the Parentes shal geue knowledge   ouernyght, or in the morning, afore the beginning of *Morning prayer* to the Curate.   And then the Godfathers,   Godmothers, and people, with the children, muste be ready at the *Fonte*,   eyther immediatly *after* the laste *Lesson* at *Morninge prayer*, or els immediatlye *after* the laste *Lesson* at Euen*inge prayer*, as the Curate by his discrecion shal appoynte.   And then

¶ When there are children to be baptized,   the parents shall give knowledge thereof over night, or in the morning before the beginning of *morning prayer*, to the Curate. And then the Godfathers and Godmothers and the people, with the children, must be ready at the *Font*,   either immediatly *after* the last *Lesson* at *morning prayer*, or els immediatly *after* the last *Lesson* ᵃat evening *Prayer*, as the Curate by his discretion shall appoynt.   And   the Priest coming to the Font (which is then to be filled with pure Water) and standing there   shall say, ᵇHath this childe been already* baptised, or No? Jf they answer, no: then shall the Priest proceed as followeth

stã̄ding there,   the Priest shal aske whether the chyldren be   Baptysed or no. H̄ they answere, no. Then shall the Priest saye thus.

DEar*ly* beloued, for asmuche as all men be conceyued and borne in synne, & that *oure Saujour Christe sayeth*, non*e*   can entre into the Kyngdome of God (excepte he be regenerate, and borne a new of water and   the holye Ghoste:) I beseche you to call vpon God the Father, throughe our Lorde Iesus Christe, that of hys bounteous mercye, he wyll graunt to these chyldren, that thyng which by nature they cannot haue,

Dear*ly* beloved, forasmuch as all men are conceived and born in sin, and that *our Saviour Christ sayth*, non*e*   can enter into the Kingdom of God except he be regenerate, and born anew of water and ᶜof the holy Ghost: I beseech you to call vpon God the Father, through our Lord Iesus Christ, that of his bounteous mercy he will grant to this Child   that thing which by nature he   cannot have,

that they maye be Baptysed with *water and* the holy ghost, and receyued into Christes holye churche, and be made   lyuelye membres of thesame.

that he   may be baptized with *water, and* the holy Ghost, and received into Christs holy Church, and be made a lively member of the same

. Then   the Priest shal saye.
¶ Let vs praye.
ALmightie & euerlastinge God, which

¶ Then ᵈshall the Priest   • say.
: Let vs pray.
Almighty and everlasting God, whoᵉ

of thy *great* mercy   diddest saue *Noe & his familie* in the Arke, *from perishing by water* : & *also*

of thy *great* mercy   didst save *Noahᶠ and his family* in the Arke *from perishing by water*, and *alsoe*

dyddest safely leade the chyldren of Israel, thy people through the redde Sea : figur*ing* ᵗhereby   thy holy Baptisme, & by the Baptisme of thy welbeloued sonne Iesus Christe,

didst safely lead the children of Israel thy people through the red Sea, figur*ing* ᵗhereby   thy holy baptism; and by the baptism of thy welbeloved son Iesus Christ   in the river Iordan

St. Mark. [Portions not found in Matthew or Luke.]	**St. Mark.** [Complete.]
	I. 1–8
1 The beginning of the gospel of Jesus Christ, the Son of God.	1 The beginning of the gospel of Jesus Christ, [1] the Son of God.
2 Even...	2 Even as it is written [2] in **Isaiah the prophet,**
Behold, I send my messenger before thy face,	Behold, I send my messenger before thy face,
Who shall prepare thy way.	Who shall prepare thy way ;
(*But the words* " Behold, I send my messenger before thy face, who shall prepare thy way " *are found in Matthew xi. 10 and Luke vii. 27*).	3 **The voice of one crying in the wilderness,** **Make ye ready the way of the Lord,** **Make his paths straight ;**
4 ...came, who baptized [?]...and...	4 **John** came, who baptized **in the wilderness** and **preached** the baptism [?] of **repentance** unto remission of sins.
5 And...all (they of Jerusalem)...	5 And there **went out** unto him **all the country** of Judæa, and all they of Jerusalem ; and they were **baptized of him** in the river Jordan, confessing their sins.
6 And...was...and did eat (Gr. *eating*)...	6 And John was clothed with camel's hair, and *had* a leathern girdle about his loins, and did eat locusts and wild honey.
7 And he preached,...stoop down and (Gr. stooping down)...	7 And he preached, saying, There cometh after me **he that is mightier than I,** the latchet of **whose shoes I am not** [3] **worthy** to stoop down and unloose.
8 ...but [? ?]...	8 **I baptized you** [4] **with water ;** but **he shall baptize you** [4] **with the** [5] **Holy Ghost.**
	[1] Some ancient authorities omit *the Son of God.* [2] Some ancient authorities read *in the prophets.* [3] Gr. *sufficient.* [4] Or, *in.* [5] Or, *Holy Spirit :* and so throughout this book.
Mark i. 8, W. & H. omit the Greek preposition in both cases.	

From: E.A Abbott and W.G.Rushbrooke, *The Common Tradition of the Synoptic Gospels* (London, 1884) in the Text of the Revised Version

St. Matthew. [*Passages parallel to Mark.*]	St. Luke. [*Passages parallel to Mark.*]
	III. 1-4, 7, 15-17.
	1 Now in the fifteenth year of the reign of Tiberius Cæsar, Pontius Pilate being governor of Judæa, and Herod being tetrarch of Galilee, and his brother Philip tetrarch of the region of Ituræa and Trachonitis, and Lysanias tetrarch of Abilene,
	2 In the high-priesthood of Annas and Caiaphas, the word of God came unto **John** the son of Zacharias **in the wilderness.**
III. 1-6, 11-12.	3 And he came into **all the region** round about Jordan, **preaching** the **baptism** [?] of **repentance** unto remission of sins ;
1 And in those days cometh **John** the **Baptist** [?], **preaching in the wilderness** of Judæa, saying,	4 As it is written in the book of the words of **Isaiah the prophet,**
2 **Repent** ye : for the kingdom of heaven is at hand.	**The voice of one crying in the wilderness,**
3 For this is he that was spoken of [1] by **Isaiah the prophet,** saying,	**Make ye ready the way of the Lord,**
The voice of one crying in the wilderness,	**Make his paths straight.**
Make ye ready the way of the Lord,	
Make his paths straight.	7 He said therefore to the multitudes that **went out** to be **baptized of him,** Ye offspring of vipers, who warned you to flee from the wrath to come ?
4 Now John himself had his raiment of camel's hair, and a leathern girdle about his loins ; and his food was locusts and wild honey.	
5 Then **went out** unto him Jerusalem, and **all** [?] Judæa, and all [?] **the region** round about Jordan ;	15 And as the people were in expectation, and all men reasoned in their hearts concerning John, whether haply he were the Christ ;
6 And they were **baptized of him** in the river Jordan, confessing their sins.	16 John answered, **saying unto them all, I** indeed **baptize you** with **water ;** but there **cometh he that is mightier than I,** the latchet **of whose shoes I am not** [1] **worthy** to unloose : **he shall baptize you** [2] with **the Holy Ghost** and *with* fire :
11 **I** indeed **baptize you** [2] **with water** unto repentance : but **he that cometh** after me is **mightier than I, whose shoes I am not** [3] **worthy** to bear : **he shall baptize you** [3] **with the Holy Ghost** and *with* fire :	17 Whose fan is in his hand, throughly to cleanse his threshing-floor, and to gather the wheat into his garner ; but the chaff he will burn up with unquenchable fire.
12 Whose fan is in his hand, and he will throughly cleanse his threshing-floor ; and he will gather his wheat into the garner, but the chaff he will burn up with unquenchable fire.	
[1] Or, *through.* [2] Or, *in.* [3] Gr. *sufficient.*	[1] Gr. *sufficient.* [2] Or, *in.*

as by its overt doctrines.

It has to be said that such a 'reading' is not encouraged
by the hitherto dominant source-critical method practised
by generations of liturgical scholars, and reflected in many
contemporary text-books.[4] Just as in the study of the Synoptic Gospels, students were indirectly encouraged to treat the
text as a pastiche of elements drawn from earlier sources,
so, in relation to the Prayer Book, extensive enquiry was
mounted into Cranmer's sources, and elaborate discussion
was undertaken of the supposed motives behind changes of
wording as between 1549, 1552 and 1661. Figure I, taken
from the work of a major Prayer Book scholar, illustrates
the point. Here, arranged in the three right-hand columns,
are the texts of 1549, 1552 and 1661, with verbal alterations
carefully indicated by the use of different kinds of type.
In the left-hand column, a series of supposed sources are
printed in Latin, German or English, enabling the student to make quick and accurate comparisons of a strictly
limited character. Figure II illustrates the same method
in its application to the Synoptic Gospels.[5] What neither
example of this method enables the student to do with any
ease is to detect the difference and similarities which arise
from a reading of a text as a whole, or from the perception
of internal rhythms created by stress or repetition.

This is not to denigrate the achievement of source-criticism, since we have independent evidence that many of
the verbal changes introduced in 1552 or in 1662 were the
consequence of argument and were plainly deliberate. But
the method presupposed a highly misleading paradigm of
the 'scientific' or 'objective' study of the text. It was as
assiduously practised on Shakespeare as upon the Bible
and Prayer Book. But, as a Shakespearean scholar was
to put it, it was a little like the enterprise of savouring a
rissole by watching the meat and onion pass through the
mincer;[6] and in due course, at least in biblical studies and
more widely in literary theory, first redaction-criticism and
later reader-response theories began to provide less sterile
perspectives.

It remains the case, of course, that there are historical
questions to put to our evidence. Cranmer's own theology

of baptism may be studied from the brief and fragmentary treatment it receives at his hands in the course of his other, major controversies.[7] It is historical enquiry which alone can assure us that the two Edwardine Prayer Books were substantially his own work.[8] Cranmer's relationship with, but independent judgement upon, German Church orders can only be evaluated from detailed knowledge of their contents, and it is highly pertinent to the changes introduced in 1552 to have considered in detail Martin Bucer's *Censura* on the 1549 Prayer Book, whether or not it was produced at Cranmer's invitation.[9] None the less it remains the case that source-criticism, with its historicist bias, remains but one of the tasks of an interpreter. Cranmer's liturgies invite a response from participators or potential participators who understand his work as worship. Ratcliff's judgment that Cranmer was 'the master, or rather the creator of English liturgical style, because he had apprehended the nature of worship'[10] – typically made at the end of a historical treatment of his work – will be the presupposition of what follows. Given that he understood worship (and here it is not necessary to suppose that he understood it *better* than any of his contemporaries, Catholic or Protestant), we shall ask what was the character he gave to the church's dramatic act of baptising infants as Christian worship.

The Structure of the Service

The basic pattern of the service, which was conceived by Cranmer as a kind of self-contained sacramental event within the pattern of Matins or Evensong, is extremely simple (see Figure III). It comprises two main elements, those of Word and Sacrament, prefaced and followed by brief transitional statements and prayers. Between the reading of the Gospel (from Mark 10), and the actual Baptism of the child, are a set of promises made by the godparents in the name of the child, which constitute a kind of hinge in the service on which entry into the grace of Baptism turns. These promises are the human response to God's promises declared in the Gospel. The whole service, therefore, has

the form of a covenant between God and the child, initiated
from God's side.

The prefatory material with which the rite begins contains a simple question whether the child has already been
baptised, a brief declaration of the necessity of Baptism and
two general intercessions for the child (the so-called 'flood'
prayer, and the 'promise' prayer). This introduction serves
two ends. It achieves, prior to the reading of the Gospel,
a focusing of the congregation's attention upon the child;
but it does so, secondly, in relation to two themes of major
importance, those of God's mercy ('which of thy great mercy
diddest save Noe and his familie in the Arke') and of his
reception of the children ('Receiue them (O lord) as thou
hast promysed'). Because structure is composed not just of
sequences, but of significant repetitions, it is as well for us
to look closely at certain recurring words.

'Reception' has already been used in the rubric at the
head of the service to describe the purpose of Baptism
('The receyuinge of them that be newely Baptysed into
the noumbre of Christes Churche'). It is now used in each
of the elements of the introductory material ('receyued into
Christes holye churche', 'receyued into the Arke of Christes
Church', 'maye receyue remission of theyr sinnes', and
'Receiue them (O lord)'). But its most striking use occurs
in the Gospel and exhortation on the Gospel. Here Christ's
action of taking the children into his arms and blessing them
is used as an analogy for Baptism.

> Doubt not ye therefore, but earnestly beleue, that
> he wyl
> lykewise fauourably receyue these present infan-
> tes, that
> he wil embrase them wyth the armes of hys
> mercye, that
> he wyll geue vnto them the blessynge of eternall
> lyfe, and make them partakers of hys euerlasting
> kingdom.

The emotionally powerful image of the child being
embraced in the arms of Jesus' mercy forms the affective heart of this liturgy. The word 'receive' significantly
continues to echo at regular intervals throughout the rest of

Figure III

PREFATORY MATERIAL

Question

invitation to prayer
flood prayer
promise prayer

THE WORD

Mark 10,   Exhortation, Prayer

address to parents about promises
demands to renounce sin, believe gospel, desire baptism
'grant' prayers

THE SACRAMENT

water prayer, baptism, signing, Lord's Prayer

POSTLUDE

prayer of thanksgiving
exhortation to godparents
extempore instruction

Figure III: The Structure of the Service

the service, in the address to the godparents, at the blessing
of the water, in the priest's declaration after Baptism (note:
'We receyue this childe'), and finally at the prayer of thanksgiving ('to receyue hym for thy owne childe by adopcion').

Excluding the rubric, there are in all no less than ten
uses of the word 'receive' in this liturgy. This, we should
note, compares with four uses in the *Alternative Service Book*'s
Baptism of Children. Cranmer's liturgy we might well conclude was, by reason of its structure, drama, and repetitions,
a liturgy proclaiming Christ's reception of little children.
When the priest at the height of the drama takes the child
into his arms he is doing what Christ himself did. The
congregation witnesses Christ's own embrace. The sacrament is God's own act ('thy holy Baptisme', in both the
flood and promise prayers). Thus the theology, Gospel reading, drama and repetitions cohere in the word 'receive' and
hence the poignancy and appropriateness of the declaration
'we receyue this childe into the congregacion of Christe's
flocke'. However, in the *Alternative Service Book*, Mark 10 is,
after centuries of usage, dropped as the Gospel, an omission
justified by the observation that the passage does not refer
to Baptism at all.[11] This is pedantry of the first order. We
already know from the text of the liturgy that the Church has
been commanded to baptise. The justification for baptising
infants lies not in any direct precedent of Christ's, but in
the quality of his response to little children, conveyed by
the phrase 'embrace with the arms of his mercy'.

The central block of the service contains Word (Gospel
reading and exposition) and Sacrament, both embodying
a mutual promising or covenant. Again the structure is
undergirded by another highly significant repetition, this
time of the word 'promise'. The second of the two opening
prayers for the child repeats the word twice, making the text,
'aske & you shal have, seke & you shal fynd', central to its
invocation, as though daring the participants in the rite to
disbelieve. The exhortation on the Gospel reinforces this
with reference to the avoidance of doubt, to earnest belief
and to being persuaded. After a brief prayer, the priest
turns to the godparents with a positive battery of references
to promise:

> Ye haue heard also that our Lord Iesus Christ hath
> promysed in hys Gospel, to graunte all these
> thinges that ye haue prayed for: which promise
> he for his parte wyll moste surely kepe & performe.
> Wherfore after thys promyse made by Christ, these
> infantes must also faithfully for theyr parte promise
> by you that be their sueties . . .

Why is so much emphasis laid upon the promise of the Gospel? The historical reason has doubtless much to do with the promissory emphasis of Luther's sacramental theology; [12] but in Cranmer's baptismal liturgy the theme of promise amounts to a structural element, not just a doctrinal allusion.

The permeation of the theme of promise throughout the service suggests that the life of the participant is itself being structured by the liturgy. Quite apart from what may feature in this particular liturgy, we could observe from the standpoint of Christian doctrine that Baptism, as the sacrament of initiation into the Church, might well be expected to express a sense of the totality of the Christian's life within the Church; or, putting it another way, that, as the sacramental incorporation into Christ, Baptism might well be expected to elicit the complete sense of fellowship with him. As it is, Cranmer makes absolutely unambiguous what he hopes that Baptism will achieve for all adult participants. In the opening rubric, he states that the point of public baptisms at main services is that 'euery man present may be put in remembraunce of hys owne profession made to God in hys Baptisme'; hence, of course, the use of an English liturgy. Furthermore the concluding exhortation to godparents offers an explicit explanation of the content of this remembrance to the following effect:

> rememberynge alwayes that Baptisme doeth represente
> vnto vs oure profession, whiche is to folowe the example
> of our sauiour Christ, & to be made like vnto him: that as he
> dyed and rose agayne for vs, so shoulde we whiche are
> baptysed, dye from synne, and ryse agayne vnto
> righteousnesse, continually mortyfyinge all oure euyll and
> corrupte affections, and daylye procedinge in all vertue and
> godlines of lyuynge.

This comprehensive summary of the Christian life constitutes the structure of the liturgy from first to last, and is
reinforced by constant repetition at every stage.

The Christian 'profession' entails a journey 'in Christ',
which begins with a dying to sin. This in itself presup-
poses that humanity apart from Christ is in a state of sin,
the information appropriately conveyed by the words with
which the liturgy begins ('Dearely beloued, for asmuche as
all men be conceyued and borne in synne'). This scriptural
reference (Psalm 51.5, Coverdale's translation) Cranmer
evidently preferred to the idea that unbaptised infants
amounted to persons possessed by demons, who must be
exorcised. Bucer had argued in the *Censura* that though
baptismal exorcism was an ancient custom, it diminished
the stature of the Gospel exorcisms.[13] Cranmer appears to
have agreed with this, and the demonology of his service is
muted and apotropaic.

Delivery from sin through the atoning death of Christ
brings the Christian into the company of those undertak-
ing the journey of sanctification, a constant further dying
to sin and growth in obedience and godliness. The final
state is that of enjoyment of the kingdom and eternal life.
Thus deliverance from sin, sanctification and entry into
the kingdom constitutes a comprehensive summary of life
'in Christ'. Because the self-same promises of the Gospel
accompany the Christian throughout his or her entire life,
Baptism is a reminder of the Christian profession, a structure and framework for the whole of Christian living.

It is not, therefore, accidental that in the pivotal address
to the godparents before they make their promises, what is
entailed in Christ's reception of and blessing of children is
spelt out as follows:

> to release them of theyr synnes [1662 adds, to sanctify
> him with the Holy Ghost], to geue them the kingdom of
> heaven, and euerlasting lyfe.

This pattern is constantly reiterated, often with only two
of the three elements being mentioned. For example, as
we have seen, the first words of the service refer to being

born in sin; this is immediately followed by a reference to being born anew of water and the Holy Ghost and thereby entering the kingdom. The 'flood' prayer which follows contains a similar sequence, washing, sanctification and final entry into everlasting life. The next, 'promise' prayer refers both to washing and entry into the eternal kingdom. The thanksgiving after Baptism contains another comprehensive brief summary of the Christian life, speaking of being buried with Christ in his death, of the utter abolition of the whole body of sin, followed by final inheritance of the everlasting kingdom.

The sense that Baptism comprehends and accompanies the whole of a Christian's life is caught in George Herbert's poem, entitled, Holy Baptisme (I). Using the traditional image invoked in the prayer before Baptism, that the baptismal waters are one with the water which flowed from the side of Christ, Herbert writes:

> O blessed streams! either ye do prevent
> And stop our sinnes from growing thick and wide,
> Or else give tears to drown them, as they grow.
> In you Redemption measures all my time,
> And spreads the plaister equall to the crime.
> You taught the Book of Life my name, that so
> What ever future sinnes should me miscall,
> Your first acquaintance might discredit all.

The efficacy of the baptismal water, like the Christian name entered into the register, accompany the believer throughout his or her life, so that 'your first acquaintance' – that is the introduction and mutual naming of a merciful, promising God to the child as his adoptive heir – is sufficient to discredit whatever shameful names subsequent sinning might seem to justify. In Baptism, redemption measures and accompanies the entire life-span of the believer.

The final thing to observe about the structure of the service is its open-endedness. Indeed it hardly ends at all. A rubric instructs the Minister to command extempore that the children be brought to the Bishop for confirmation at the proper time. The 1549 rubric, instructing the congregation to depart in the name of the Lord, was omitted in 1552.

It is wholly appropriate that there should be no formal
closure, because the liturgy itself opens out on to the daily
service of the church, the life of growth in all virtue and
godliness of living. Naturally enough, the congregation's
hope and expectation that the infant will grow physically
and mentally becomes the implicit metaphor for Christian
life ('that al thinges belonginge to the spirite, may liue &
growe in them'). There is reference to increased 'power
and strength', to manhood and warfare, and to the anticipated learning of which the infant is shortly expected to be
capable. The simultaneous address to the assembled adults
of these evocations of the basic metaphor of growth becomes
explicit in the prayer after the Gospel:

> We geve thee humble thankes, that thou haste vouch-
> safed to call vs to knowledge of thy grace & fayth in
> thee, encrease this knowledge, & confirme this faythe in
> vs euermore.

In other words, this liturgy is characterised by a structure
and a pattern of repetitions expressive of the way in which
a Christian becomes involved in the divine plan, and the
consequence of having done so. The structure focuses the
drama upon the child, deploying the powerful thought of
divine tenderness towards small children, but at the same
time addresses adult participants through the metaphor of
growth to maturity. It deliberately sets out to remind all
present of the fundamental character of their own Baptism,
and to reinforce and encourage Christians in the profession
of their faith.

The Drama and Symbols of
Baptism

In his liturgical work Cranmer intended above all else
to be faithful to Scripture, and the Scriptures lack any
explicit description of the rituals of early Christian Baptism. The general aim of simplification imbibed from the
continental Reformation inclined him against a plethora

of dramatic or symbolic rituals, even when these were capable of perfectly acceptable evangelical interpretation. Bucer was of the opinion that proper teaching about the use of these rituals was a distraction from the main aim of a simple instruction in the faith, at least for the time of pastoral emergency in which he lived. He seems not to have considered the possibility that the symbols might be capable of speaking for themselves without extensive verbal interpretation, or that they had arisen from meditation upon the Scriptures.[14] At all events Cranmer's liturgy represents in itself a dramatic reduction of ritual actions, as compared with the medieval Sarum rite.

But it is not devoid of drama, nor is its language symbolically impoverished. The liturgy contains no less than ten images of Baptism, namely, washing, drowning or rescuing from being drowned (as in the cases of Noah or the children of Israel at the Red Sea), deliverance from wrath and condemnation, reception into (the ark of) the Church, being embraced by Christ, becoming a living limb or member of the body, being born again, burial and resurrection with Christ, the imagery of the sacrificial blood and water from the side of Christ, being grafted into Christ, and being adopted as a child of Christ. Ample use has, therefore, been made of the rich possibilities provided by the Scriptures for the interpretation of Baptism.

The rituals themselves are simply those of baptising by dipping the child into the water (presuming a certain measure of undress) or, in the case of certified weakness, sprinkling it with water, and signing it with the sign of the cross. By 1552 the drama of exorcism ('the priest lokyng vpon the children', 1549) has been abandoned, as has the ceremonial blessing (with use of the sign of the cross) of the water. In 1661 the latter was to be partially restored by the insertion into the prayer before Baptism of the words 'Sanctifie this Water to the mystical washing away of sin', an inclusion which incidentally reinforced the threefold pattern of deliverance from sin, sanctification and entry into the kingdom.

But even the ritually low-keyed version of 1552 is not without verbally reinforced drama. As we have argued, the centre or hinge of the service is the point at which the covenant is made. Here, at the moment when godparents make their promises as sureties for the child, Cranmer has placed a series of ejaculatory prayers, each beginning with the word 'grant'. In 1549 these were added to the blessing of the font and were eight in number. By 1552 they had been reduced to four. Their origin may have been in part from the *Missale Mixtum*, a Spanish book edited in 1500 by Cardinal Ximenes, and the *Missale Gallicanum vetus*.[15] It was Cranmer's genius, however, to pick from the texts the major dramatic themes of burial of the old Adam and resurrection of the new, of death to the flesh and life in the spirit, and of warfare and triumph over the devil, the world and the flesh; and to heighten their impact with repetition of the word 'grant'. It may not be too much to say that the effect was calculated to compensate for the loss of the drama of exorcism, and to substitute a sense of radical movement from an old to a new condition, a major feature of rites of passage.

But it would be inappropriate at this point not to comment on the losses entailed in Cranmer's 1552 efforts at simplification. If we inspect the rituals from the perspective provided by the anthropological theory of *rites de passage*,[16] what is most strikingly absent is the sense of the separation of the baptisand from the structures of society. In the Sarum rite this is amply provided for by the order for the making of a catechumen, with its very extensive and elaborate preliminary rituals. The exorcism and administration of salt to make the candidate hungry for spiritual food, the separate rituals for male and female children, and the adjuration and exorcism of the devil, are all conceived of as forms of preparation so that the candidate may be ready to approach Baptism and fit to receive its grace. They separate the child from its natural community for adoption within the new covenant.

In Cranmer's first revision of Sarum in 1549, the first half of the baptismal order was, according to the rubric, to be conducted at the church door. This has the consequence that the opening prayer, signing with the cross, exorcism, proclamation of the Gospel and profession of the creed could

all be regarded as preparation (and thus separation) before
arrival at the font. But so attenuated a residue of the rite of
separation had, plainly, lost its *raison d'être,* and it fell victim
to Bucer's reductive observation that the practice amounted
simply to a sign of the fact that children are conceived and
born in sin.[17] Since, he argues, that is admitted in so many
words in the text and 'since a multitude of signs does not
become a new people', nothing would be lost by having the
entire Baptism at the font. Cranmer concurred with this
reasoning in 1552; but we in our day may beg to disagree.
In a secularised culture there is everything to be said for a
solemn rite of separation, a reminder to both parents and
godparents that their renunciations may have costly consequences in their daily lives. Discussion of the retention of
exorcism in such a context presents specialised and complex
problems, into which it is impossible to enter here.

Baptism and the Lord's Supper

It remains to ask what connection Cranmer envisaged or
established between his two liturgies, of Holy Baptism and
Holy Communion. Irrespective of what we may actually
find to be the case, the question is forced on us by our
observation of the pattern which Baptism places upon the
living of the Christian life. We are bound to enquire whether
the Order for the Eucharist is consistent with this pattern,
whether it reflects and embodies the same fundamental
convictions about the character of the covenant between
God and humankind.

On the connection between Baptism and Holy Communion Cranmer himself occasionally commented in his
eucharistic writings. For example, in the 1550 *Defence
of the True and Catholic Doctrine of the Sacrament,* he relates
Baptism and Eucharist as different modes of the one, divine
action; 'Our Saviour Christ is both the first beginner of our
spiritual life (who first begetteth us into God his Father),
and also afterwards he is our lively food and spiritual life.'[18]
Again, subsequently, Cranmer discusses a passage from
Hilary's *De Trinitate* which, he asserts, makes no distinction

between the believer's union with Christ in Baptism and in the Eucharist. Both affirm Christ's 'natural' presence in us, a oneness of the believer with Christ and of Christ with the believer, which can only be spoken of as a spiritual union.[19] The purpose of the argument is to overthrow the case from tradition for transubstantiation, which he understands to be the doctrine of a real and corporal presence of Christ in the bread of the sacrament. But, replied Cranmer, if we truly partake of Christ at Baptism we do so without any miraculous change of the water. The indwelling of Christ in the believer as a result of Baptism is both true and 'natural'. But because it is a mutual indwelling, involving the believer in being in Christ, as Christ is in him or her, it should be not spoken of as corporal but as spiritual.

Though the confusion of the terminology is considerable, Cranmer's intention is perfectly plain. It is to focus attention on the convenantal aspect of the eucharistic rite. Just as in Baptism Christ meets the believer through his or her response to his promise, so, through faith in the promise, precisely the same encounter is to take place at the Eucharist. The 'presence' is neither greater nor less in one case or in the other. The most striking evidence, therefore, that Baptism and Eucharist are conceived on the basis of the same ground-plan, lies in the renewal of the mutual promising which, as we have seen, is the hinge between word and sacrament in the baptismal rite. We should not, therefore, be surprised to find the same movement in the order for Holy Communion, articulated in an absolution which directly refers to the same comprehensive summary of life in Christ as found expression in Holy Baptism. The absolution recalls that the God of mercy has promised forgiveness of sins to all who turn to him with repentance and true faith. Such a God will pardon and forgive sin, will confirm and strengthen in all goodness, and will bring the believer to everlasting life. These are his sure promises, and in the light of them the believer may be lifted up in heart and mind to feast with Christ at his table in the heavens.[20]

But 'everyone of us must be guests and not gazers'.[21] This fundamental affirmation of the *Homily of the Worthy Receiving and Reverent Esteeming of the Body and Blood of Christ* is pertinent to the issue of growth in understanding which we have seen to be an important metaphor through which adult participators in the baptismal liturgy are addressed. Infants are to be brought to a state of comprehension of what it is that the Eucharist recalls, so that they may feast at the Lord's Table with understanding. Like the passover feast, partakers must be instructed in the cause and end of the Eucharist; otherwise there can be no true memorial of the death of Christ. Because that death accomplished a complete atonement for sin, the remembrance of it entails both a serious calling to mind and a thorough repentance of our own sins. The Eucharist is the 'nourishment and augmentation' of what was begun in Baptism because in it, adults lay hold of forgiveness. Forgiveness, both forgiving and being forgiven, is the means by which Christians are to grow into an ever more complete union with Christ; 'that we may euermore dwell in hym, and he in us'.

It is for this reason that so profound – even terrifying – an emphasis is placed upon 'worthy reception'. The Exhortations in Cranmer's 1552 eucharistic rite place believers in a double bind. They will be punished if they fail to examine themselves before receiving the Eucharist; they will also be punished if they fail to come to the Eucharist. 'Worthy reception' of the Eucharist is, however, merely identical with what the Article XXVII 'of Baptism' refers to as right reception. Because there is a continuing requirement deriving from participation in Baptism, Baptism and Eucharist are inseparable from each other. Those who receive Baptism rightly are those who have come to understand for themselves the terms of the new covenant in the blood of Christ. The incompleteness of the rite of infant Baptism points forward, therefore, to a true partaking of the spiritual food of the most precious Body and Blood of Christ, to lively membership of the mystical body of Christ and to the promise of the inheritance of his everlasting kingdom.

Our review of the text of Cranmer's liturgy of Public Baptism has revealed a depth and subtlety of content and structure which it might be tempting to contrast with the 'alternative' service. It is, however, sufficient

to add that that service is indeed, alternative, and that
the norm of its interpretation remains the *Book of Common Prayer*. Precisely because Baptisms are public rituals
it remains possible for parishes to recapture the substance
of what Cranmer achieved, even whilst using the modern
text. Instruction, choices of readings and hymns, and the
organisation of processions give parishes the opportunity
to establish those patterns and resonances so important to
the liturgy of 1552. It is to be hoped that future revisers
of the alternative services will be less dominated by the
historical and source-critical school of liturgiology, and will
lay securer hold upon the texts as worship.

Notes

1. Canon *A5* of the Church of England reads thus: 'The doctrine of the
   Church of England is grounded in the holy Scriptures, and in such
   teachings of the ancient Fathers and Councils of the Church as are
   agreeable to the said Scriptures. In particular such doctrine is to be
   found in the Thirty-nine Articles of Religion, the Book of Common
   Prayer and the Ordinal.'
2. Canon C15, Of the Declaration of Assent.
3. See P.H.E. Thomas, 'A Family Affair: The Pattern of Constitutional
   Authority in the Anglican Communion' in *Authority in the Anglican
   Communion*, ed. Stephen W. Sykes (Toronto, 1987), pp. 119–43.
4. To a very large extent the pattern was set by Francis Proctor's
   History of the Book of Common Prayer (London, 1855), a work revised
   and rewritten by W.H. Frere in 1901, and published in successive
   impressions until 1961. There was a dogmatic motive reinforcing the
   trend towards historical and source-critical treatment of the *Book of
   Common Prayer*, in that Anglican writers influenced by the Oxford
   Movement greatly preferred the 1549 Prayer Book Eucharist to that
   of 1552, and had an apologetic interest in demonstrating the continuity of Anglican forms with earlier Catholic models. Most liturgical
   scholars have been Anglo-Catholics.
5. The tradition of printing the text of the Gospels in parallel columns
   goes back beyond the early critical work of Griesbach (1745–1812) on
   the synoptic problem, to the ancient tradition of Gospel harmonies.
   The extract from Abbott and Rushbrooke illustrates well how theory-
   laden these apparently objective comparisons actually are. I am
   grateful to Mr Peter Head, of St Edmund's College, Cambridge,
   for his observations on this point.
6. 'Analysis of the creative act is fascinating in its own right; but it tends
   to present great art as a rissole one learns to savour by watching meat

and onion through the mincer', D.L. Frost, *The School of Shakespeare* (Cambridge, 1968), p. 23.

7. See G.W. Bromiley, *Thomas Cranmer, Theologian* (London, 1956), ch. V.

8. E.C. Ratcliff, 'The Liturgical Work of Archbishop Cranmer' in E.C. Ratcliff, *Liturgical Studies*, ed. A.H. Couratin and D.H. Tripp (London, 1976), pp. 184–202.

9. Or that of Bishop Goodrich of Ely, as seems probable: see C. Hopf, *Martin Bucer and the English Reformation* (Oxford, 1947) and E.C. Whitaker, *Martin Bucer and the Book of Common Prayer*, Alcuin Club Collections 55 (Great Wakering, 1974).

10. Ratcliffe, p. 199.

11. R.C.D Jasper and P.F. Bradshaw, *A Companion to the Alternative Service Book* (London, 1986), p. 350.

12. See especially Luther's treatise, *The Babylonian Captivity of the Church* (1520), and *The Large Catechism* (1529).

13. J.D.C. Fisher, *Christian Initiation: The Reformation Period*, Alcuin Club Collections 51 (London, 1970), pp. 101f.

14. *The Rationale of Ceremonial* produced in England sometime between 1540 and 1543 had provided an explanation of the baptismal rituals of the Sarum manual in terms undoubtedly uncongenial to Cranmer at the time.

15. Fisher, p. 151.

16. Classically formulated by A. Van Gennep in 1908, in a subsequently translated work, *The Rites of Passage* (London, 1960).

17. Fisher, p. 98.

18. *The Work of Thomas Cranmer*, ed. G.E. Duffield (Appleford, 1964), p. 69. The passage is from Book I, ch. X.

19. *The Work of Thomas Cranmer*, p. 175. The passage is from III, ch. XV.

20. See Peter Brook's suggestive discussion of what he calls 'the *sursum corda* approach to the heavenly Christ', in *Thomas Cranmer's Doctrine of the Eucharist* (London, 1965), pp. 101f.

21. *The Two Books of Homilies* (Oxford, 1859), p. 439. The Homily in question, from the second collection of 1563, is generally ascribed to Bishop John Jewel.

IX

Music and English Liturgy
Margot Johnson

The Reformation in England brought not only English Liturgy, but a fresh approach to church music. Many supporters of the reforming party, believing that sung services had become so complex and difficult as to inhibit both lay understanding and participation in worship, sought a new simplicity and dignity in church music.

John Merbecke (*c*. 1510–*c*.1585), a man of Calvinist views, is remembered today chiefly for his composition of a simple and dignified setting for the service of Holy Communion in the First English Prayer Book of 1549. He appears to have spent the whole of his life at Windsor, where he became organist at St George's Chapel.

The post of organist had become increasingly common from the late fifteenth century, and Merbecke held this post from at least 1541–2 (records are incomplete). Bishop Burnet called him a 'singing man'; and in the petition of 1 December, 1547, drawn up by the minor canons and lay clerks of St George's Chapel and presented to the new Commissioners of Edward VI, Merbecke's name heads the list of fourteen lay clerks, the third name being that of George Thaxton, his fellow organist. Merbecke's name first appears in both the Precentor's rolls and the Treasurer's rolls as receiving payment as organist in the financial year 1541–2; but as the records are defective, it is impossible to tell whether he took up the post in that year, or had held it earlier. Probably by then he would be Master of the Choristers, responsible for rehearsing the services, teaching the boys music, and giving organ lessons, as was the custom elsewhere (e.g. Rochester in 1543, and York Minster in 1552). This arrangement altered the old provision for teaching elementary reading and writing and giving basic instruction in music in the Song Schools, whose foundation in many places (e.g St Paul's, Rochester and York) can be traced well before the Norman Conquest.

John Merbecke's *The Book of Common Praier noted* was printed in 1550 by Richard Grafton, the King's printer, but whether or not this implies official recognition is a matter for debate. The simple music is adapted from plainsong to suit the new English words, following the custom of 'for every syllable a note'. As in the 1549 Prayer Book itself, it is clearly intended that the priest and clerks shall sing, rather than the congregation.

In a short preface, Merbecke sets out the notes he has used and their values:

In this booke
is conteyned so muche of the Order
of Commō prayer as is to be song in
Churches: wherin
are vsed only these
iiii. sortes of notes,
The first note is a strene note and is
a breue. The second a square note,
and is a semy breue. The iii, a pycke
and is a mynymme. And when there is a
prycke by the square note that prycke
is halfe as muche as the note
that goeth before it. The
iiii. is a close, and is
only vsed at yᵉend
of a verse.

The 'pycke' was so called because of its shape like a pikehead; and the 'prycke' is a point, which became the 'dot' in modern notation.

Merbecke used the customary black notation with staves of four red lines. The C clef was used in various positions at the beginning of each stave, with the F clef as an occasional variant; and when a flat was needed in the signature (e.g in the *Kyrie* and the Creed), it was printed without a clef in the top space of the stave.

By these means he obtained variety. The priest was
to intone the Preface and the special Prefaces in C;
the Prayer for the Church, and the prayers following,
including the Consecration Prayer, were to be intoned
on A, modulating on the closing words before the Lord's
Prayer to almost the key of G, followed by the opening
words 'Our Father' on B natural. As in other Tudor
church music, there are no bar lines; but Merbecke
inserted a single bar line after each of the three parts
of the *Kyrie,* in the *Sanctus, Benedictus,* and *Agnus Dei.*

The value of the note for the priest intoning the
prayers is the 'pycke' or minim, while the unit note for
the clerks is the semibreve.

The effect of Merbecke's settings sung by unaccompanied men's voices in unison was one of great simplicity
and dignity, and in marked contrast to what had gone
before. The words were given a natural rhythm in
accordance with their sense, and melodic changes indicated the moods of different parts of the service.

It has been supposed that Cranmer encouraged
Merbecke to produce this book, as it has been
conjectured that the two collaborated in the Litany.
Unfortunately, only circumstantial evidence exists for
their acquaintance and association. Cranmer probably
encountered him at the meeting of 1548 at Windsor;
and earlier would know of his trial for heresy, with three
others from Windsor, in July 1543.

Merbecke had taken advantage of the English Bibles
set up in churches in 1538 and began to write out his
own copy. Richard Turner, a perpetual chantry priest
at Windsor from 1535 or 1536, discovered this self-
appointed task, and proposed a better use of time and
talent in compiling an English Bible concordance. In the
following two years Turner, who held reformed views,
encouraged Merbecke in biblical study. When Merbecke
published *A Book of Notes and Common Places* in 1581, it
included long quotations from Turner's unpublished
lectures on the epistles to the Ephesians and to the
Hebrews, and on the epistle general of James, delivered
at Basle during exile in Mary's reign. At the time of

the Windsor meeting, Turner was Cranmer's chaplain; and in view of Merbecke's competent compositions and reformed opinions, might well have proposed him as a composer of music for a vernacular liturgy.

Merbecke's arrest followed the unwise behaviour of Robert Testwood, another lay clerk of reformed views, who, besides causing excitement by altering the Latin words of what he was expected to sing, struck off (with a key he carried) the nose of an alabaster figure of the Virgin Mary reverenced by pilgrims. A lawyer, William Simons, retrieved the nose and Merbecke, Testwood, and two others were arrested and their houses searched.

Merbecke's *Concordance* was found and confiscated (it had reached L, every word with its Latin equivalent). Also found were his notebook on the Bible, and a letter of John Calvin against the Mass, copied for another man, as he pleaded at his trial, before the Six Articles became law. Merbecke had admirers: two of the judges favoured him – Sir Humphrey Foster, who spoke up for him, and Dr Capon, Bishop of Salisbury; Dr Skip, Bishop of Hereford, warned him of a trap during the interrogation; Dr Goodrich Bishop of Ely, admired his *Concordance*. In spite of this and his obvious integrity, Merbecke and the other three were condemned to the stake; but the sentence was delayed on the day of execution. Bishop Capon of Salisbury had written to Dr Gardiner, Bishop of Winchester, who had interrogated him, requesting a pardon. Gardiner, evidently under pressure, went to the King and obtained a reprieve; but the other three perished next day. After a period of imprisonment in the Marshalsea, Merbecke returned to his post at Windsor and began his great *Concordance* over again. This, the first to cover the whole Bible in English, was published in 1550, the same year as *The Book of Common Praier noted*.

In 1549, Merbecke is said (by Wood) to have supplicated for the degree of Bachelor of Music at Oxford, but whether he received it is not known. The records are incomplete. However, in 1550, in the Preface to his *Concordance* he wrote of his life as formerly 'vainly consumed . . . in the study of Music and playing on Organs'.

Under the influence of Swiss reformed views, organ music was now falling into disfavour as a distraction from worship. It was suppressed at New College, Oxford, in 1549, at St Paul's Cathedral and York Minster in 1552, and other churches followed suit.

Royal Injunctions (8 February, 1550) ordered the number of choristers to be reduced at St George's, Windsor, and vacancies to be filled by men with good voices, 'having always regard to their virtue and learning than in excellency in music', and suitable for ordination. The same year, on 20 October, a further injunction provided that John Merbecke and George Thaxton (his fellow organist) were to continue to receive their fees 'as if organ playing had still continued in the church'. The number of services was lessened drastically and choristers reduced to ten. The singing seems to have been unaccompanied. Music, apart from worship, was still valued and performed, and Merbecke probably taught music from 1551 in the Dean and Chapter's School at Windsor. The organs were dismantled probably late in 1550 or early in 1551; and in 1552 the King's Commissioners asked the Chapter what had become of the 'organes and pipes'. When the Second English Prayer Book was published in 1552, Merbecke's settings to the 1549 Prayer Book needed adaptation to accommodate the changes; but after Edward VI's premature death in 1553 it became impossible to consider a second edition.

It is not known how Merbecke, holding Calvinistic views, survived Mary's reign (1553–58); but he remained at Windsor when the Latin Mass and its elaborate music were revived. Possibly he taught music in the school, but the only references to him in surviving records are for work as a copyist in 1553–4; again in 1555–6 for examining and correcting choir books; and in 1557–8 for copying, for John Somer, one of the Canons, a *Collectarium*, or book of liturgical collects. Copies were rare and this was probably the manuscript listed in an inventory of 1385.

In 1558–9, at the beginning of Elizabeth's reign, Merbecke was paid again as Master of the Choristers and for 'playing on the organs', the first time surviving accounts show payments to him for both duties in the same year. In the following year, 1559–60, new regals (portable reed organs) were purchased for his use, although the accounts show that others had been bought for the Chapel as recently as 1555. In 1564, Merbecke had five shillings 'for pricking songs this quarter' and ten shillings for playing the organs. He is not known to have composed any more music. He devoted his time to religious writing; and published six works besides his *Concordance* and *The Book of Common Praier noted*.

Merbecke's loss of interest in liturgical music reflected contemporary attitudes. It was due largely, if not wholly, to the influence of the more advanced Continental Reformers, and exemplifies the inter-relation of music with the theological movements of the period.

Before the introduction of the First English Prayer Book, in 1549, his position at Windsor had familiarised him with the numerous books used in the performance of the Roman liturgy.

The developed Roman rite was used throughout England, Wales and Scotland before 1300. There were two groups of service books: one for the eight daily services; another for the sacraments and other offices. The first group included: the Psalter (containing Psalms and Canticles); the Antiphonary (antiphons and anthems); the Responsary (responds to lessons); the Bible (for lessons); the Homiliary (sermons); the Hymnary (hymns); and others besides. In the second group were the Sacramentary (prayers at the Eucharist and other services); the Gradual (the parts of the Eucharist sung by the choir); the Lectionary (lessons and epistles at the Eucharist); and the Gospel Book (gospels). The two groups were linked by the Ordo, providing rules for singing the services.

Later, the contents of these books were re-arranged for convenience; and by 1500 they consisted of the Portifory (containing everything for Divine Service, and so-called because it was small enough to be carried about); the Missal (all for the Eucharist); the Manual (all the offices used in a parish church); the Processional (litanies and other material for processions); and the Pie, containing rules for singing the services in the preceding four books. There were two other books: the Pontifical (everything used by the bishop) and the Primer (an official book of private prayers).

The rites varied in different places and by the early sixteenth century York, Lincoln, Hereford, Exeter, Salisbury, Aberdeen and Bangor, besides some monastic churches, had their own Uses. The liturgy was so complex that a great desire arose for liturgical reform, both on the Continent and in England by the second decade of the century. Many ancient customs had been allowed to fall into disuse, to be replaced by new rites and ceremonies. As the services, including hymns and readings, were in Latin, which few could understand, they had become in the main musical performances of trained singers in larger churches, with lay people as mere spectators.

In early times, services had been sung in plain-chant, which was always unaccompanied and in unison. In Rome it developed as Gregorian chant, based on the *Cantilena Romana* evolved by the papal choir in the fifth and sixth centuries, codified in the time of Pope Gregory, and brought to England by the Roman mission in 597, where it gradually replaced older forms.

From these beginnings, the use of music in services became increasingly elaborate. The use of antiphons is an example. From the fourth century, the custom grew of chanting the Psalms responsively (or antiphonally, to use the term in a modern sense) by dividing the choir into two parts.

A later variant was the introduction, between the chanted verses, of refrains or antiphons always sung to tunes (i.e melodic) governed by the first (and not the dominant or reciting) note of the respond or original Psalm verse. In time, the refrain disappeared except for processional use and in the choir offices, where it tended to be dropped except in a shortened form after the first verse, and in full after the last verse of the psalm.

Psalms were chanted also at Mass, at both the Introit and the Communion, but at the latter were reduced eventually to one or two verses only, before being dropped entirely, leaving only the antiphon. Some elaborate antiphons arose independently with no reference to psalms, and were sung especially in processions; while others kept the idea of the psalm verse, but were sung to melodies instead of the psalm chant. These were used generally at the Offertory.

Gregorian chant thus embraced both the original plain song and developed responsorial or antiphonal singing.

The words of antiphons were usually Biblical and, in the Daily Offices, sung before and after the canticles and psalms. Those sung before the *Benedictus* at Lauds, and the *Magnificat* at Vespers, came from the gospel for the day; and verses chosen for the antiphons of the weekdays following, continued the Gospel's teaching. For example, the antiphons before the Christmas psalms were: before Psalm 2, 'Thou art my Son, this day have I begotten thee . . .'; before Psalm 19, 'The Lord cometh forth as a bridegroom . . .'; and before Psalm 45, 'Full of grace are Thy lips . . .'

Similar anthems called *Invitatories* were sung before the *Venite* (sometimes called the Invitatory Psalm, and in Henry VIII's Primer 'A song stirring to the praise of God'). They were repeated in the course of it either in whole or in part, and were intended to emphasise the theme of the day's services. For example, the Invitatory for the first Sunday in Advent was: 'Behold the King cometh, let us go to meet our Saviour', and sung in full before verse 1, and after verses 2, 7 and 11. After verses 4 and 9, this was shortened to 'Let us go to meet our Saviour'; but the entire Invitatory was repeated after the *Gloria*. In practice, this scheme was too complex for an ordinary congregation and found to detract from worship. The Sarum Use, imposed on the whole Southern Province by the Convocation of Canterbury in 1542, had a different Invitatory for each day of the week.

The words 'O Sapienta', printed beside 16 December
in the *Book of Common Prayer* calendar, mark the
first of the nine days until Christmas Eve, which had
special Antiphons to the *Magnificat*. They were called
the great Oes, from their opening words: O Sapientia;
O Adonay; O radix Jesse; O clavis David; O Thome
Didime (on the Eve of St Thomas, 20 December); O
oriens Splendor; O Rex Gentium; O Emmanuel; O
Virgo Virgintum. (St Thomas' day fell on 21 December until 1980.) O Sapientia (16 December) was the sig-
nal for medieval revelry which at Salisbury, for example,
led to lay abuse ruled against by the Cathedral Statutes.
Extra payments were made to the choristers there 'pro
le O' on 16 December long after the Reformation; but
by 1624 the origins were so far forgotten that the words
were corrupted to 'cum leo'!

Antiphons, originally intended to involve congregations in repetitive devotional singing when books were
scarce, few could read, and Latin was spoken, had
become so complex by the sixteenth century that many
thinking Christians considered they hindered rather
than enhanced worship. The music demanded trained
singers; and the Latin words were unintelligible to a
largely illiterate laity.

Hymns had been known since New Testament times.
Written at first for lay participation when their original
Greek or Latin was universally understood or spoken,
their use passed gradually to trained choirs, monks and
clergy who, in the Western Church, continued to sing
them in Latin, with one exception, and so excluding the
laity. Many ancient hymns were in metre; and each choir
office came to have its special hymn. These were revived
in translation by the Tractarians in the nineteenth century.
Other ancient hymns or canticles became integrated into
the liturgy itself, and included the *Te Deum Laudamus*,
the *Gloria in excelsis*, the *Sanctus*, the *Agnus Dei*, and
the *Quicumque Vult*, all sung in Latin except the *Kyrie
Eleison*, which was always sung in Greek.

In the Sarum Breviary, the *Quicumque Vult* was appointed to be sung daily at Prime, after the psalms and

before the prayers. It had its own varying antiphons and was concluded by the *Gloria Patri*.

The *Te Deum*, whose form suggests it was originally intended to be sung by a choir, and which, in the Roman Breviary, was entitled 'Psalm Te Deum', was used in the Latin Mass on special occasions; but set to elaborate music it could form a separate service.

Before the Reformation, new feasts introduced into monastic churches were each accompanied by special antiphons and fresh music. Musical standards rose, and polyphonic music developed both in popularity and complexity as the services themselves became more elaborate. Unfortunately, however, the sense of the words was sacrified frequently to satisfy musical considerations and much was omitted. The Preface to the 1549 English Prayer Book refers to this practice and to the daily psalms, of which a few were said or sung and the rest 'utterly omitted'.

Erasmus wrote with feeling of the dominance of musical considerations to the neglect of essential elements in worship. The Creed was shortened, the Lord's Prayer inaudible, the singing of the Prosa too long; words were compressed or omitted to suit the music; and, especially when faburdons were sung, they produced 'a tremendous tonal clamour, so that not a single word is understood'.

Continental changes began in the 1520s with Lutheran vernacular services; and there were papal attempts to revise and shorten Latin rites. The Roman Breviary (or abridgement of the Daily Offices), drawn up originally under Pope Hildebrand (Gregory VII, 1073–1086), was reformed and revised in 1516; and in 1541 the Salisbury Breviary was issued, further reformed. The similar attempt of Ferdinandez Quiñones, the Spanish cardinal, to introduce a further compression and revision of the Roman Breviary (at the request of Pope Clement VII) in 1535, and again revised the following year, was so well received that it was reprinted six times between February 1535 and May 1536. A second edition was reprinted 20 times before its suppression in 1566.

Continental reformed teaching, and especially that of
Martin Luther, was much discussed in Cambridge in
the early 1520s in a group which included a number
of future bishops and probably Cranmer himself. When
he visited Germany in 1532, he attended reformed services and afterwards kept himself informed on Lutheran
ideas and experiments, as well as those of the Catholic
tradition.

A comparison of the views of Zwingli, Calvin and
Luther on church music reveals the concern about its
effects on comprehension, participation and devotion.

Zwingli, the most musically gifted of the three, was
the most radical, considering music to be a distraction
in Christian worship, and congregational hymn singing
unscriptural. By 1525, all music, as well as ceremonial,
was removed from Zurich churches; and in 1527 the
organ in the Grossmünster was dismantled. In contrast, Zwingli recognised the value of religious music
played or sung in private.

Calvin shared many of Zwingli's views, but believed
that music had a proper place in worship within certain
limitations. He allowed the unaccompanied singing of
metrical psalms in unison by the whole congregation,
but polyphonic music was forbidden on the grounds
that the words could not be heard distinctly, and the
congregation had to remain passive during its performance.

Martin Luther's approach was different. He wanted
all the arts, and especially church music, to be used in
the service of God, and therefore in worship. Later
Lutherans, following his lead, developed a distinctive
instrumental and choral tradition of church music.

A little later the English Thomas Becon expressed in
The jewel of joys (1553) views similar to those of Zwingli.
While approving of sacred music in private, he too was
concerned about church music as a distraction from the
simple proclamation of the Gospel through preaching
and the Sacrament.

When Thomas Cranmer was consecrated Archbishop
of Canterbury on 30 March, 1533, he was well equip-

ped to forward reform when given the opportunity; but Henry VIII's objections to liturgical change made progress difficult. Yet in 1537, he ordered Bibles in Latin and English to be placed in every church, while continuing to forbid the use of English during the services. With the King's sanction, in 1542 a Committee of Convocation was set up consisting of two bishops and six other clergy. It was to consider the whole question of revising the service books, especially missals, antiphoners and portifories or breviaries; to eradicate all reference to the Bishop of Rome; to remove all apocryphal or legendary material, the names and memorials of saints not mentioned in Scripture or in the ancient doctors of the church, and all 'superstitious oraisons' (prayers), collects, versicles and responses. The breviary had been used mainly by religious orders, by then abolished, and it was felt that a prayer book for more general use was needed. The Commission began by simplifying the numerous and complex rubrics. Its work was impeded by the Act of Six Articles of 1543, which made reformed teaching impossible, under pain of severe penalties. Little was achieved during the King's lifetime, although in 1542 the use of the Sarum Breviary was imposed throughout the Southern Province, so ending much diversity; and in 1543 a chapter of the Bible was commanded to be read in English after the *Te Deum* at Matins and after the *Magnificat* at Evensong.

Meantime, Cranmer was working on English 'processions' or litanies. In June 1544, he received from the King a letter directing the use of a 'procession' or litany in all parish churches because of 'the miserable state of all Christendom' which was 'so plagued with most cruel wars'. England was at war with Scotland and Henry VIII was preparing to invade France with Charles V. Litanies on such occasions were customary and many Primers had included litanies for over 150 years. The letter itself appears to be Cranmer's, written with the King's assent.

Forasmuch as heretofore the people, partly for lack of good instruction and calling, partly for that they

understood no part of such prayers or suffrages, as
were used to be sung and said, have used to come
very slackly to the procession, when the same have
been commanded heretofore: we have set forth certain godly prayers and suffrages in our native English
tongue.

It was 'to be sung or said, as the number of the quire
shall serve', and came to be included (apart from clauses
invoking the Virgin Mary, saints, patriarchs, prophets
and apostles), in every edition of the *Book of Common
Prayer*.

The main sources were the Sarum *Processionale* (itself
based on a Greek liturgy brought to England about 700)
with many saints' names omitted, petitions grouped,
and versicles and responses added; a Latin litany of
Luther; a collect from the Latin version of the Liturgy
of St Chrysostom; and some additions of Cranmer himself.

The Litany in English was first sung in procession
in St Paul's Cathedral on St Luke's Day, Sunday 18
October, 1545. It was published as *An exhortation unto
prayer, . . . to be read in every church afore processyons. Also
a letanie with suffrages to be said or song in the tyme of the
said processyons*. Of seven editions known to have been
published in octavo in 1544, three have music and four
are without, while another, undated, but probably of the
same year is 16° in format and has no music. Two more
editions appeared in 1545 without music; and a further
two editions, also lacking music, were printed in 1546.
The original music consisted of simple syllabic melodies;
but soon the English Litany was sung to uncomplicated
four-part settings.

It has been conjunctured (without firm evidence) that
Merbecke was associated with Cranmer in producing
the Litany, and adapted the music to Cranmer's text.
Merbecke's talent was already recognised through his
known surviving works: two Latin motets, an English
carol, and a polyphonic Mass for five voices.

Later in 1544 Cranmer wrote to Henry VIII about

verse translations of several more 'processions'; he suggested they might be set to 'some devout and solemn note' and that they should 'not be full of notes, but, as near as may be, for every syllable a note, so that it may be sung distinctly and devoutly'. He was referring to the practice, usual at the period, in connection with the canticles but laying down no rule, and alluded to his attempt (not very successful) to translate the Latin hymn *Salve sancte dies* into English.

At this time, Cranmer was already working on other English services, adapting for general use the eight choir offices which were, by then, often recited in two groups for morning and evening use respectively.

Immediately after the King's death, Convocation resolved that the works of the 1544 Committee should be laid before them; the offending Statute of Six Articles was repealed; and Cranmer produced two tentative schemes for the Daily Offices. The work of revision was completed in 1548; and the first English Prayer Book was authorised by Convocation, the King in Council, and then by Parliament. It was ordered to be used in all churches after Whitsunday 1549. In its preface, much of which derives from Quiñones' revised Breviary, Cranmer refers to the number and hardness of the rules called the Pie, which were so hard and intricate 'that many times there was more business to fynd out what should be read than to read it when it was found out'. He concludes by saying that the services shall be read and sung in English 'to thende y^t the congregacion maie be thereby edified'.

Although each medieval Office had its hymn in metre, no hymns were included in the new book (perhaps because the Committee lacked poets); but the 1549–50 Ordinal, issued separately, contains the longer translation of the *Veni Creator* which is probably, but not certainly, Cranmer's work. He had admitted he had no facility in verse in his letter to Henry VIII quoted above:

But by cause mine English verses lack the grace and

facility that I would wish they had, Your Majesty may cause some other to make them again, that can do the same in more pleasant English and phrase.

Clearly, the priest and clerks (choir) were to sing the English services. There was no direction, as yet, for the congregation to join in. At Matins, the parts to be said or sung were the *Venite* in English, the proper psalms, the other canticles, and *Gloria*. At Evensong the directions were similar, with the *Quicumque Vult* to be 'song or sayd' after the *Benedictus* at Christmas, Epiphany, Easter, Ascension, Pentecost and Trinity. The rubrics for Holy Communion direct the clerks to sing a special psalm as Introit, followed by the *Kyries* (in English) and the Offertory sentences; and the priest is to 'saye or syng' the Prayer for the Church Militant, down to the consecration. After the Lord's Prayer, the priest says 'The peace of the Lord be always with you', and the clerks answer (?sing) 'And with thy Spirite'. During the Communion, the clerks are to sing 'O lamb of God . . .' and the Scripture sentences of the post-Communion. The Litany is to be said or sung on Wednesdays and Fridays. In the marriage service, there is provision for the clerks to sing the psalm or canticle as the priest leads the couple into the quire. At a burial, the opening sentences may be sung by priest and clerks together, and the verse 'I heard a voyce from heaven . . .', before the graveside prayers, is to be sung also. A separate injunction ordered the Litany to be sung also on Sundays before High Mass by the clerks and clergy kneeling.

Although the words were now in English, contemporary church music had been composed to suit Latin words. Only the English Litany was provided with its own music from the first; but the directions for singing in the 1549 Prayer Book anticipated the provision of the new setting which Merbecke was to provide in 1550.

Unfortunately, when the Second English Prayer Book was published in 1552, Merbecke's settings were outdated and fell into disuse. Services with a minimum of music had now become the ideal and no second edition was prepared. Merbecke's work was generally forgotten until it was rediscovered and revived in an adapted form in the nineteenth century.

The Royal Order of 1561, commanding the removal of everything above the breast-summer (the load-bearing beam) of rood screens, often affected musical performance. Besides the crucifix, attendant figures, and sconces, the gallery and both parapets must be taken down although the screen itself (perhaps decorated with a coat of arms) remained to divide chancel and nave. As, in many churches, both organ and singers (facing the congregation) had occupied the rood-loft, it was often re-erected for them at the west end, or a new gallery built there. The congregation 'faced the music' for some sung parts of the service, especially (a little later) the metrical psalm after the third collect. An alternative was to place the organ and singers at the side of the nave. In Wales, the Order was much ignored. Singers, musicians and organs occupied the rood-loft in some places until this century.

Clergy exiled in Geneva during Mary's reign were strongly under Calvinistic influence. They returned to England objecting to the 1552 Prayer Book, the use in worship of organs and other musical instruments, and antiphonal singing, alluded to as 'the singing, ringing and trowling of Psalms from one side of the choir to the other'. Their disapproval resulted in a motion brought before Convocation in 1562, proposing the abolition of organs and 'curious music'. It was defeated by only a narrow majority.

Because many thought it profane to sing during divine service anything not directly derived from Scripture, collections of versified psalms became popular. In 1561, William Kethe published a Genevan Psalter containing 87 psalms; and a complete French Psalter appeared in Geneva in 1562 containing some translations by the French poet Marot (1497–1544) and a number of good tunes by Louis Bourgeois. Thomas Sternhold had produced nineteen metrical psalms in 1549, to which John Hopkins and others made additions to complete

The Whole Book of Psalms, published in 1562. Originally
a different tune was intended for each psalm, but the
idea petered out for later psalms. Tunes borrowed
from Bourgeois, originally written for elegant French
verse, were poorly adapted to less sophisticated English
translations; and much of the verse was poor; but the
book appealed to a largely illiterate laity who could learn
the words and sing them to simple tunes, especially those
well written by composers such as Thomas Tallis.

Day's Psalter of 1561 was less famous; but the edition
of 1562 was the first complete and harmonised Psalter. It contained metrical psalms by Thomas Becon,
and Edmund Grindal (1576–83), who was successively
Bishop of Salisbury and Archbishop of York, and followed Matthew Parker at Canterbury in 1575. Both were
returned exiles who disapproved of organs and choral
music.

There was much borrowing of material. Sternhold
and Hopkins had borrowed from the 1561 Psalter of
William Kethe, whose eighty-seven metrical psalms, with
forty-two from Sternhold and Hopkins and twenty-one
new ones were adopted by the Scottish Presbyterians
to form their Metrical Psalter, still in use. Psalm 124
was versified by William Whittingham (the Presbyterian
Dean of Durham), with a tune by Bourgeois, whose *Old
Hundredth* is still sung to 'All people that on earth do
dwell', the metrical version of Psalm 100.

Thomas Tallis contributed some tunes to Archbishop
Parker's metrical Psalter of *c.*1567; but as this was not for
congregational use, Sternhold and Hopkins remained
in vogue in ordinary parish churches until the 'New
Version' of Tate and Brady appeared in 1696.

The 'Old Version' of Sternhold and Hopkins (1562)
included the *Te Deum,* the *Nunc Dimittis,* the Athanasian
Creed, the Lord's Prayer, and the Ten Commandments
all in metre, besides eight hymns. This small hymnary
was copied and expanded later in the metrical Psalters of
Tate and Brady, Ravenscroft, and Playford, and others
in the following century. The advocates of only words
paraphrased from Scripture became fewer, and slowly

hymns as we know them came to be generally accepted.

Meantime, in cathedrals, collegiate churches and parishes with good choirs, an English school of church music was developing. Later in Elizabeth's reign it became part of the great outburst of talent in literature, music and art.

Queen Elizabeth herself was a skilled performer on the lute and virginals, and it is possible that had it not been for her love of music and encouragement the great choral tradition, as we now know it, might never have taken root and flourished. Elizabeth herself was reticent about her religious views; but while she would not allow the elevation of the Host in her royal chapel, she wished to worship with a certain amount of ceremonial before an altar furnished with crucifix and candles, and with clergy wearing traditional vestments. These had to be accepted as private preferences by the Puritans who disapproved. Although sympathising with reformed teaching in moderation, she refused to admit the more advanced views imported from Geneva.

Some of the most distinguished composers of the day were associated in some way with the royal chapel. The 'Chapels Royal' were (and are) composed of clergy and choristers directly in the service of the monarch and the court, and travelled about with them when required. Merbecke's appointment at Windsor was to the 'Royal Free Chapel', a separate foundation serving the Order of the Garter and the residents in Windsor Castle. There, in the Upper Ward, is the chapel royal, independent of St George's Chapel. Sometimes the staff of the chapel royal joined with the singing men of St George's Chapel on particular occasions, and are known to have done so in Merbecke's time. This may explain in part why Merbecke's talents were not revived in the new movement, quite apart from his disinclination on theological grounds, and his increasing deafness.

Among the earliest composers associated with the chapel royal to take up the new style of simple music was Christopher Tye (c. 1500–72), who began the fashion of writing four-part anthems, which could be sung by non-professional singers. He was a choirboy in Cambridge, but in 1553, when he published his *Actes of the Apostles,* he was attached to the chapel royal and music tutor to Edward VI. Tye was a prolific composer, circulating his compositions in manuscript.

Another composer was Thomas Tallis (*c.*1505–85) who, although not directly connected with the chapel royal, obtained royal favour. He was organist at Waltham Abbey at the dissolution in 1540. Although he composed mostly for Latin words, he took up the fashion for simpler music tending to lay performance and congregational worship. Some of his compositions appeared in Day's Psalter. In 1576, he and William Byrd were granted by Queen Elizabeth a monopoly for music printing for twenty-one years; and in the same year published *Cantiones Sacrae.* His 'First Service' was printed in 1641; and the Oxford Movement led to the publication of many of his works. He wrote a gigantic motet for forty voices; but perhaps he is best remembered for his settings for the responses, which became much loved and used almost universally,

William Byrd (*c.*1538–1623) was 'bred up to musick' by Thomas Tallis and was organist of Lincoln Cathedral from 1563, succeeding to a vacancy in the chapel royal in 1569. Besides music for virginals, he composed much sacred music, including three Masses. In contrast to his Latin music, much of his English work was not printed in his life-time, although it was known in many places. This was due to the 'circulating library' system of co-operation between cathedrals and collegiate foundations. A composer sent round the vocal score and usually a sketchy organ part of a service or anthem, and each church had transcribed each voice part separately into its own proper voice book, and the organ part into the organ book, before forwarding the manuscript to the next cathedral or other church. Most of such manuscripts wore out in use, those for the treble or boys' parts suffering most. The complete text of Byrd's Great Service was discovered among the manuscript choir books of Durham Cathedral in the early 1920s, and is now preserved as one of the sets in Durham Cathedral Library. It was thus retrieved for publication.

A pupil of William Byrd, Thomas Morley (1557–1604), was organist of St Paul's Cathedral in 1591–2 before becoming a gentleman of the chapel royal from 1592–1602. His *Plaine and Easie Introduction to Practicall Musicke* (1597) long remained a standard authority. He wrote profusely, published several collections, and was granted a monopoly for printing music, following that of Tallis and Byrd, in 1598.

Orlando Gibbons (1583–1625) was organist of the chapel royal before 1606 until leaving the post before 1622. His madrigals, anthems and hymns are master-pieces of their kind, and he is associated with the development of music for stringed instruments, writing music in three parts for viols.

Another composer who did much to enrich church music was Thomas Weelkes (d.1623). He first appears in connection with his first book of madrigals for three, four, five and six voices (1597). In a Book of *Balletts and Madrigals,* published in 1598 and dedicated to Edward Darcye, groom of the Privy Chamber, he alludes to his 'yeeres yet unripened' and it has been conjectured that he was born between 1570 and 1580. Weelkes was organ-ist at Winchester College, and on 16 July, 1602, took the degree of Mus.B. from New College, Oxford, after which he became organist of Chichester Cathedral. He had published two sets of madrigals in five and six parts in 1600. A six-part madrigal of his appeared in a volume by Thomas Morley, to whose memory he paid tribute in 'a Remembrance of his friend Thomas Morley' in *Ayeres or Phantastique Spirites* (1608). In the latter part of his life he composed much church music, including thirty-two anthems and six services.

It is clear from these examples that appointments to the chapel royal were closely connected with the flower-ing of choral music for the enrichment of worship; while the granting of monopolies to print music to gifted musicians in the same sphere helped to promote the new compositions. Without such royal patronage, and

exposed to Puritan disapproval, the performance of the
liturgy and its music would have been the poorer.

Summary and Conclusion

Under Cranmer, the English church achieved a Reformed liturgy based on ancient precedents, presented as
one simple book for clergy and laity alike, to replace
a multiplicity of books. Portions of its services were
intended to be sung by clerks or choir, and its use of
English ensured lay understanding (with exceptions, for
example, in colleges where Latin was still the learned
language). Although most of Cranmer's own work on
litanies, sung by clergy and laity together, was never
used, it confirms the impression that he hoped for
a means of lay participation. The desired hymns in
translation were missing because not only did the 1544
Committee lack the talent, but failed to grasp their value
for worship, mutual edification and teaching, points
recognised long ago by St Ambrose. Growing Puritan
opposition prevailed. Yet Cranmer's words, following
ancient traditions of liturgical writing, had an intrinsic
musical rhythm and natural beauty which made them
easily memorable, so that they were absorbed into the
minds of generations of English-speaking people. The
prayers and collects became their own; and words and
phrases repeated in ordinary social intercourse fulfilled,
in part at least, the purpose of the primitive hymns.

Clearly Cranmer did not intend the abandonment
of good liturgical music, but, influenced by Puritan
fear of its associations with unreformed doctrine, others
cast out the ancient legacy of plainsong, polyphony
and hymnody which might have been adapted and
developed for English words and lay participation.

Merbecke himself failed to adapt his settings to the
1552 Prayer Book because of his Calvinistic views on
music. The poor quality of some of the metrical psalms,
inserted to meet a need for lay sung participation, combined uneasily with the dignity and beauty of Cranmer's

English. More than a hundred years passed, including the Commonwealth period when the Prayer Book was abandoned, before English services began to take the shape a more perceptive Edwardian Committee might have forged.

The revival of English worship, which lasted well into the present century, comprised many factors: the gradual growth of successful hymnody through writers such as Milton, Vaughan, Bunyan, Herbert, the Wesleys, and others; new translations of the ancient Latin hymns; the rediscovery of Merbecke's work in the nineteenth century and its adaptation to the 1662 Prayer Book; while, after robed choirs were introduced into parish churches (beginning at Leeds in 1841), anthems and settings, well within their scope, became readily available, many of these from competent new composers.

Today, much of this material is discarded in favour of a transient modernity. The late twentieth century poor standard of English and passion for 'relevance' to secular attitudes combine to give the impression of a lack of confidence in the Christian message. The worshipper is faced again with more than one service book and many complicated alternatives; a common 'Use' has been lost; and even, in a few instances, Latin words have been reintroduced (meaningless to almost everyone, however beautifully enunciated). In following the current fashion for the service of 'Parish Communion', especially in one of the forms in the *Alternative Service Book*, many good settings are neglected, particularly for Prayer Book Mattins; and because of its lack of memorable words and phrases, poetical quality, and natural word rhythms, worthy new music is in short supply. The material does not encourage composition.

The old pattern of rejection has been repeated in recent attempts at liturgical reform, and perhaps with even less satisfactory results when Cranmer's superb gift for musical and memorable English has been ignored. The qualities of a modern Cranmer are needed to select from, re-interpret, and develop, our even richer heritage of words and music for the lasting worship of the contemporary church, otherwise there will be little to hand down to future generations.

Acknowledgment

Grateful thanks are due to Dr Peter Le Huray, who kindly read the draft text of this essay and made many helpful suggestions. Any faults are those of the author.

Select Bibliography

Fellowes, E.H., *The Office of the Holy Communion* as set by John Merbecke (Oxford, 1949).

Fellowes, E.H., *Organists and Masters of the Choristers of St George's Chapel in Windsor Castle.* 2nd edition (Windsor, 1979).

Hunt, J.E., *Cranmer's* First Litany, 1544, and *Merbecke's Book of Common Prayer noted*, 1550 (London, 1939).

Leaver, R.A., *The Work of John Marbeck* (Sutton Courtenay, 1978).

Moorman, J.R.H., *A History of the Church in England* (London, 1953).

X

Prayer Book Catholicism
Sheridan Gilley

The displacement of the *Book of Common Prayer* from its central place in the worship of the Church of England over the past two decades may obscure the fact that the Prayer Book has been challenged before, and that even while its content has remained virtually unchanged since 1662, there is a sense in which its significance has been different for each successive generation. This paper considers the reasons why the Prayer Book survived largely unscathed through the nineteenth century, in spite of one of the biggest transformations of Anglican worship in the Church of England's history. What it seeks to show is how the Prayer Book was made a vehicle for these changes; for the book's survival was due in good part to the fact that it was able not only to accommodate change, but to provide an argument for it.

Take an ordinary Anglican church in 1800. Its central feature was probably a three-decker pulpit, for parson and clerk, dominating and perhaps obscuring the small communion table behind or even beneath it. Indeed the medieval chancel might well have been shut off and used as a storage room or day school. Otherwise, the chief features of the building were its classical wall memorials and the high box pews which were very often the 'appropriated' rented or private property of leading families in the congregation, while most of the remaining seating was also let for a fee. More seating was available in the large modern galleries which ran round three sides of the building and sometimes four. The walls were whitewashed, and, if there was any stained glass, it was almost certainly medieval; the windows were nearly all made of clear leaded glass without colour or distinctive ecclesiastical symbols or decoration. The church was manifestly a preaching box, with the Word exalted over the Sacrament, with weekly celebrations of Matins and Evensong, and with Communion services only perhaps four times a year; while preaching the clergyman might wear a black Geneva gown. The choir might well perform with an orchestra of flutes and fiddles in the west gallery, its stock repertoire still being the metrical psalms, as popular hymnody was only just beginning to make its big advances into Anglican worship, and there were only the two metrical hymns, and those only for ordinations and episcopal consecrations, the two translations of the *Veni Creator*, 'Come Holy Ghost', in the *Book of Common Prayer*.[1]

Take the same church in 1900. The pulpit is less prominent and the chancel is again in use, its dominant feature being the vested altar surmounted by a carved stone or marble or wooden reredos and standing in full sight of the congregation. If the church is a fairly high one, there will be two lighted candles on the altar – a crucifix and six candles denotes highness indeed – but in a great many churches, the altar will be 'garnished', that is, decorated by the ladies with vases, foliage and flowers. A pitiless incumbent has swept the box pews away, and replaced them with free and open seating. The galleries may have been demolished, and the walls scraped clear of whitewash, and perhaps even adorned with Gothic stencilling. Most of the windows contain bright modern stained glass by Kempe and Clayton and Bell. Significantly, the whole atmosphere has changed. The church has now clearly become a sacrament house, the centre of the eucharistic cultus, and the preaching of the Word has been demoted to an equal if not to second place. The clergyman wears a stole and surplice at Communion and faces east; in the mission chapel for the poor down the road, his curate is more daring and wears a chasuble. The surpliced choir occupies new or refurbished stalls in the chancel, and the orchestra has given way to a properly ecclesiastical organ. The Greek and Latin hymnody of Byzantium and of medieval and modern Rome has been ransacked by Anglican translators, pre-eminent among them John Mason Neale, to furnish the materials for congregational singing, now made available in *Hymns Ancient and Modern*. But though the appearance of the service has been changed utterly, the clergyman and congregation are still using the same form of words in 1900 as in 1800. They are possibly now being chanted rather than simply read, but are only decked out with Roman interpolations in those few churches which attain the very heights of highness. All seems to have changed – but one thing has not: the clergyman and congregation have held on to their ancient heritage, the words of the *Book of Common Prayer*[2].

Of course, this transformation was by no means universal. It was for long resisted by Evangelicals, and only occurred in many churches in this century. It is strange to recall that the legality of lighting candles on the altar for a ceremonial as distinct from a utilitarian purpose, to indicate a Real Presence in the Sacrament, was really resolved by Archbishop Edward White Benson's Lincoln Judgment at late as 1890. Reserving the Blessed Sacrament only spread during and after the First World War. Yet there are now few churches with old-fashioned box pews, and I know of only one with a great central pulpit, the Sailors' Church at Whitby, if you except the elegant manorial arrangements of Gibside Chapel. But it is surely remarkable that the Anglo-Catholic rebuilders of the Victorian Church of England were able to achieve their revolution essentially within the forms of the old words, and indeed they created a lasting liturgical tradition, the Prayer Book Catholic tradition, which has only suffered eclipse in the last decades of this century.

One reason for this lies in the Anglo-Catholic loyalty to the *Book of Common Prayer*. From the seventeenth century, it was the particular pride of High Churchmen to hold to the words and worship of the Prayer Book, as an authentic statement of the faith of the undivided Church of the early Christian centuries. The book had, moreover, been consecrated, firstly by Puritan abuse of it in the sixteenth century, as 'an unperfect book, culled and picked out of that popish dunghill, the Mass book full of all abominations,'[3] then by the Puritan ban upon it during the Interregnum, and by the blood of the martyrs, Archbishop William Laud and King Charles I, who were held to have died for it. King, bishop and Prayer Book were the three pillars of the Restoration Settlement in 1660; indeed 2,000 Puritan clergy who refused to use the book in its amended form were expelled from their parishes in 1662. The celebrated preface to the ordination services already restricted the Anglican ministry to the three Catholic orders of bishops, priests and deacons who had been episcopally consecrated or ordained; but the preface was now interpreted not only to guarantee that the Church of England was an episcopal church, but also led into the High Anglican view that churches without bishops, like the Presbyterian and Independent, had no valid ministry and sacraments, and were therefore not churches. Thus loyalty to the Prayer Book and the ministry ordained according to its rites was the special mark of the Churchman, against the Papist and Dissenter; and against Dissenters especially, a true Anglican was one who was loyal to the *Book of Common Prayer*.

Thus the significance of the Prayer Book was different after 1662 from what it had been before 1640; attitudes had hardened on both sides, and Cosin's revised book of 1662 defined with a new clarity the Anglican Churchman against the non-Anglican Dissenter. Indeed, the radical Puritan and Protestant unease with certain aspects of the Prayer Book is the source of one tradition of dissent from it *within* the Church. The other tradition of dissent arose after 1690, and was especially widespread by 1830, as liberal clergy found a new ground for objection, in the Trinitarian forms of the Doxology, the imprecatory or cursing psalms, and the damnatory clauses of the Athanasian Creed. To some extent, the two traditions of dislike of the Prayer Book, the Protestant and the liberal, coalesced, as liberals worried about traditional dogma also tended to be sensitive to Protestant dissenting objections;[4] but Church and

State under the four Georges were generally not to be
fussed with such controversies, and when in the 1790s,
English Churchmen closed ranks against the ideas of
revolutionary France, there developed an even more
marked unwillingness to abandon the sacred Prayer
Book text. Even many of the new Anglican Evangelicals
championed the Prayer Book, like the clerical leader of
the Evangelical party, Charles Simeon, who declared the
Prayer Book 'as superior to all modern compositions as
the work of a philosopher . . . is to that of a school-boy'.[5]
We could even describe the Prayer Book in the period of
the French wars as a counter-revolutionary document,
declaring the Churchman's opposition to Gallic atheis-
tic and republican regicide, a new enemy to put beside
the Papists, the Dissenters, and the English infidels and
Deists, who also looked with hope to events across the
Channel.

In fact, however, the years after 1790 saw the beginnings of the mushroom growth of Dissent in England
and the first political stirrings of Roman Catholicism
in Ireland. Dissenters were given the permanent and
formal right to sit in the British legislature in 1828, the
Roman Catholics were admitted in 1829; and a Parliament containing non-Protestants and non-episcopalians
now had a supreme authority over the Protestant episcopal Church of England. The crisis in Church–State relations came to a head in 1833, when the Whig government, supported by radicals, Dissenters and Roman
Catholics began to reform the small and unrepresentative established Church of Ireland, which had been
united with the Church of England under the Act of
Union in 1800. It was this crisis that produced the
Oxford Movement or Anglo-Catholic revival, under
the leadership of a small group of clergymen academics
in the University of Oxford: John Keble, John Henry
Newman, Edward Bouverie Pusey and Richard Hurrell
Froude. In the first instance, their enemies were the
old High Churchman's enemies: the Dissenters, Roman
Catholics and political radicals and infidels outside the
Church, and the liberals and Evangelicals inside it.

And so, we find the Prayer Book in the 1830s assuming a still more complex role, as an authority to be defended against non-Anglicans, Papists and unbelievers, *and* Anglican Liberals and even Evangelicals, on the principle that it was the Prayer Book which was the ark of the covenant of the faith and worship of the Church of England.

That defence, however polemical, could only be mounted in the conviction that the Prayer Book was a spiritual treasury second in the English language only to the King James Bible itself. The Oxford Movement's most senior figure was an old-fashioned 'hereditary High Church' country parson of Jacobite non-Juring sympathies, John Keble; but Keble was also Professor of Poetry at Oxford, and a friend of William Wordsworth; and his first great service to Anglican Christianity was to show that there was a devotional depth in the Prayer Book which was in harmony with the deeps of contemporary Romantic experience. To the old-fashioned High Churchmen of the generation before 1830, Romantic feeling was often repudiated with anathemas as enthusiasm, and they had reason to look unfavourably on the Romantic poets. After all, Southey, Coleridge and Wordsworth had begun their public careers as Unitarians and sympathisers with revolutionary France, and though Wordsworth outgrew his flirtation with Gallic radicalism and with the young French lady who had borne him a child, and though all three of these 'Lake Poets' had become defenders of the Church of England in middle age, the conservative suspicion of Romanticism was confirmed by the atheism of Shelley and the profligacy of Byron. Keble, however, adapted the Wordsworthian model to the Anglican needs of his time by writing a collection of verses called *The Christian Year* published in 1827, one poem for each service, Sunday and red letter saint's day of the *Book of Common Prayer*. Some of these verses have become familiar to everyone as hymns – 'New every morning is the love' and 'Bless'd are the pure in heart' are the best known – and in the nineteenth century, the habit grew up in devoutly High Anglican households of reading Keble's verses before the morning service. Keble's poetry adorned the Prayer Book with the fascinations of the romantic mood; to use a word which Keble's friend and disciple Newman helped to give its currency in modern English, *The Christian Year* subtly changed the Anglican ethos, the atmosphere in which Anglicans said their prayers. Newman said that Keble 'woke up in the hearts of thousands a new music'.[6] A mere historian might say that he restored the Prayer Book to its central place in the mainstream culture of the age.[7]

Yet even Keble's poetry was not innocent of a polemical or controversial intent. In the Preface to *The Christian Year*, he declared that while the Church of England sets a 'sober standard of feeling in matters of practical religion', 'in times of much leisure and unbounded curiosity, when excitement of every kind is sought after with a morbid eagerness, this part of the merit of our Liturgy is likely to be lost . . .' This is a repudiation of the 'excitement' and 'morbid eagerness' of the revolutionary atheism of France and Shelley, and of the extra-liturgical preaching of the Evangelicals, whom the new High Churchmen especially despised and disliked for the vulgar display of emotion which was beneath the notice of a gentleman. To these excitements, to be considered both vulgar and immoral, Keble opposed the Prayer Book's '*soothing* tendency' and as Professor of Poetry at Oxford, he enunciated in his *Lectures on Poetry* a total aesthetic in which the Prayer Book had an essential place. In this, Keble trod a strait and narrow path. On the one hand, he wanted to arouse the devotional senses in worship. But he felt that such feelings are the profounder, indeed the more intense, if strictly controlled within a set of old liturgical forms. Emotion in both religion and politics is dangerous and anarchic, a threat to Church and State; it requires the discipline of an established and accepted sound form of words, and against the wild excesses of Dissenting and radical enthusiasm, against the preaching of the village Ranters

and the oratory of democratic and trade union politicians, it was this control over the emotions that the forms
of the Prayer Book were fitted to supply.

This strong sense of the need for a discipline on the
emotions passed into the Oxford Movement's teaching on 'reserve' in communicating religious knowledge.
Following the teaching of the Alexandrian Fathers Clement and Origen, Newman believed that as our Lord had
taught under the veil of parables, so the early church
in the first Christian centuries had withheld the central
truths of Christianity from its initiates or catechumens
until they were held to be sufficiently spiritually and
morally enlightened to understand them in the fullness
of faith. Indeed the primary Christian truths were mysteries only partly disclosed by God, and beyond complete
human understanding; and the fullest understanding
possible to weak human minds is only accessible to men
and women who have a measure of holiness of life. The
knowledge of God is too great for us, and sacred truth
is only partially revealed even to the holy. But if this
is so, then Evangelicals profane the mystery of Christ's
most sacred death by preaching it before the infidels
and scoffers who are by their very character least fitted
to receive it. Only the spiritually enlightened can grasp
spiritual truth. But this is also an answer to liberals who
think that religion is a matter of public reason and proof
and argument:

> Bless'd are the pure in heart,
> For *they* shall see our God . . .

It is the pure in heart who see God; not the intellectual,
not the academic, not the philosopher: 'not many wise
. . ., not many mighty, not many noble'. How indeed
could it be otherwise with a God who had chosen the
poor and simple? The convert responds not in reason
on its own but in the stillness of the awakened heart. But
this, indeed, is the very claim of the Prayer Book, that it
speaks neither in proof nor in the wild clamour of exciting preaching, but by the authority of the slow action of
hallowed words with hallowed associations over a whole

life-time of repeating them. Indeed in joy or sorrow or bereavement, their very familiarity lends them a novel force, as the threads of half a century of faith draw together and coalesce around the soul. Treat the truth in terms of quiet, though it is tremendous; and *then* it will strike home into the heart.

The Oxford Movement, therefore, approached the Prayer Book on its knees, as a book of worship containing the best means for teaching the Christian faith, on the principle that we get our understanding of religion from the way in which we say our prayers. Religion for Newman begins for all believers in devotion, as it began in apostolic devotion to the person of Christ; and theology is the rational explication of this devotion, as faith, using reason as its instrument, seeks out an understanding of itself. Thus, as Newman explains the matter in his *Lectures on the Prophetical Office*, which defines Anglicanism as a *via media* or middle way between Popery and popular Protestantism, it is the *lex orandi* or law of prayer which determines the *lex credendi* or what you must believe; or putting it more simply, the kind of God in whom you believe is the God to whom you say your prayers.

Thus the Christian religion is wholly contained within the Prayer Book, as it is wholly contained in the life of prayer. As Newman explains in his *Lectures*, the Church

transmits the ancient Catholic Faith simply and intelligibly. Not the most unlettered of her members can miss her meaning. She speaks in her formularies and services. The Daily Prayer, the Occasional Offices, the Order of the Sacraments, the Ordination Services, presents [*sic*] one and the same strong, plain, edifying language to rich and poor, learned and unlearned, and that not as the invention of this Reformer or that, but as the witness of all Saints from the beginning. The very titles of the prayers and creeds show this; such as, 'the Apostles', and 'the Nicene Creeds', 'the Creed of St Athanasius', 'the Catholic Faith', 'the Catholic Religion', a 'Prayer of St Chrysostom', and

the like. It is undeniable, that a stranger taking up the
Prayer-Book would feel it was no modern production;
the very Latin titles to the Psalms and Hymns would
prove it. It claims to be Catholic; nor is there any
one of any party to deny, that on the whole it is.
To follow the Church, then, in this day, is to follow
the Prayer-Book, instead of following preachers, who
are but individuals. Its words are not the accidental
out-pouring of this or that age or country, but the
joint and accordant testimony of that innumerable
company of Saints, whom we are bound to follow.
They are the accents of the Church Catholic and
Apostolic as it manifests itself in England.[8]

It was, then, in the worship and devotion of the
Prayer Book that the Catholic faith was to be learned
and understood, not in argument or academic learning
or fine preaching, but in simple humility and holiness
of heart.

There was, however, another polemical argument in
this: that the Oxford Movement appealed to the Prayer
Book as the repository of the whole Catholic sacramental
system which Anglican Protestants had neglected or
forgotten. The movement got the nickname Tractarian,
because its principal figures expounded this teaching in
ninety tract manifestos, written 'against Popery and Dissent', and published between 1833 and 1841. The very
first tract, by Newman, is a defence of the doctrine of the
Apostolic Succession as contained in the threefold ministry of bishop, priest and deacon, and quotes the words of
commission of the ordination service: 'Receive the Holy
Ghost for the office and work of a Priest in the Church of
God, now committed unto thee by the imposition of our
hands: whose sins thou dost forgive, they are forgiven;
and whose sins thou dost retain, they are retained.'
These words established for the Oxford Movement
that the priest is uniquely and divinely commissioned
to declare the forgiveness of sin, a doctrine confirmed
by the form of absolution in the Visitation of the Sick:
'Our Lord Jesus Christ, who hath left power to his Church

to absolve all sinners who truly repent and believe in him, of his great mercy forgive thee thine offences: And by his authority committed to me, I absolve thee from all thy sins . . .' Indeed this led straight on to the later Anglican revival of auricular confession in a Roman form almost unknown to the English Church since the Reformation, and to a wave of liberal and Evangelical revulsion which then produced new demands for Prayer Book reform.

Thus the Oxford Movement took its stand against such reform in principle. Newman's Tract 3, 'Thoughts . . . on Alterations in the Liturgy', was obviously voicing his own opinion when it referred to the objection to 'the imprecatory Psalms' 'as savouring of the shallow and detestable liberalism of the day' and went on to stigmatise these cavillers as 'worldly men, with little personal religion, of lax conversation and lax professed principles'. Such men were to be identified 'with this great Statesman, or that noble Land-holder', a clear reference to sceptical Whig grandees like Lord Melbourne who, according to legend, once declared that he supported the Church, not 'as a pillar', but 'as a buttress . . . from the outside', and is supposed to have left an Evangelical sermon, declaring, 'Things have come to a pretty pass when religion is allowed to invade the sphere of private life.'[9] Again, Newman thought that such men of the world 'dislike the *doctrine* of the liturgy'.[10] They 'do not like the Anathemas of the Athanasian Creed'; and indeed it was the Athanasian Creed, a particular liberal bugbear, which was to become the special symbol of Anglo-Catholic resistance to liturgical change. In his *Grammar of Assent*, Newman memorably describes the Creed as

the war-song of faith, with which we warn first ourselves, then each other, and then all those who are within its hearing, and the hearing of the Truth, who our God is, and how we must worship Him, and how vast our responsibility will be, if we know what to believe, and yet believe not . . . For myself, I have ever felt it as the most simple and sublime, the most devotional formulary to which Christianity has given birth . . .[11]

Indeed like the imprecatory psalms, the Athanasian Creed speaks of the holy otherness of God, who is not to be bound by merely human thought about him, but stands as the *mysterium tremendum et fascinans*, forever beyond our total grasp. It is in this sense that the Tractarians thought that Liberalism, in rejecting the imprecatory psalms and the Athanasian Creed in which God stands over and above us, diminished the Christian doctrine of God.

On the other hand, Newman was equally scathing of those Evangelical churchmen who like the Puritans and Presbyterians of the seventeenth century, objected to the charitable presumption in the burial service that the dead Christian was saved, and who doubted that the child at the font was regenerate or born again in Baptism: a doctrine defended from the literal meaning of the text in the baptismal service, 'Seeing now, dearly beloved brethren, that *this child is* regenerate . . .' and reinforced by the rubric, 'It is certain by God's Word, that children which are baptised, dying before they commit actual sin, are undoubtedly saved.' As a young Evangelical, Newman had denied the doctrine of baptismal regeneration. His growth into High Church opinions had taken the form of coming to believe the doctrine; indeed it was a kind of key belief for the High Churchmen even in the generation before the Oxford Movement, and was taken up by the most learned of the Tractarians, Edward Bouverie Pusey, for fifty-four years Christ Church Professor of Hebrew, and the author of a massively learned work comprising numbers 67, 68 and 69 of the *Tracts, Scriptural Views of Baptism*. In fact, Evangelical opinion on the matter was complex and confused, but it was essentially concerned to deny an *ex opere operato* Catholic understanding of the working of the sacrament, and to interpret the Prayer Book text, according to a wide range of theories, as describing a partial or ecclesiastical or conditional regeneration which would only be complete at a later conversion. Under Tractarian insistence, the Evangelical tendency was increasingly to deny the obvious literal meaning of the service and simply to identify regeneration with conversion. It can, therefore, be seen that on these points, the Prayer Book could be taken as a declaration of High Church doctrine against Anglican liberals and Evangelicals. Indeed, by insisting on the Prayer Book's literal meanings, the Catholics of the Oxford Movement could claim to be English Catholics or Anglo-Catholics, not Roman ones, teaching in simple loyalty to the doctrine of the Church of England.

There were, however, difficulties with the Anglo-Catholic position which arose from the drift of some of the High Churchmen towards Rome. This took two forms: a doctrinal unease about the Thirty-nine Articles in the Prayer Book and attempts to dignify Anglican ceremonial with borrowings from Roman Catholic ritual. The doctrinal difficulty surfaced first, in Newman's Tract 90, in 1841, in which the author tried to reconcile some, if by no means all, of the Articles with the Canons of the Roman Council of Trent. So Newman wrote of

> our present scope, which is merely to show that, while our Prayer Book is acknowledged on all hands to be of Catholic origin, our Articles also, the offspring of an uncatholic age, are, through God's good providence, to say the least, not uncatholic, and may be subscribed by those who aim at being catholic in heart and doctrine.[12]

The double negative 'not uncatholic' in the sentence indicates a distinct unease. One difficulty here is Newman's tendency to equate Catholic and Roman Catholic; and I think that it would be generally acknowledged that Newman denied the obviously Protestant meaning of some of the Articles, which, like those on justification and 'the sacrifices of Masses' (XXXI), were written specifically to exclude Roman Catholic positions. In doing so, Newman forged a dangerous weapon for the liberals, as some of them recognised by showing how

apparently binding doctrinal statements can be interpreted in an heretical sense quite unintended by their
framers. It is significant of this Anglo-Catholic difficulty
with the Articles that Tract 90 was the last of the Tracts,
and that in 1845, Newman became a Roman Catholic.
Newman himself noted elsewhere the old jibe that the
Church of England had 'Calvinistic Articles, and a Popish
Liturgy',[13] and he thought that as a set of local, solely
Anglican ordinances, the Articles had less authority than
the Catholic Creeds, but he was opposed to the liberal
remedy, to relax the terms of subscription to make it
easier to believe. We could say that the liberals have
applied his method of giving a sound form of words
an unintended sense to the Catholic creeds in our own
day.

The second difficulty arose from the new emphasis
after 1840 on ritual. In 1839 two Cambridge students,
J.M. Neale and Benjamin Webb, founded the Camden
Society, later the Ecclesiological Society, to urge the
return or re-creation of a medieval architectural and
artistic setting for Anglican worship.[14] It coincided with
a massive boom in church building and church restoration, which wanted expert guidance on what to do; and
so successful were the society's recommendations that
the great majority of Anglican churches were built or
restored in the nineteenth century in a neo-medieval
style, especially in the middle-pointed or Decorated
Gothic, which became almost a defining characteristic of the buildings of the Church of England. The
church building boom produced a host of new accesso-
ries: encaustic tile floors, stone altars, brass and marble
altar rails, brass candlesticks and eagle lecterns, Gothic
choir stalls, stained glass windows, restored chancels and
surpliced choirs, and organs along the lines described in
the opening remarks of this paper. A small minority of
churches, some of them nationally famous or notorious,
even pioneered the introduction of vestments, lights
and incense. It is difficult now to recapture the pain
and disturbance which these innovations caused, from
the riot over the Bishop of Exeter's instructions to his

clergy to wear the surplice in 1845, through the mayhem in St George's-in-the-East in 1859–61, to the Public Worship Regulation Act of 1874, after which five clergymen were sent to prison for ritual offences.[15] If the Oxford Movement restored the Church's dogma, the Cambridge Camden Society gave it its clothing; and certainly the symbolic changes amounted to a new height in the Anglican understanding of the doctrines of church, ministry and sacrament, in a more clerical Church, in which the sacramental function of the priest as the indispensable channel of divine grace revolutionised and re-religionised the rather secular and utilitarian view of the clergyman's role in later Georgian England.

This development had, however, a number of weaknesses which reflect on the Church's present condition. The Oxford Movement was a largely clerical one; and we all know the pain inflicted by clergymen who want to impose liturgical change upon us with theological arguments which we may feel unable to refute. Liturgical scholarship is a highly specialised discipline, in which the few acknowledged experts should *not* be allowed the last word; they are no more and no less prejudiced than the rest of us, and I feel the deepest sympathy with Victorian Protestant congregations outraged in their most heartfelt convictions by the authoritarian behaviour of Catholicising clergymen, with the unfair advantage, in the nineteenth century, of having the best liturgical scholarship on their side. There is a related point to be made about High Church resentment of the authority of an increasingly non-Anglican state over the Church, as an interference by Caesar with the things of Christ, for by the things of Christ was too often meant the power of the clergy. Parliament's refusal to pass the rather moderate proposals of the 1928 Prayer Book was in part inspired by a wholesome conservative dislike, especially among Evangelical Protestants, of the Anglo-Catholic clerical professionals; and when at last the professionals escaped the state's controls in the 1970s, we saw the lamentable results in the *Alternative Service Book*. There is, then, a sense in which the Oxford Movement's exaltation of the clerical office against the state has been the *magna carta* of our own liturgical reformers, and ultimately a disaster for the Church. Religion is too important to be left to priests. It says much about the theological ignorance of ordinary Anglican layfolk that they all too often allow the terrible folly of letting the clergy have their own way.

Indeed, we may now wonder if the nineteenth-century changes in worship were not too abrupt a break in Anglican continuity, justifying similar ruptures in our own day. This was certainly not true of the leaders of the Oxford Movement, as Keble, Pusey and Newman had *not* been ritualists; but the ritualist tendency was to adopt Roman customs which had no Prayer Book sanction or to revive medieval ones disused for centuries. This was in part perfectly justifiable and understandable: thus the new Anglican religious orders had no choice but to adopt or adapt the Roman Breviary for the offices of a full monastic observance, for which the Prayer Book made no provision; and the addition of the occasional services of blessing in a volume like the Rev F. G. Lee's *Directorium Anglicanum* [16] was an obvious outgrowth of the new interest in sacramentals, itself the product of a fuller sacramental theology. But the ritualist tendency here was to argue that the Prayer Book, though good enough as far as it went, was deficient if not supplemented from other sources; and – especially among some Evangelicals who had become High Churchmen – the Prayer Book was simply not exciting enough. This was especially felt in working-class parishes in which the priest was also an evangelist, and defended the colour and excitement of ritual as a means of converting the poor. The cast of mind here was often as much Roman and Evangelical as High Anglican. The young ex-Evangelical Frederick William Faber, son of the secretary of a Bishop of Durham and nephew of the Evangelical Master of Sherburn Hospital, having written a tract in the manner of John Keble arguing that the Prayer Book was our safeguard against spiritual excitement, went on to become a Roman Catholic and to fuse the excitements of

Evangelical conversionism and Baroque devotionalism as first Superior of the Brompton Oratory.[17] For popular Romanism, much of the intensity of worship took place not in the Mass but in the Adoration and Benediction of the Blessed Sacrament and the extra-liturgical recitation of the Rosary; and these practices also began to find their admirers in the Church of England. I would defend the perfect propriety, indeed the value, of such forms of worship myself; but they obviously laid Anglo-Catholics open to Protestant charges of disloyalty to the Prayer Book. Even more odd was the basis on which many of the changes were justified – the Elizabethan ornaments rubric, that the ornaments of the church and minister should be those in use 'in the Second Year of the Reign of King *Edward* the Sixth'. This was clearly a muddled mistaken interpolation by the Elizabethan reformers, and for three centuries no one interpreted it as a justification for restoring the whole paraphernalia of medieval worship. Indeed, such ritual could only be introduced by defying the authority of the bishop, on the authority of an infallible priest-pope in every parish, whose defiance contributed to that collapse of Anglican authority in Church and State which now seems to leave even bishops free to teach and preach almost anything. In short, ritualist lawlessness made an important contribution to the collapse of authority in the Church of England. There was a further danger in the Anglo-Catholic appeal away from the local diocesan bishop to the vaguely stated usages of the Western Church as this could only mean the Holy Roman one. This meant Anglicans adopting a Roman liturgical standard without reference to the native genius of their own liturgical tradition, a principle faithfully observed by those among our own clergy who formerly followed Rome up and have now followed her down.

It is difficult to state what has been lost in that revolution, in which the Roman model was such an influence. It was undoubtedly the product of increased liturgical knowledge; but there was no reason why liturgical change should have taken the

form of radical modernisation, except the conviction that such modernisation was culturally required
by contemporary need. There is, however, another,
more domestic, explanation. Unfortunately, the ideal of
reforming the liturgy took shape in that strange period
of English history which began with Dr Beeching's cuts
to the railways, proceeded through the white heat of
Mr Wilson's technological revolution and Mr Heath's
expansion of hospital administration and reorganisa-
tion of local government; a period which has left us
the tower block slums as its enduring memorial, and
which had an office block for a soul. By a mysterious
process, the Church capitulated to this wider cultural
collapse and the Prayer Book suffered the fate of the
Euston Arch. The revolution in modernity was especially
dramatic in the realm of language. The reform of the
school curriculum in the state system set out to abolish
what was left of Greek and Latin and the teaching
of formal grammar, while the threshold of boredom
among the nation's youth was dramatically lowered by
the impact of a culture of instant gratification, impatient
of anything that could not be immediately consumed or
understood. Even the great tradition of English religious
poetry, which began with Caedmon, seemed to die with
T. S. Eliot. In short, the time was not propitious for
liturgical reform. It called for a great prose poet like
Cranmer. What it got was Ronald Jasper.

In that evil hour, the Church resolved to sacrifice
the distinctively Anglican language of its worship (on
ecumenical grounds, it seems to me) to the ICET and
ICEL translations, a strange compromise between the
English of the airport lounge and mock-Tudor, so that
the special literary genius of Anglican spirituality and
devotion was lost. Of course the new services appear
formally orthodox. The difficulty is that dogma is given
and received at a deeper level than the intellectual in
worship, and it is at this deeper level that an impoverished liturgy, which is formally orthodox, may fail to
teach the dogma by failing to move the heart. Indeed,
confronted by a tremendous mystery like the Blessed

Trinity, a preacher can only hope that the poetry of the service has risen to the height of the dogma, which is unlikely to receive the whole measure of its due from his own inadequate and faltering words about it.

In brief, what has altered, and for the worse, is what the Oxford Movement called the 'ethos' of Anglican worship, its distinctive feeling and atmosphere. There is a range, a variety, in the way we talk to other people; and there must be a distinctive way or ways in which we talk to God. I do not mean by this a liturgy of fear, though to 'serve God acceptably with reverence and godly fear' is a good biblical phrase (Hebrews 12.28); but Christian worship must speak of sin, hell, death and judgment, and worship must convey the awe, the mystery and the wonder of God. One interesting local instance of this tendency to minimise the Last Things lies in the diminution of the eschatological element in the St Chad's College Advent Procession in Durham Cathedral, in a manner which has resulted in its attenuation and impoverishment.

Thus it seems to me that liturgical revision and the new services in their flat bad English have reduced the needed elements of eschatology and self-abasement before the transcendent God of glory who is enthroned above the cherubim, and replaced him with a cosy middle-class community God, in a kind of internal secularisation of religion, mirroring the secularisation of the wider society. Does your priest face God or the people? On the face of it, the question is nonsense: God is everywhere, and *in* the people. But the priest, in facing east, symbolically proclaims that God is supremely transcendent in glory beyond them, and if we lose that perception of divine transcendence, we lose the very conception of the God of Abraham, Isaac and Jacob, and of our Lord and Saviour Jesus Christ. Indeed, a one-sided emphasis on immanence lies behind the Modernist Liberal Protestant heresies. Yet there is nothing wrong with the immanentist emphasis in itself. The Oxford Movement and the ritualists placed as strong an emphasis on immanence as on transcendence. No one was as insistent as Newman that the believer must first discover the God within himself, and Keble's verses gave a new tenderness to popular devotion to Christ. The Tractarians also laboured to restore to worship the sense of mystery; but that sense of the divine mystery was already implicit in the splendour of the Prayer Book language and gave it life. And with the modern shift of ethos away from the Prayer Book has departed what the Oxford Movement most prized, the insensible action of lovely and hallowed words with hallowed associations on the life of the believer. The new liturgies, I think, lack not only numinosity and transcendence and excitement; they do not contain a single striking phrase to stir the mind or touch the heart. At one time, Anglicans could hope to grow slowly over a long lifetime into the spiritual stature of the Prayer Book phrases; how is this possible today?

I am not, of course, recommending a return to old embattled positions. The Evangelical has as good a claim to the Prayer Book as the Anglo-Catholic, and indeed receives from it the same fundamental Catholic truths of a 'mere Christianity' which Christians everywhere receive. Despite my reservations about modern worship, I honour the perfect orthodoxy of many of those, Catholic and Evangelical, who employ it. I can endure Rite B, in which much of the old language is retained. Unlike the past Anglo-Catholic champions of the Prayer Book, I would not even insist on the Athanasian Creed, which though magnificent and true, so far as tongue can utter truth about such things, is not universally accepted in the Christian East or used in the services of the Roman Catholic Church. Nor do I wish to contest the validity of the ministries and sacraments of Dissenters or deny that they have Christian churches. Indeed, I have more in common with a Salvation Army captain who has no sacraments but believes the Apostles' and Nicene Creeds than with a validly ordained and consecrated Bishop of Durham who denies them. But my argument has been that the Prayer Book survived in the past because it served a religious and theological purpose; and if the Prayer Book is not to be a museum piece in a dying religious culture, that purpose today must be an ecumenical one. It is the tragedy of liturgy that the modern liturgists have hijacked the ecumenical movement, but then, it could be asked, why should Roman Catholics or Dissenters feel any enthusiasm for a Prayer Book which was the standard for opposing and even persecuting them in the past?

The answer can only be that for certain universal prayers, which are Catholic, and not just Anglican, for the *Pater Noster*, the Creeds, Prefaces, *Sanctus* and *Gloria*, for the *Magnificat, Nunc Dimittis* and Psalter, indeed for much of the devotion of the ancient Catholic Church, the Prayer Book contains the very finest versions in our tongue. Take the Collect for the Annunciation, which comes from the Gelasian Sacramentary, and is universally known as the prayer concluding the *Angelus*. Any treasury of Christian devotion would include some of the Prayer Book collects. *Nothing* sets out more bluntly and powerfully the purposes of marriage than the old wedding service, so uncongenial to modern sensibilities, while the burial service contains thoughts too deep for tears. If the whole Prayer Book cannot be saved, these at least must be saved; for these are, as Newman called them, the 'accents' of the Church 'Catholic and Apostolic in . . . England', and until another Cranmer arises, nothing will replace them. Again, the Prayer Book liturgy is an *English* one, though it has been valued wherever the English language has been valued. Catholic Christianity is universal; but it permits us the love of our native place, and to love the universe, you must love one part of it first. I am not being a Little Englander in preferring the majestic English that nurtured Shakespeare to that of the airport lounge, and surely even our ecumenists must tire of the airport lounge and return to *the* English national liturgy. The Prayer Book Catholic tradition contains the profoundest combination of what is Catholic and universal. Let us worship in the language in which Shakespeare worshipped – giving back to God the noblest of his gifts, our worship in the finest of our mother tongue. No sensible person gets rid of his antique furniture to buy the modern rubbish sold today; but my argument is not against modern liturgy in principle, but against the third-rate one we have been given. It is a natural instinct to preserve what we have, until something better comes along. If this means preferring the production of a past age to one of the present, we have C. S. Lewis's apology, 'On a Vulgar Error',[18] to remind us of our spiritual impoverishment today:

> No. It's an impudent falsehood. Men did not
> Invariably think the newer way
> Prosaic, mad, inelegant, or what not.
>
> Was the first pointed arch esteemed a blot
> Upon the church? Did anybody say
> How modern and how ugly? They did not.
>
> Plate-armour, or windows glazed, or verse fire-hot
> With rhymes from France, or spices from Cathay,
> Were these at first a horror? They were not.
>
> If, then, our present arts, laws, houses, food
> All set us hankering after yesterday,
> Need this be only an archaising mood?
>
> Why, any man whose purse has been let blood
> By sharpers, when he finds all drained away
> Must compare how he stands with how he stood.
>
> If a quack doctor's breezy ineptitude
> Has cost me a leg, must I forget straightway
> All that I can't do now, all that I could?
>
> So, when our guides unanimously decry
> The backward glance, I think we can guess why.
>
> Or as Hilaire Belloc put it more simply,
>
> And always keep a-hold of Nurse,
> For fear of finding something worse.

Acknowledgement

I am grateful to my colleague Gerald Bonner for reading and commenting on this paper, which has been read to meetings of the Anglican Society, the Prayer Book Society and the Cosin Club.

Notes

1. G.W.O. Addleshaw and Frederick Etchells, *The Architectural Setting of Anglican Worship* (London, 1948), describes a wider variety of usage than this, but I am trying to state a general norm. The members of Durham's Cosin Club suggested other examples of eighteenth-century survivals.
2. Peter F. Anson, *Fashion in Church Furnishings, 1840–1940* (London, 1965).
3. Cited S.T. Bindoff, *Tudor England* (London, 1952), p. 229.
4. 'Between 1662 and 1800, therefore, attempts at liturgical revision were mainly the work of Latitudinarians who hoped thereby to secure the comprehension of Dissenters.' R. C. D. Jasper, *Prayer Book Revision in England 1800–1900* (London, 1954), p. 5.
5. Cited Arthur Pollard and Michael Hennell (eds.), *Charles Simeon (1759–1836)* (London, 1959), p. 84.
6. J.H. Newman, *Apologia pro Vita Sua* (New York, 1950), p. 47.
7. See my essay, 'John Keble and the Victorian Churching of Romanticism', in J.R. Watson, *An Infinite Complexity: Essays in Romanticism* (Edinburgh, 1983), pp. 226–39.
8. J.H. Newman, *Lectures on the Prophetical Office of the Church, viewed relatively to Romanism and popular Protestantism* (London, 1837), pp. 313–14.
9. *The Oxford Dictionary of Quotations* (London, 1966), p. 335. The first remark was also applied to Lord Eldon. See *D.N.B.*
10. William G. Hutchison (ed.), *The Oxford Movement. Being a Selection from Tracts for the Times* (London, 1906), pp. 18, 20.
11. J.H. Newman, *An Essay in Aid of a Grammar of Assent* (Notre Dame and London, 1979), pp. 117–18.
12. Hutchison, p. 190.
13. *Tract 38*; Hutchison, p. 136.
14. James F. White, *The Cambridge Movement* (Cambridge, 1962).
15. James Bentley, *Ritualism and Politics in Victorian Britain; The Attempt to Legislate for Belief* (Oxford, 1978).
16. (London, 1865.)
17. As I have argued in 'Vulgar Piety and the Brompton Oratory, 1850–60', in Roger Swift and Sheridan Gilley (eds.), *The Irish in the Victorian City* (London, 1985), pp. 255–66.
18. Cited Philip Larkin, *The Oxford Book of Twentieth Century English Verse* (Oxford, 1973), pp. 314–15.

XI

Cranmer and the Evangelical Revival
James P. Hickinbotham

If you wanted a name for a Church of England college with an Evangelical outlook, what would you call it? For months the *mot juste* eluded us. At last someone said, 'Why not Cranmer Hall?' and everyone answered, 'You've got it. That's it.' And it was so.

It suited, first, because Cranmer made the Church of England what it is. He was its 're-former' *par excellence*, the man who gave it a new form and shape, a unique character which in substance has lasted down the centuries and has given Anglicanism its distinctive place among the confessional traditions of Christendom.

It suited, secondly, because Cranmer was motivated by three dominant religious convictions, which have also motivated the evangelical movement in the Church of England. To some other churchmen Cranmer has been an embarrassment. Not sharing his convictions or at least the proportions in which he held them, they wish he had shaped the Church differently. They emphasise most some elements in it which to him were secondary, while playing down some that to him were crucial. Evangelicals have felt a kinship of spirit with Cranmer and have been at home with his proportions of the faith. Not that they idolise him or think his work perfect or unchangeable. But they would change it by giving better expression to his basic convictions, not by departing from them.

Cranmer's dominant convictions were three. First, he believed in the Bible as the standard and source of Christian faith. At Cambridge he was one of the circle, inspired partly by Erasmus, who sought to get behind the contemporary church's distorted presentation of Christianity to its authentic pristine presentation in the Bible studied in the original languages with the best known text. It was (as C. S. Lewis observed about a modern translation) as if an ancient portrait smothered by layers of dirt and varnish was cleaned and shone out bright and clear. And the portrait came alive to them, so to speak. God's word written became God's living word. The Bible was not only the standard of the Church's faith but also the source of the individual's faith. It fed his soul as well as his mind.

Secondly, Cranmer believed in the gospel of salvation by grace, through faith in Christ and his all-sufficient atoning death ('justification by faith' for short), as central in the Bible and in effective Christian living. The Cambridge circle, inspired partly by Luther, found here the unifying theme which runs through the Bible, and a glorious release from the contemporary church's presentation of the way of salvation as a matter of winning one's way to God's eventual favour through good works and through paying for one's sins by penances here and the tortures of purgatory (described in similar terms to hell except for the duration) hereafter. Small wonder that those who took their religion seriously were anxious and often near despair. Contrariwise, to know that God in Christ has dealt completely with sin, that God offers you a right standing ('justification') with him as his beloved, forgiven and accepted children here and now, as a free gift ('by grace'), to be trustfully accepted as such ('through faith') is gospel indeed. And you can't take such love without being moved to gratitude and the desire to love and serve God in the growing holiness which leads on to heaven. Good works are never the grounds of our justification, but they are its inevitable result. It is all summed up in three modern aphorisms: 'I contribute nothing to my own redemption except the sin from which I am redeemed' (William Temple). 'The justifying verdict is nothing more than the "best robe" and the "ring" and the "fatted calf" of the parable' (Sanday and Headlam). 'The Christian life is vocation based on gratitude' (who first said that?).

Thirdly, Cranmer believed in the church as the creation and the vehicle of the Gospel. If the church is to be God's salvation community and not a bogus imitation, it must draw its life from God who gives himself to us in the gospel. He comes to us through the ministration of the word of God and the sacraments which Christ instituted to encapsulate and convey the gospel. The true church, accordingly, is recognised by the use of these means of grace, not by attachment to the Papacy. God gives life to the church, nourishes it, and builds it up in holiness by the means of grace. The church's calling is to receive God's grace in faith and to live in grateful obedience to him, so that through its life his will may be done on earth.

Cranmer formed these convictions early. As a Cambridge don he was noted for promoting biblical studies. In 1532 he married the niece of Osiander the Lutheran divine, which was inconceivable unless he believed their central doctrine, justification by faith. That he stuck his neck out by defying the law of clerical celibacy shows that he discerned some of the practical implications of his convictions, as do his prayers from 1525 onwards, against the Pope's jurisdiction; but that Cranmer would become a great reformer seemed, even after his surprise nomination to the primacy, wildly improbable. What the Bible said of Moses applied much more obviously to him: 'Now the man was very meek'; splendidly meek towards the truth, feeling his way slowly, never jumping to conclusions, a humble learner all his life. But that meant he was only beginning to see where his convictions would lead, and he had no programme. Only just before Henry's death did he change his eucharistic belief. Charmingly meek towards other people, it was said of him, 'If you do my Lord of Canterbury an injury, you will make him a friend for life.' But that does not make for strong leadership. Misguidedly meek towards the monarch, to him the 'Lord's anointed', he accepted Henry's pace, which meant little more than the break from Rome, and the English Bible authorised and set up in churches. Meanwhile he minded the shop and thought his thoughts.

But the delay paid off. When Edward's Protectors gave him the chance of reforming the Church thoroughly, he was ready with a comprehensive plan for a new framework of doctrine, liturgy and order. He needed the state's support. So, for that matter, did Luther and Calvin. He had collaborators and consultants in plenty. But as principal composer and editor-in-chief of the Forty-two Articles, the Homilies, the Second Prayer Book, and the Ordinal, he imposed on the church a new framework and a new shape which was substantially his own creation. Someone else might have done a better job; but it would have been a different job. We know of no one who would have shaped the Prayer Book and other formularies as Cranmer did. Without him, what we know as Anglicanism would probably never have existed. His formularies cover a vast range of subjects; but they form a coherent whole, because at every point they reflect Cranmer's intention to bring the whole life of the church under the control of Scripture, and the gospel of justification by grace through faith. Nothing is to be an article of the faith or necessary for salvation except what can be proved by Scripture. In lesser matters, tradition may be followed providing it is not contrary to Scripture (e.g, the Creeds because provable by Scripture, episcopacy because its antiquity is proved, not by Scripture alone, but by Scripture and ancient authors). This allows for continuity and also for drastic change (e.g. the Pope goes, General Councils have erred, the liturgy is re-made). The Homily 'Of Salvation' fully expounds justification. The Articles treat the sacraments as instruments as well as symbols of God's grace; but the divine gift conveyed by them is received only by faith. In speaking of a 'spiritual', instead of a 'real' eucharistic presence, Cranmer is struggling to present God's dealings with us in terms of personal relationships, instead of the medieval categories of substance and accidents. God makes himself available to us for communion and fellowship, not in the elements, but by the use of them in the sacramental action; but we can reject his gift of himself ... to our loss. The two Daily Offices provide for more Scripture reading than in any other church; and the ideal of a celebration of Holy Communion together with the Offices every Sunday provides a full and balanced ministration of word and sacrament. Worship is made congregational and corporate by being in English, simple in structure, the same everywhere, and mostly unchanging Sunday by Sunday, and therefore easily memorable; the laity as well as the priest communicate. Dom Gregory Dix describes the Communion rite as 'the only effective attempt ever made to give liturgical expression to the doctrine of justification by faith alone'. It was certainly not the *only* effective attempt, but it was a very effective one. We approach in the Humble Access prayer depending entirely on grace. We proclaim the 'full perfect and sufficient' sacrifice of the cross, and his institution of the sacrament, with the prayer that as we obey his command to 'do this' we may be partakers of his body and blood. We obey his command immediately by receiving the sacrament and then offer our sacrifice of praise, thanksgiving and self-oblation. The order is: our need, Christ's redemptive act, his giving the redemptive gift to us, our receiving of it, our responsive giving to him. This is the typical pattern of the gospel. God does all for us. Only then can we do something for him. The Communion must be sacrament first (receiving the benefit of his sacrifice) and only then becomes a sacrifice offered by us. A similar pattern governs the Preparation, from invitation to confession and absolution, confirmed by the gospel promises, to the offering of adoration. Likewise the Offices: invitation, confession and forgiveness make us God's family (Lord's Prayer) and lead to two-way communion through our praise (psalms, canticles and creed) and God's word, and so to our offering of ourselves in intercession (second Lord's Prayer and versicles) and petition (collects). In the Prayer Book, prayers for the faithful departed consist of thanksgiving for, and affirmation of, their blessedness, our present unity with them in Christ and our joyful expectation of joining them in heaven. Intercession is excluded because it implies uncertainty about their state, whereas we know through the promises of the gospel that they are 'in joy and felicity'. Here is the New Testament note of assurance and joy in God's salvation, which the medieval church lacked, but which is our privilege through the gospel.

Queen Mary swept away the entire Reformation and tried to destroy the integrity and repute of its main architect and symbol; but finally meekness towards the claim of truth overcame meekness towards the monarch's authority, loyalty to which probably did more than fear of death to elicit the recantations. Cranmer died more a martyr than a renegade. Elizabeth restored his entire church framework almost word for word. The sovereign became Governor not Head; the positive divine gift in the Eucharist was underlined by omitting the Black Rubric and joining the 1549 words of administration to those of 1552. The Articles were revised and some asperities were softened. Thus the emphasis was shifted slightly, but substantially Cranmer's settlement was restored, this time for good.

For almost a century the Cranmerian settlement kept almost all the nation under its umbrella, and signally proved its worth. The Bible and Prayer Book bit deeply into people's consciousness. Standards of religious knowledge and understanding, public worship and private prayerfulness, and of character and behaviour, improved dramatically. The second century was less happy. Weary of mid-century political and religious strife, England settled in 1688 for a quiet life. Parliament dismissed an autocratic king and clipped his successors' wings. The Church of England swallowed the pill of limited toleration for dissenting churches outside the Establishment, and the Puritans settled for that half-loaf as better than no bread. The Age of Reason dawned. Deists openly

denied the whole Creed except for belief in one distant God and a life after death. The Latitudinarian
church relaxed its discipline and zeal, and instead
of preaching the gospel read Tillotson's moralisings
from the pulpit. Vice went public both among the
rich and the poor, whose numbers swelled, and
whose living conditions became more and more appalling as the Industrial Revolution got into gear (see
Hogarth).

To this situation the Evangelicals, that section of
the revival movement which remained in the Church
of England, addressed themselves. As their nickname
'Evangelicals', i.e. 'Gospel people', suggests, they shared
Cranmer's basic convictions. The Bible, and the gospel of
justification through the cross which it proclaimed, were
their life. They gave themselves to making it also the life
of the church and nation. They stayed in the Church
of England because they thought Cranmer's framework
was the best available expression of their convictions.
They loved the Prayer Book because it communicated
the gospel so clearly and profoundly. They valued the
parochial system because it offered Christian ministry
for every citizen. They scrupulously observed church
discipline, even when it hindered their work; with few
exceptions they renounced itinerant preaching outside
their own parishes and holding unlawful 'conventicles'
within them. Cranmer the re-former had given the
Church a form and framework well fitted to nour-
ish spiritual life within and through it. But in their
time the life had gone out of it. Their job was to be
re-vivalists: not to change the framework, but to put
new life into it. 'Can these dry bones live?' 'Yes', said
the Evangelicals. That, by God's grace, was to be their
job. But ironically, by doing their job, they showed up,
often without noticing that they were doing so, major
blemishes and limitations in Cranmer's framework and
the need for new ways of expressing the gospel through
the church in a different age. It happened in four areas.

First the area of evangelism.

Cranmer's framework assumed that all citizens were

church members from infancy. Their need was for teaching and pastoral care, from Baptism, via Catechism, to Confirmation and life as responsible worshippers. Steady growth, not sudden conversion was the aim, and apart from the Ordinal's lovely sentence about the duty of priests 'to seek for Christ's sheep that are dispersed abroad' the formularies ignore the church's evangelistic ministry. The Evangelicals, however, were first and foremost evangelists. Their aim was to confront both spiritually unawakened conformists, 'formal professors' as they called them, and the openly irreligious, with the gospel of justification by grace through faith in Christ crucified, with a call to a clear-cut personal response of turning to Christ, accepting him as Saviour, and committing themselves to him as Lord. Their aim was inwardness, an experienced personal relationship with Christ; the way to it was conversion, a once for all closing with God's offer of salvation. For some this was a dramatic change. For others it was the step forward from an unselfconscious and unthought-out faith to a conscious and deliberate commitment. What mattered was to belong to the Lord and to know that you belonged to him.

Their central method was preaching, Sunday by Sunday, gospel-centred sermons, relevantly and clearly applied, prayerfully prepared, and delivered from the heart. Live preaching, with reverently conducted worship, and the introduction of the great new evangelical hymns transformed worship. Its climax was Holy Communion, deeply loved by the Evangelicals as the sacrament of our redemption. Celebrations became frequent and communicants multiplied. The Archbishop of York, investigating a criticism of Grimshaw, learnt that during his ministry at Haworth numbers had risen from twelve to over three hundred in winter and over a thousand in summer. 'We can find no fault in Mr Grimshaw,' he concluded, 'seeing that he is instrumental in bringing so many to the Lord's Table.'

Teaching and pastoral care, visiting, praying with people, and teaching them to pray, prepared for evangelism and also built up converts in a strong, practical holiness.

Above all, the Evangelicals brought the Bible to the people. Mass circulation was promoted through the interdenominational Bible Society so that everyone who could read might ponder a passage daily during the private prayer time by which the Evangelicals set such store. An astonishingly successful circulation of millions of cheap tracts helped to get biblical religious and practical teaching across. Evangelicals played a major part in the Sunday School movement which did so much to bring the gospel, the Bible, and the ability to read the Bible, to generations of children, for many of whom it was their only chance of religious and general education.

Secondly, the area of world mission.

Cranmer's England had almost no contact with the non-Christian world and felt no missionary responsibility towards it. Prayer Book intercessions are exclusively concerned with Christendom; but now commerce and colonialism had widened the horizon. SPCK and SPG had started work overseas, but very little, and mostly among our own settlers; but once evangelism became a priority, it could not be confined to home. Like others in the revival, Evangelicals responded to the imperative 'Go and make disciples of all nations'. In 1799 they founded the Church Missionary Society for Africa and the East. It was to be 'missionary', evangelising the heathen; with almost unlimited geographical commitment, 'Africa and the East'. It was also to be 'Church', because the aim was to form converts into structured churches and they believed that their own church framework was the best. After a slow start, Evangelical parishes were drawn into a great network of communication, prayer, and giving, so that the Church became involved at grass roots; missionaries and Bible translations multiplied; schools and colleges nurtured Bible-reading converts and an indigenous ministry. The aim was not 'missionary imperialism', but, in CMS Secretary Henry Venn's phrase, 'self governing, self supporting, self extending' churches. Soon CMS became much the largest Church of England missionary agency and remained so throughout the 'Great Century' of missionary expansion and beyond.

Thirdly the area of social concern.

Like almost everyone from Constantine's time to his own, Cranmer assumed that church and state should be interwoven in a single *respublica Christiana* in which the state would protect the church, and the church would be the state's conscience, and would Christianise society at every level. It was a noble ideal, with the Old Testament People of God as its precedent; but in practice the officially 'godly prince' wielded the power, and brooked no interference from clerics or Christian laymen in his management of affairs. The Cranmerian settlement taught the duty of obedience to the Crown, but not the duty of criticism. The church was to support the social order, not change it. However, since 1688 government had been more relaxed. In Parliament and outside, middle- and upper-class Englishmen had a say in public life. Justification by faith implied that all Christians have equal access to God and are equally called to serve him, the clergy in their gospel ministry, the laity in christianising their families, businesses, and society generally. Leading Evangelical laymen saw here their vocation. 'My business is in the world,' wrote Wilberforce, the MP who sacrificed dazzling political prospects to lead the campaign against the slave trade and then slavery itself, 'and I must mix in the assemblies of men or quit the part which Providence seems to have assigned to me.' He and Shaftesbury, the industrial and social reformer, were the best known leaders among great numbers of evangelical lay men and women who found their vocation in making Christian standards of integrity, justice and compassion effective in the political, professional, industrial, commercial and social life of the nation.

Fourthly, the area of voluntary association.

Cranmer believed in the spiritual unity of all believers within the one church of God, even when they were outwardly divided, and that this should be expressed in Christian fellowship. Hence his friendship with the Lutheran and Reformed Churches and his plan, with Melanchthon's and Calvin's help, to arrange a council to strengthen their unity. But at home, unity was to be expressed only in the Church's official liturgical and other activities within the legally enforced framework. The Evangelicals shared Cranmer's attitude to foreign Protestants, welcomed them as visitors to Communion as all Anglicans before the Oxford Movement did, and communicated with them when abroad. They also worked closely with Dissenters (new since Cranmer's time), welcomed them (as everyone else did) to occasional Communion and treated them not as schismatics, but as partners in the gospel. The Evangelicals realised the need for structured and disciplined church life; but they used the greater freedom of their day to found, either by themselves or with Dissenting partners, a host of voluntary societies, for mutual edification (such as the clerical societies) or for fellowship in common enterprises (such as the missionary and Bible societies, or the societies for educational and charitable work and for social reforms). Some even included foreign Protestants. CMS followed SPCK's example of staffing its Indian mission with Lutherans, by employing German Lutherans in that country and Sierra Leone. It is too little known that the Anglican churches in South India and West Africa were founded and nurtured by non-episcopalian fellow-Christians. The societies brought together men and women, clergy and laity, Church people and Dissenters in a way which profoundly deepened their spiritual unity, and tapped and piped into the service of the gospel and of humanity vast hidden reserves of spiritual energy which could not be reached by the official structures.

'It is very remarkable,' Mr Gladstone somewhat incautiously remarked in 1884 about his government's reforming record, 'so remarkable that it leaves nothing to be done.' Cranmer and the early Evangelicals left much to be done; but what they did was indeed very remarkable and is still relevant to the on-going work of the church today.

Cranmer's dominant convictions have been challenged and exhaustively re-examined. They have stood the test. There is nothing inconsistent in accepting the conclusions of modern scientists and responsible biblical critics on the one hand and the authority of the Bible as God's word on the other. Indeed, it enlarges our understanding of the Bible. Nor does modern scholarship support the liberal substitution of 'the human Jesus' for the gospel of redemption. That gospel is the basis of the Gospels as well as the Epistles, and the horrors of our time shout that redemption is what we need. The unfinished task is to persuade the public that to believe in the authority of the Bible and its gospel is neither childish nor intellectually dishonest.

Cranmer's framework has continued to be gently loosened to help the Church to express the gospel effectively in changing circumstances.

Church and state have moved further apart, because in a largely non-Anglican and non-Christian England all citizens ought to have equal rights irrespective of religion, and the Church ought not to be governed by those who do not share its faith. The Church remains established, with a spiritual mission to the nation and its citizens; and the state in this way acknowledges the Christian basis of national life. But the Church now has full synodical self-government, subject to Parliament's right to refuse the legal status of Acts of Parliament to proposals of Synod, and the Crown's right to select for bishoprics either of two persons nominated by the Church as suitable and acceptable. The Church is thus assured of its right, both to govern its own life under Scripture and to continue its calling to be the Church of the nation, inclusive and outward-looking in spirit, and not an introverted episcopalian sect. It continues officially to welcome to Baptism all children whose sponsors, after instruction, wish to make the promises, just as it welcomes to Communion all confirmed people and leaves their sincerity to their own consciences.

The *Alternative Service Book* authorises much more varied ways of worship. It worships and reads the Bible in contemporary English, the 'vulgar tongue' on which Cranmer insisted. It prays for the whole world. It is not inconsistent with the Prayer Book, though sadly the new Communion rites abandon Cranmer's basic pattern instead of adapting it creatively, and thereby lose something of his clear affirmation of salvation freely given through the cross of Christ. Too many options, and specially too many versions of the Bible will, however, prevent the liturgy and the Bible from becoming familiar, easily remembered, and able to sink deeply into people's minds. Moderate uniformity educates.

The progressive opening to women of official ministries in the Church has arrived at their admission to Holy Orders as deacons. The Church has agreed that there is no fundamental theological objection to their ordination as priests. Indeed, it seems to follow from justification by faith. In Christ there is neither Jew nor Gentile, slave nor free, male nor female; for we are all one in him. All alike receive his grace and communicate it to others. He treats us on the basis not of our distinguishing marks but of our common redeemed humanity. If we cannot say that on principle he excludes the Gentiles or slaves from his call to the ordained ministry neither can we say it of Christian women.

If reunion into one visible church is to happen, the framework must be stretched much further. The experience of the Church of South India and other united churches indicates that if the authority of Scripture, the gospel of justification by grace through faith in Christ crucified, and the ministry of word and the gospel sacraments are made basic in the constitution, the united church will not go far astray. Alas that because of timidity about theological technicalities we have missed the opportunity to reunite with the Methodists or enter into covenant with them and most of the other English churches with whom we share loyalty to the Bible, the gospel, and the church as living by and under them.

Cranmer's dominating convictions stand, as stand they must if the faith is to be the faith and the church the church. Cranmer's framework, modified to meet new needs and increasingly flexible to allow more room for Christian freedom in the Spirit, can still serve us well.

But we have left to the last by far the most remarkable and important thing. If it were not so familiar it would thrill us. It is that the concerns of the Evangelical Revival, evangelism and world mission, social responsibility and voluntary association for Christian fellowship and action, have moved from being at best peripheral to being central in the life of almost all churches. Here is the Spirit pouring new spiritual life into the churches and through them to the world. Frameworks and outward forms exist only so that the Spirit may fill them and work through them. We shall only get our structures right if we put them to the test of whether they foster and liberate or smother and cramp the vitality the Spirit gives to the church. Reformation is for revival. This was Cranmer's perspective. His times and his office made him a reformer. But his purpose was that through reform the Spirit and the Word of God should have free course throughout the Church, and access in life-giving power to all people. That was the perspective of the Evangelical Revival, and has been the perspective of Evangelicals in the Church ever since. That is why Cranmer, the father of Anglicanism in general, is in a special sense the father of Anglican Evangelicalism. And that is why I think it was a good idea to call our College Cranmer Hall.

XII

Charles Wesley's Hymns and the *Book of Common Prayer*
J.R. Watson

A great deal of attention has been paid to Charles Wesley's use of the Bible in his hymns. Henry Bett, for example, claimed that 'the hymns, in many cases, are a mere mosaic of biblical allusions,'[1] while J. Ernest Rattenbury went so far as to claim that 'a skilful man, if the Bible were lost, might extract much of it from Wesley's hymns;[2] similarly, John W. Waterhouse, in a pamphlet entitled *The Bible in Charles Wesley's Hymns*, noted 'how delicately he makes his allusions and how adept he is in finding just *the* word or phrase from the Bible to enshrine his themes.'[3]

Perhaps because most of the commentators on Charles Wesley's hymns have been Methodists, anxious to establish his uniqueness and individuality, this attention to the Bible has seemed to be a fine example of a Methodist independence; and there has been less attention paid to Charles Wesley's very Anglican attachment to the *Book of Common Prayer*. But, as Henry Bett pointed out, the Wesley brothers (who were, of course, priests of the Church of England) knew the Prayer Book well,[4] and frequently made use of it in their hymn writing:

> They often used, and sometimes deliberately preferred to use, the older version of the psalms (substantially Coverdale's) which is retained in the *Book of Common Prayer*. As devout churchmen they had been familiar with this from childhood, and in many cases their use of it was doubtless merely casual. But there are other instances in which they remembered both versions, and combined or contrasted them.[5]

As an example of the use of the Prayer Book version, Bett quotes Psalm 45.4: 'Gird Thee with Thy sword upon Thy thigh, O Thou most Mighty, according to Thy worship and renown', which becomes:

> Gird on thy thigh the Spirit's sword,
>   And take to thee thy power divine;
> Stir up thy strength, almighty Lord,
>   All power and majesty are thine:
> Assert thy worship and renown;
> O all-redeeming God, come down!
>   (HP,[6] 799)

The whole hymn, beginning 'My heart is full of Christ, and longs/ Its glorious matter to declare' is a paraphrase of verses 1–4 of the psalm in the *Book of Common Prayer* version; but the interesting thing about the paraphrase is not the way in which Charles Wesley echoes the very phrase of the psalm, as in

> My ready tongue makes haste to sing
> The glories of my heavenly king

which echoes 'My tongue is the pen: of a ready writer'; so much as what Charles Wesley adds to his originating text. From Isaac Watts he learned the trick of altering the psalms, to make David 'speak the language of a Christian'; thus on this occasion the King is, from the very first line of the hymn, Christ, and the third verse ends with the reference to the 'all-redeeming God'. The fourth verse makes this explicit:

> Dispread the victory of thy cross,
> Ride on, and prosper in thy deed;

so that the hymn, which originates with the God of might in Psalm 45, also includes the redemptive power of Christ and the workings of the Holy Spirit:

> Gird on thy thigh the Spirit's sword . . .

This line transforms verse 4 of the psalm by fusing it with Ephesians 6.17: 'And take the sword of the Spirit'.

Henry Bett was right, therefore, to point to this and other debts to the *Book of Common Prayer:* but the significant and creative element of Charles Wesley's hymnody is his ability to take a familiar phrase or idea from the Bible or the Prayer Book and transform it, to use it in a way which 'de-familiarises' it or gives it new and unexpected meaning. It is not, therefore, the actual repetition or seizure of a phrase which is important, but the felicitous development of it.

There are three elements of the *Book of Common Prayer* which were used by Charles Wesley: the prayers and orders of service (principally for the Holy Communion); the psalms; and the collects. It is also necessary to see the part which the *Book of Common Prayer* played in the shaping of the Wesleys' theology to understand fully their commitment to it and their use of it.

Charles Wesley's attachment to the prayers in the *Book of Common Prayer* is illustrated by his use of the General Thanksgiving. His paraphrase of it is one of three thanksgiving hymns, written in the same 10.10.11.11. metre and found in *Hymns and Sacred Poems* (1742). It begins with a reference to 'Almighty God, Father of all mercies', but expands it to draw out the meaning of 'all thy goodness and loving kindness to us, and to all men' into a metaphor of the generous and benevolent storekeeper with his abundance of riches:

> O heavenly King, look down from above;
> Assist us to sing thy mercy and love:
> > So sweetly o'erflowing, so plenteous the store,
> > Thou still art bestowing, and giving us more.
> > > (1780:191;HP,504)

Similarly, the next section, 'We bless thee for our creation, preservation, and all the blessings of this life' is given an extra emphasis to underline the 'here and now' element of the prayer, the thanksgiving for present blessings in this life, and the evangelical need to make this known to all people:

> O God of our life, we hallow thy name:
> Our business and strife is thee to proclaim.
>> Accept our thanksgiving for creating grace;
>> The living, the living shall show forth thy praise.

The 'preservation' element of this part of the General Thanksgiving is reserved for the next verse, together with 'all the blessings of this life'; again God is transformed into the 'donor', the bountiful giver:

> Our Father and Lord, almighty art thou;
> Preserved by thy word, we worship thee now;
>> The bountiful donor of all we enjoy,
>> Our tongues, to thine honour, and lives we employ.

The last line here jumps forward in the prayer to the hope 'that we shew forth thy praise, not only with our lips, but in our lives'. The next verse, which deals with the redemption, should (if following the General Thanksgiving exactly) have preceded this; but it is held back by Charles Wesley in order to make a climax to the hymn, a forward movement of increasing power, which corresponds to the lines in the prayer following 'all the blessings of this life':

> ... but above all, for thine inestimable love in the redemption of the world by our Lord Jesus Christ; for the means of grace, and for the hope of glory ...

Charles Wesley spots the 'above all', and uses it with an exclamation, 'O' ('Oh!' in the original text) to indicate amazement and wonder:

> But O above all thy kindness we praise,
> From sin and from thrall which saves the lost race;
>> Thy Son thou hast given the world to redeem,
>> And bring us to heaven whose trust is in him.

There are echoes here of John 3.16: 'For God so loved the world, that he gave his only begotten Son, that whosoever believeth in him should not perish, but have

everlasting life.' That this is the climax of the hymn is
suggested by the final verse, which is dependent upon
it:

> Wherefore of thy love we sing and rejoice,
> With angels above we lift up our voice;
>   Thy love each believer shall gladly adore,
>   For ever and ever, when time is no more.

This is the equivalent of 'walking before thee in holiness
and righteousness all our days; through Jesus Christ our
Lord, to whom with thee and the Holy Ghost be all honour and glory, world without end . . .'; but by making
this verse so closely linked with the preceding one,
Charles Wesley is re-structuring the General Thanksgiving to give more prominence to the redemption.
The original prayer asks God to 'give us that due sense
of all thy mercies, that our hearts may be unfeignedly
thankful'; the hymn foregrounds the supreme act of
redemption as the great cause for thanksgiving. To be
sure, the prayer does say 'above all'; but the hymn really
does sharpen that awareness of salvation by its structure
and shape.

   The General Thanksgiving is used in other places, for
example in a hymn of dedication and thanksgiving at the
beginning of a new year, 'Sing to the great Jehovah's
praise':

> Our lips and lives shall gladly show
>   The wonders of thy love,
> While on in Jesus' steps we go
>   To see thy face above.
>
> Our residue of days or hours
>   Thine, wholly thine, shall be,
> And all our consecrated powers
>   A sacrifice to thee.
>   (HP, 360)

The reference to 'lips and lives' is unmistakably from
the General Thanksgiving, and 'on in Jesus' steps' is
a rendering of 'walking before thee in holiness and

righteousness all our days', taking the metaphor of walking and adapting it so that the progress of this life becomes a preparation for the next; what remains of our time on earth is to be employed in 'giving up ourselves to thy service'. Charles Wesley's word 'sacrifice' (echoing Romans 12.1) stiffens the original 'giving up ourselves' and makes it more demanding; just as his final four lines (which are no longer sung in modern hymn books) emphasise the greatness of the final reward:

> Till Jesus in the clouds appear
>   To saints on earth forgiven,
> And bring the grand sabbatic year,
>   The jubilee of heaven.

It is typical of Charles Wesley that he should have added this verse: it could be said to be an expansion of the phrase 'the hope of glory', but its florid expression takes it far from the original into the imaginative world of Charles Wesley's individual vision. As so often, his hymn begins on earth and ends with an anticipation of heaven.

Other hymns are influenced by phrases from the Order of Morning Prayer, such as the lines from 'All glory to God in the sky' which echo the second collect, for Peace – 'O God, who art the author of peace and lover of concord' –

> Receiving its Lord from above,
>   The world was united to bless
> The giver of concord and love,
>   The prince and the author of peace.
>   (1780:211; HP, 400)

Here the original metaphor 'author of peace' has been preserved, and 'lover of concord' has been expanded to make God the giver of concord rather than the lover of it. At other times the metaphors are suppressed, as in one of the several borrowings from the *Te Deum* in the Order for Morning Prayer, where the word 'sharpness' disappears from 'When thou hadst overcome the sharpness of death, thou didst open the kingdom of heaven to all believers':

> When thou hadst all thy foes o'ercome,
> Returning to thy glorious home
> Thou didst receive the full reward,
> That I might share it with my Lord,
> And thus thine own new name obtain
> And one with thee for ever reign.
>
> (1780:70)

The 'new name' is from Revelation 3.12, which is the principal text for this hymn, 'Saviour on me thy grace bestow', from *Short Hymns on Select Passages of the Holy Scriptures* (1762); it suggests that the borrowing from the *Te Deum* was a passing reference, as it was elsewhere. But there are echoes of other orders of service in Charles Wesley's hymns, such as the reference to the Litany in 'Would Jesus have the sinner die?', a dramatic hymn on the sufferings of Christ:

> Thou loving, all-atoning Lamb,
>   Thee – by the painful agony,
> Thy bloody sweat, the grief and shame,
>   Thy cross, and passion on the tree,
> Thy precious death and life – I pray,
> Take all, take all my sins away!
>
> (1780:32; HP, 185)

This is a clear echo of 'By thine agony and bloody sweat; by thy cross and passion; by thy precious death and burial . . .' but Charles Wesley transforms the original prayer by enclosing it within a structure that emphasises, in the first and last verses especially, the saving power of Christ and loving mercy of God. The first verse begins

> Would Jesus have the sinner die?
>   Why hangs he then on yonder tree?
> What means that strange expiring cry?

This is to counter one question with two others, both of which are rhetorical, and affirm the place of the Passion in the scheme of redemptive action; and in the final verse, the hymn ends with a prayer for redeeming love:

> O let thy love my heart constrain,
>   Thy love for every sinner free,
> That every fallen soul of man
>   May taste the grace that found out me;
> That all mankind with me may prove
> Thy sovereign, everlasting love.
>
> (1780 text)

Thus the phrases from the Litany are carried within a structure which emphasises the redemption; it is as though the penitence of Ash Wednesday is surrounded by the assurance of Good Friday and Easter Day. Similarly, in 'Out of the deep I cry' (a first line taken from Psalm 130 in the *Book of Common Prayer* version), the reference to the Litany is intersected with phrases which remind the reader of the love of God and the ransoming of souls:

> Thy love is all my plea,
>   Thy Passion speaks for me!
> By thy pangs and bloody sweat,
>   By thy depth of grief unknown,
> Save me, gasping at thy feet!
>   Save, O save thy ransomed one!
>
> (1780: 145)

This passage from the Litany is used on several occasions, sometimes with an assurance of God's saving power in Christ Jesus, and sometimes in prayer and penitence. In both kinds of hymn Charles Wesley uses the passage from the Litany to add vigour and realism to his sense of the price to be paid in suffering. Thus in 'Thou Man of griefs, remember me', which appears in *A Collection of Hymns for the use of the People called Methodists* (1780) in the section 'For Believers Convinced of Backsliding', the first verse begins without any of the confidence of the questions in 'Would Jesus have the sinner die?':

> Thou Man of griefs, remember me,
>   Who never canst thyself forget!
> Thy last, mysterious agony,
>   Thy fainting pangs, and bloody sweat!
>
> (1780:174)

The additions to the Litany here are two-fold: there is first the 'fainting pangs', to add to the realism with which the crucifixion is portrayed; then there is the crucial word 'mysterious', which carries the meaning not only of something incomprehensible but also of some great and holy mystery. As Charles Wesley says elsewhere, 'Tis mystery all: the Immortal dies!', and the word 'mystery' contains the sense of a God whose actions are mysterious in that they are wonderful, but also because they are impenetrable and holy. The Greek word *mysterion* is here echoed in its sense of something holy and arcane: and the hymn ends with a prayer which is moving because it has none of the customary assurance (though it does have a fine piece of precise vocabulary):

> I deprecate that death alone,
>   That endless banishment from thee:
> O save, and give me to thy Son,
>   Who trembled, wept, and bled for me.

The balance between penitence and thankfulness in the hymns which include echoes from the Litany is even more marked in the hymns which are concerned with the Holy Communion. Most of these are to be found in a publication of 1745, *Hymns on the Lord's Supper*. This contains some of Charles Wesley's finest hymnody, and demonstrates his intimate knowledge of the Order of Service for Holy Communion in the *Book of Common Prayer*. In this case, however, the story is complicated by an intermediate influence, Dr Daniel Brevint's *The Christian Sacrament and Sacrifice*. Brevint was an Anglican divine of the seventeenth century, whose work was published in 1673: it was one of a number of devotional texts which John Wesley admired, and abridged so that it could be distributed to his followers. In this case, John Wesley's abridgement was used as a preface to a collection of hymns which was issued more times in the eighteenth century than any other collection of Wesley hymns.

The complete work is available in a modern edition, J. Ernest Rattenbury's *The Eucharistic Hymns of John and Charles Wesley*, published in 1948. Rattenbury there described the relationship between Brevint's prose and Charles Wesley's verse with a fine rhetorical flourish:

> Charles Wesley gives Brevint wings, and adds very significantly the confirmation of Methodist experience to Brevint's doctrine. In some of his verse he turns the devotional theology of a High-Church Caroline divine into the flaming Methodist Evangel without losing Anglican values.[7]

There are 166 hymns in the book, corresponding to the various sections of Brevint's work and John Wesley's abridgement; a study of the whole book reveals the depth of feeling and complexity of understanding of the Holy Communion found in it. In particular there are certain hymns which are directly related to moments in the service, such as 'Meet and right it is to sing' (1780:212; HP, 501), which has its origin in 'It is very meet, right, and our bounden duty, that we should at all times, and in all places, give thanks unto thee, O Lord ...'; this relationship between certain Wesley hymns and the various stages of the liturgy from the *Book of Common Prayer*, has been helpfully studied recently by Kathryn Nichols, and her article shows clearly the way in which Charles Wesley's hymns are not only related to specific phrases in the Prayer Book, but are also thematically related to stages in the service such as the Exhortation and the Confession.[8]

In the space available here it will only be possible to consider two representative hymns as demonstrating Charles Wesley's knowledge of the *Book of Common Prayer* and of Brevint's interpretation of the sacrament of Holy Communion. The first is one of the few Wesley hymns that is better known outside Methodism than within it, because it was included in the second edition of *Hymns Ancient & Modern* (1875):

Author of life divine,
    Who hast a table spread,
Furnished with mystic wine
    And everlasting bread,
Preserve the life thyself hast given,
And feed and train us up for heaven.

Our needy souls sustain
    With fresh supplies of love,
Till all thy life we gain,
    And all thy fullness prove,
And, strengthened by thy perfect grace,
Behold without a veil thy face.

                                        (HP, 596)

This hymn is associated with the two alternative prayers
after Communion, especially in verse 1 with the second prayer: '. . . we most heartily thank thee, for that
thou dost vouchsafe to feed us, who have duly received
these holy mysteries, with the spiritual food of the most
precious Body and Blood of thy Son, our Saviour Jesus
Christ . . .' and in verse 2 with the first prayer: 'And here
we offer and present unto thee, O Lord, ourselves, our
souls and bodies, to be a reasonable, holy, and lively
sacrifice unto thee; humbly beseeching thee, that all
we, who are partakers of this holy Communion, may be
fulfilled with thy grace and heavenly benediction . . .'.
But the hymn is also based on the following passage from
Brevint:

And as bread and wine keep up our natural life,
so doth our Lord Jesus, by a continual supply of
strength and grace, represented by bread and wine,
sustain that spiritual life which He hath procured by
His Cross . . .

Once again it is noticeable that Charles Wesley takes
these antecedent passages and transforms them. He
uses the principal metaphor of feeding from the Prayer
Book service, but he deliberately develops the reference to the 'spiritual life' of which Brevint speaks: the
hymn becomes a true exploration of the holy mysteries,

because those mysteries lead the Christian to life and to heaven. The first line, 'Author of life divine', anticipates the other references to life, and it is made clear that such life leads ultimately to the fullness of Christ and the joy of heaven. The partaking of Holy Communion is the receiving of 'fresh supplies of love', as if from some celestial quartermaster whose store is always open and whose table is forever spread; and that love leads to life, to the administration of perfect grace, and to heaven itself.

Charles Wesley has therefore taken Brevint's original commentary, which lines up the comparison between 'natural life' and 'spiritual life', and developed it to show the progression from earth to heaven. We may also notice the beautiful and unobtrusive art of the two stanzas, especially the way in which each is a complete sentence, working gracefully through the four short lines (rhyming ABAB) and then coming to a climax in the longer couplet at the end: the structure of the verse form is used with consummate tact and skill to lead the reader (or singer) towards the promise of heaven at the end of each verse.

The second hymn from *Hymns on the Lord's Supper* which I wish to discuss briefly is 'Jesu, we thus obey', a beautiful exercise in Double Short Metre:

> Jesu, we thus obey
>> Thy last and kindest word;
> Here, in thine own appointed way,
>> We come to meet our Lord.
> The way thou hast enjoined
>> Thou wilt therein appear;
> We come with confidence to find
>> Thy special presence here.
> Our hearts we open wide
>> To make the Saviour room;
> And lo! the Lamb, the Crucified,
>> The sinners' friend, is come!
> His presence makes the feast;
>> And now our bosoms feel
> The glory not to be expressed,
>> The joy unspeakable.

With pure celestial bliss
He doth our spirits cheer;
His house of banqueting is this,
And he hath brought us here.
He doth his servants feed
With manna from above,
His banner over us is spread,
His everlasting love.

He bids us drink and eat
Imperishable food;
He gives his flesh to be our meat,
And bids us drink his blood.
Whate'er the Almighty can
To pardoned sinners give,
The fullness of our God made man
We here with Christ receive.
(HP, 614, with restoration of original verses)

This is based on Part IV of John Wesley's abridgement of Brevint, entitled 'Concerning the Sacrament, as it is a Means of Grace'. It runs as follows:

> As He offers Himself to man, the Holy Sacrament is, after the sacrifice for sin, the true sacrifice of peace-offerings, and the table purposely set to receive those mercies that are sent down from His Altar. Take and eat; this is My Body, which was broken for you; and this is My Blood, which was shed for you.
>
> Here then I wait at the Lord's Table, which ... offers me the richest gift which a saint can receive on earth, the Lord Jesus crucified.

But in addition to their source in Brevint, Charles Wesley's lines are also a commentary on the Prayer of Consecration in the *Book of Common Prayer*. The first lines are, perhaps surprisingly, dramatic: they indicate the movements of human characters in the process of coming to partake of the Holy Communion, and they bring out the latent drama of the situation. This is present at every moment of the order of service, and is especially noticeable at certain points, such as the prayer beginning 'We do not presume to come to this thy Table, O merciful Lord, trusting in our own righteousness . . .'. In the hymn such a dramatic speech is equalled by Charles Wesley's sense of movement: the participants 'come to meet' their Lord, and suddenly, it seems, the Lord is present with them:

> And lo! the Lamb, the Crucified,
> The sinners' friend, is come!

The sense of a moment of encounter is brilliantly set out here: not only is there the sudden 'lo!' but the hymn also combines the qualities which inspire awe – the Lamb, the Crucified – with those which remind us that Christ was the friend of publicans and sinners (Matthew 11.19). It is thus a hymn which addresses itself with a profoundly accurate intuition to the central mystery of the Holy Communion, the institution itself: as Christ was about to undergo his suffering on the cross for our redemption, and make

> (by his one oblation of himself once offered) a full, perfect, and sufficient sacrifice, oblation, and satisfaction, for the sins of the whole world;

in the midst of this amazing and earth-redeeming action, he also instituted something very simple, a breaking of bread and wine as natural and as spiritual food. In Charles Wesley's expression, this was his 'last and kindest word':

> Take, eat, this is my body which is given for you: Do this in remembrance of me. . .Drink ye all of this . . .

Charles Wesley's hymn therefore brings out, in all its force, the dramatic possibilities of the Holy Communion: the meeting of Christ and the sinner, the contrast

between the immense and demanding power of Christ
and his tender mercy, the complexity of God made man,
and the simplicity of eating and drinking. At the Holy
Communion we are bidden to eat and drink, but the
food is 'imperishable food', the bread of life (John 6.35)
which is Jesus himself: 'He that cometh to me shall never
hunger; and he that believeth on me shall never thirst.'

The hymns which are influenced by the Order of Service for Holy Communion show Charles Wesley's ability
to give shape and point to the original wording, to bring
out its hidden significance. His treatment of the psalms
is similar, although he is closer to Isaac Watts here in his
practice of giving a New Testament significance to Old
Testament material. He had subscribed to Article VII
of the Thirty-nine Articles on becoming a priest: 'The
Old Testament is not contrary to the New: for both in
the Old and New Testament everlasting life is offered
to Mankind by Christ, who is the only Mediator between
God and Man, being both God and Man . . .'. So Charles
Wesley takes Psalm 48 and boldly alters it in the very first
line. The psalm begins:

Great is the Lord, and highly to be praised: in the city of our
God, even upon his holy hill.
The hill of Sion is a fair place, and the joy of the whole earth:
upon the north-side lieth the city of the great King; God is
well known in her palaces as a sure refuge.

Charles Wesley turns this into robust verse, in a rather
unusual 7.6.7.6.7.7.7.6. metre, which gives an additional
weight at a crucial point in the second half of the verse:

> Great is our redeeming Lord
>   In power, and truth, and grace;
> Him, by highest heaven adored,
>   His church on earth doth praise.
> In the city of our God,
>   In his holy mount below,
> Publish, spread his name abroad,
>   And all his greatness show.
>   (HP, 438)

The surprise here is the insertion of 'redeeming' in line 1, which transforms the traditional imagery which comes after it. Similarly, in the last verse, the psalmist's 'For this God is our God for ever and ever: he shall be our guide unto death' is given an entirely new pattern of meaning:

> Zion's God is all our own,
>   Who on his love rely;
> We his pardoning love have known,
>   And live to Christ, and die.
> To the new Jerusalem
>   He our faithful guide shall be:
> Him we claim, and rest in him,
>   Through all eternity.

It is now the love of God which is presented, the pardoning love in Christ Jesus. It is this love which penetrates the whole being of the Christian: 'For whether we live, we live unto the Lord; and whether we die, we die unto the Lord: whether we live therefore, or die, we are the Lord's' (Romans 14.8). Charles Wesley has expanded the ideas of the psalmist to take in these profounder reverberations; and while God is still a 'guide unto death', the way is now seen as leading to the new Jerusalem.

Such subtle and intricate handling of the psalms is typical of Charles Wesley's use of the *Book of Common Prayer*. At other points, it can be seen that elements of his phraseology, such as 'the Lord is King' (Psalm 99.1), or 'out of the deep' (Psalm 130.1), or 'open my eyes that I may see' (Psalm 119.18), emerge quite naturally from the mind of one who had been accustomed to singing the psalms from childhood. At other times, his poet's love of unusual vocabulary delights in words such as 'minished' (Psalm 12.1):

> The faithful, whom I seek in vain,
> Are minished from the sons of men.
>   (1780:16)

He also extracted homely words from the psalms, such as 'simpleness', from Psalm 69.5, 'God, thou knowest my

simpleness and my faults are not hid from thee'. This
becomes (in an address to Jesus):

> Whom man forsakes thou wilt not leave,
> Ready the outcasts to receive,
> Though all my simpleness I own
> And all my faults to thee are known.
>
> (1780:157)

The same verse from the psalm opens another hymn:

> Jesus, thou know'st my simpleness,
>   My faults are not concealed from thee...
>
> (1780:170)

Wesley's consciousness of the vocabulary and phrasing
of the psalms is also indicated by the way in which
he uses verses as titles. Thus a hymn beginning 'Jesu,
my Advocate above' (1780:97), which refers to 1. John
2.1, used as some of the 'comfortable words' at the
Holy Communion, was entitled (in some editions) 'Psalm
139.23. Try me, O God, and seek the ground of my
heart'; and another, 'Lord, how long, how long shall I'
(1780:150) was entitled 'My soul gaspeth for thee, as
a thirsty land', from Psalm 143.6. Interesting though
these are as evidence of his general awareness of the
psalms, the most notable use of them occurs when he
takes phrases from a psalm and gives them new life by
putting them in a fresh context, both theologically and
poetically. In his *Short Hymns on Select Passages of the
Holy Scriptures* (1762), for example, there is a one-stanza
anapaestic hymn on Psalm 39.8: 'And now, Lord, what
is my hope: truly my hope is even in thee':

> What now is my object and aim?
>   What now is my hope and desire?
> To follow the heavenly Lamb,
>   And after his image aspire.
> My hope is all centred in thee;
>   I trust to recover thy love,
> On earth thy salvation to see,
>   And then to enjoy it above.
>
> (1780: 360)

The verse from the psalm acquires strength and meaning from its expansion: meaning from the interpretation which Charles Wesley gives to the original, almost as if he were producing an exposition of a text; and strength from the impassioned rhythm of the verse. In the 1780 *Collection* John Wesley joined this to an even stronger verse, from Psalm 42.2: 'My soul is athirst for God, yea, even for the living God: when shall I come to appear before the presence of God?' The transformation is startling but also full of energy:

> I thirst for a life-giving God,
>   A God that on Calvary died,
> A fountain of water and blood
>   Which gushed from Immanuel's side!
> I gasp for the stream of thy love,
>   The spirit of rapture unknown,
> And then to re-drink it above,
>   Eternally fresh from the throne.

The presence of God has now become the saving water and blood from the Crucifixion: the image of thirst is given extraordinary life by the suggestion that the sinner will drink it on earth, and then re-drink it in heaven, eternally fresh, a stream of living water and blood. Similarly, a phrase such as 'the fierceness of man shall turn to thy praise: and the fierceness of them shalt thou refrain' (Psalm 76.10) is the source of a 'Hymn for the Kingswood Colliers', beginning 'Glory to God, whose sovereign grace', written in the early years of the Methodist revival and published in 1740. At the end of the hymn that verse from the psalm is given an authentic but lurid eighteenth-century actuality:

> Suffice that for the season past
>   Hell's horrid language filled our tongues,
> We all thy words behind us cast,
>   And lewdly sang the drunkard's songs.
>
> But, Oh! the power of grace divine!
>   In hymns we now our voices raise,
> Loudly in strange hosannas join,
>   And blasphemies are turned to praise!
>   (1780:195)

This is an example of the way in which a phrase from a psalm may be used to end a hymn. More often it provides the initial impulse, the starting point for a searching meditation or a profound development:

> I will hearken what the Lord
>   Will say concerning me!
> Hast thou not a gracious word
>   For one that waits on thee?
>   (1780:175)

This comes from Psalm 85.8: 'I will hearken what the Lord God will say concerning me: for he shall speak peace unto his people, and to his saints, that they turn not again.' As so often, Charles Wesley takes the second part of this verse and gives it a New Testament significance:

> Speak it to my soul, that I
>   May in thee have peace and power,
> Never from my Saviour fly,
>   And never grieve thee more.

The same thing happens with another opening, from Psalm 99.1: 'The Lord is King, be the people never so impatient: he sitteth between the cherubims, be the earth never so unquiet.' The hymn follows the psalm quite closely in verse 1, getting the plural of cherub right, then switches abruptly to a phrase from Matthew 28.18:

> The Lord is king, and earth submits,
>   Howe'er impatient, to his sway;
> Between the cherubim he sits,
>   And makes his restless foes obey.

> All power is to our Jesus given;
>   O'er earth's rebellious sons he reigns;
> He mildly rules the hosts of heaven,
>   And holds the powers of hell in chains.
>   (1780:217)

Charles Wesley's treatment of the psalms does not have the force and grandeur of some of Watts's incomparable versions; but Wesley's texts have energy and variety in abundance, and are a testimony to his intimate knowledge of the *Book of Common Prayer*, although he

would have known them as well from the Authorised
Version of the Bible. From the Prayer Book, however,
he undoubtedly took his knowledge of the collects.

As with the psalms, there are phrases in the collects
which enter Charles Wesley's mind spontaneously and
naturally, and are part of his poetic resources. These
include 'Pardon and peace in Jesus find' (1780:4, from
Trinity 21) and 'Thou hatest all iniquity/But nothing
thou hast made' (1780:262, from Ash Wednesday), or
'Thou didst the meek example leave/ That I might in
thy footsteps tread' (1780:321, from Easter 2). However, the influence of the collects is greater than these
individual examples suggest, if only because one of the
recurring structural patterns in them is that of a prayer
for good conduct on earth followed by the hope of an
everlasting life in heaven: '. . . Grant, we beseech thee,
that we may so faithfully serve thee in this life, that we
fail not finally to attain thy heavenly promises' (Trinity
13). Charles Wesley's hymns often follow the same pattern: there is a progress very frequently from life on
earth to love in heaven, for example in 'Love divine, all
loves excelling' where the soul is finally

> Changed from glory into glory,
>   Till in heaven we take our place,
> Till we cast our crowns before thee,
>   Lost in wonder, love, and praise!
>   (1780:374; HP, 267)

It is not possible to attribute this to the collects with any
certainty; indeed the endings of Charles Wesley's hymns
often owe more to the Book of Revelation than to anything else; but it is possible that the *Book of Common
Prayer* may have been an influence on this very powerful
pattern of movement. It is found, certainly, in 'And let
our bodies part', where the fifth verse is as follows:

> O let our heart and mind
> Continually ascend,
> That haven of repose to find
> Where all our labours end!
>   (1780:521)

This comes from the Collect for Ascension Day: '...
so we may also in heart and mind thither ascend, and
with him continually dwell, who liveth and reigneth with
thee and the Holy Ghost, one God, world without end
...'. This is a pivotal verse in a hymn of twelve verses,
which begins with a portrayal of Christians at work in
the various vineyards of the world and ends with seven
verses describing the joys of heaven; apart from one
verse, the hymn shows no debt to the *Book of Common
Prayer*, unless it is seen as imaginatively constructed on
the same pattern as the collects. Similarly, the hymn 'Ye
faithful souls who Jesus know' is a tissue of biblical ideas
interwoven on a design from the Collects for Ascension
Day and the Sunday following:

> Ye faithful souls who Jesus know,
>   If risen indeed with him ye are,
> Superior to the joys below,
>   His resurrection's power declare.
>   (1780:408; HP 751)

The verses which follow are related to the Collect for the
Sunday after Ascension Day:

O God the King of glory, who hast exalted thine only
Son Jesus Christ with great triumph unto thy kingdom
in heaven; We beseech thee, leave us not comfortless;
but send to us thine Holy Ghost to comfort us, and
exalt us unto the same place whither our Saviour
Christ is gone before, who liveth and reigneth with
thee and the Holy Ghost, one God, world without end.
Amen.

The crucial words here are 'glory' and 'exalted', which
underpin verses 2 and 3:

> Your faith by holy tempers prove,
>   By actions show your sins forgiven!
> And seek the glorious things above,
>   And follow Christ your Head to heaven!
>
> There your exalted Saviour see,
>   Seated at God's right hand again,
> In all his Father's majesty,
>   In everlasting pomp to reign.

The phrase, 'in heart and mind thither ascend, and with him continually dwell', from the Collect for Ascension Day itself, occurs in verse 4:

> To him continually aspire,
>   Contending for your native place;
> And emulate the angel choir,
>   And only live to love and praise.

These Ascension-tide Collects are of particular importance to Charles Wesley, because they help to release his verse into its most visionary and exalted descriptions of heaven. But that theme is balanced, as it is here, by an equally vigorous moral and pastoral concern, by the requirements of Christian behaviour:

> Your faith by holy tempers prove,
>   By actions show your sins forgiven!

The action which John and Charles Wesley were most deeply engaged in throughout the years following their conversion in 1738 was the revival of the Church of England (not the separation from it). They saw themselves as breathing new life into a decaying and feeble body, and the Collect for the Twenty-fifth Sunday after Trinity was a crisp expression of their aim:

> Stir up, we beseech thee, O Lord, the wills of thy faithful people; that they, plenteously bringing forth the fruit of good works, may of thee be plenteously rewarded; through Jesus Christ our Lord. Amen.

In view of the actual course of their lives, it is not surprising that the phrase 'stir up' should occur on several occasions in Charles Wesley's hymns. One example, 'Stir up thy strength, almighty Lord' has already been quoted at the beginning of this essay. Another occurrence is in a hymn on prayer, 'Jesu, thou sovereign Lord of all':

> Pour out the supplicating grace,
> And stir us up to seek thy face!
>   (1780:285)

The most celebrated example, however, is from a hymn that has become familiar to most denominations, 'O thou who camest from above':

> Still let me guard the holy fire,
> And still stir up thy gift in me;
> (1780:318; HP, 745)

The metaphor of fire, the emblem of the Holy Spirit, is used with beautiful precision here; as Henry Bett pointed out, Charles Wesley is using the English equivalent of the Greek word *anazopurein*, meaning specifically 'to stir up a fire'. He may have taken it from Paul's letter to Timothy (2 Timothy 1.6), but he would certainly have been aware of its presence in the *Book of Common Prayer,* where it is wonderfully placed at the end of the Sundays after Trinity, trembling with expectation for Advent Sunday and the beginning of the new Christian year. The moment in which the old year is about to become the new year, the stirring of the new at the end of the old, the sense of potential and renewal, would have been deeply attractive to the Wesleys.

Both John and Charles Wesley were conscious of the value of the *Book of Common Prayer* to the Church of England; and while John was bolder in his innovations and procedures, Charles had 'an inviolable attachment to the Church of England'9 and continued to oppose any movements among the Methodist people towards separation. It is only to be expected, therefore, that he should have made use of the Prayer Book in his hymns: sometimes in a formal and conscious way, and at other times in ways that suggest an almost unconscious reliance on phrases and cadences that he had known since childhood. Perhaps the most remarkable feature of his borrowings from the Prayer Book, however, is not the borrowings themselves, but the extraordinary ways in which the metaphors deepen and expand in meaning in Charles Wesley's handling of them.

In a moving and eloquent essay on Charles Wesley, written in the early 1960s, in W.F. Lofthouse had a vision of Anglican-Methodist unity based on a mutual respect for the finest literature of each denomination:

To the Church of England man, worship finds its finest manual in the language of the prayer-book. The

Methodist has been brought up to find his prayer-
book, or its equivalent, in Wesley's hymns. But the
Book of Common Prayer is more than a sectarian manual
of worship. It is one of the noblest expressions of
our English religious life. John Wesley set it, with
a few inevitable alterations and omissions, with both
of which most Anglicans today would probably agree,
before all his societies, in this country and America.
It has been used regularly in Methodist worship overseas, and there seems no reason why, with the growing
interest in liturgical forms for prayer, it should not
regain the place it occupied in our chapels sixty years
ago. As for Charles Wesley's hymns, no one was ever
more passionately devoted to the Church of England,
as he conceived it, than their author. Some of them
are already enshrined in the worship of the Church
of England. No selection of hymns could provide a
more adequate expression of that orthodoxy which is
so precious to the Anglican . . .

If there were a proper concern for unity, Lofthouse continued:

Then, surely, with the prayer-book in the form to
which the larger part of Methodists were accustomed
for a century, and with the modifications in the hymns
which all Methodists now accept, an atmosphere might
be created, with a common *lex orandi* and *lex credendi*,
which could make union in some form both possible
and desirable to all.[10]

This vision, in all its optimism and nobility, now seems
sadly in the past. The unity schemes fell in ruins in the
1970s, and the two great forces on which Lofthouse
based his hopes, the *Book of Common Prayer* and
Wesley's hymns, are now having to fight to survive; at
the present time, perhaps the most painful thing about
a study of the relationship between them is that such an
enquiry is in danger of becoming little more than an
essay in history. The *Book of Common Prayer* is now
frequently unused, its incomparable language neglected

and forgotten; while in many places the Methodists are abandoning the hymns of Charles Wesley in favour of modern songs, which may make the Gospel seem attractive on a superficial level, but which are characterised – it has to be said – by doubtful theology and unbelievable triviality (not to mention their lamentable poetry). It is heartbreaking to think that the influence of the *Book of Common Prayer* on the hymnody of Charles Wesley will soon be a matter of academic interest alone.

Notes

1. Henry Bett, *The Hymns of Methodism in their Literary Relations* (London, 1913, revised and enlarged edition, 1920), p. 71.
2. J.E. Rattenbury, *The Evangelical Doctrines of Charles Wesley's Hymns* (London, 1941), p. 48.
3. John W. Waterhouse, *The Bible in Charles Wesley's Hymns* (London, 1954), p. 3.
4. For a full discussion of John Wesley's treatment of the *Book of Common Prayer* and his attitude towards it, see Frank Baker, *John Wesley and the Church of England* (London, 1970), pp. 234–55.
5. Bett, *The Hymns of Methodism*, p. 17.
6. The texts of Charles Wesley's hymns are taken from two sources: 1. *A Collection of Hymns for the use of the People called Methodists* (1780), using the modern edition edited by Franz Hildebrandt and Oliver A. Beckerlegge (Oxford, 1983). I am greatly indebted to this edition, and to its index, for help in identifying many of the borrowings from the *Book of Common Prayer* in Charles Wesley's hymns; 2. *Hymns & Psalms*, the current hymn book of the Methodists Church (1983). The two books are abbreviated as '1780' and 'HP' respectively. Where a hymn appears in both books, I have generally used the modern punctuation, on the grounds that it is more accessible to the reader.
7. J.E. Rattenbury, *The Eucharistic Hymns of John and Charles Wesley* (London, 1948), p. 13.
8. Kathryn Nichols, 'Charles Wesley's Eucharistic Hymns: Their Relationship to the *Book of Common Prayer*', *The Hymn* (published by the Hymn Society of America), Vol. 39, no. 2, April 1988, pp. 13–21.
9. Thomas Jackson, ed., *The Journal of the Rev. Charles Wesley, M. A.*, (London, 1849), I. 320.
10. W.F. Lofthouse, 'Charles Wesley', in *A History of the Methodist Church in Great Britain*, ed. Rupert Davies and Gordon Rupp (London, 1965), pp. 115–44 (p. 144).

XIII

One Dissenter's thoughts on the *Book of Common Prayer*
Charles E. B. Cranfield

Among English Nonconformists the *Book of Common Prayer* tends to be an acquired taste rather than an immediate favourite. Even for those of us who find its language no obstacle it has much to live down, in particular its association with the Act of Uniformity, the Great Ejection, the Conventicle Acts, the Five Mile Act, the Test Acts, etc. And if the copy we use happens to be one which, for good measure, includes the Elizabethan Act of Uniformity, this hardly helps matters. Yet, in spite of the difficulty of dissociating the Prayer Book altogether from these bitter things, some of us have a warm regard for it, and much of the real affection which we feel for the established Church of our country is closely, if not inseparably, bound up with it. Perhaps a Nonconformist's comments on it may be not altogether without interest. The very distance from which we view it may just possibly enable us to notice some things which those who are much nearer to it may miss.

I shall attempt first to make some more general observations and then to offer a few remarks about particular services in the *Book of Common Prayer*. I begin by referring to some things which strike me as blemishes.

I mention first the tendency to what seems to me excessive repetition. In this connection I sympathise with the comment made by Karl Barth: 'I went to an Evening Prayer at which the Lord's Prayer was said twice and the *Gloria* five or six times. I said to them afterwards, 'If I were the good God, I would reply to you in a voice of thunder, "All right, that will do, I've heard you! . . ."'[1]

More serious, if I am right in detecting it, is the rather

grudging and minimal obedience to the 'for all men' of I Timothy 2.1. The church's obligation to embrace all humankind in its prayers gets some recognition in, for example, the Collect for all Conditions of men, the General Thanksgiving and the Litany; but it seems scarcely more than a passing nod. In the prayer for the Church Militant in the Communion Service the words of 1 Timothy 2.1. are quoted, but the 'for all men' seems to be quickly lost sight of. The civil authorities prayed for are those that are 'Christian'. Whether 'all them, who in this transitory life are in trouble, sorrow, need, sickness, or any other adversity' was intended – and is generally thought by worshippers – to include non-Christians I am not clear. I miss an unambiguous, resolute and whole-hearted acceptance of the New Testament's 'for all men'.

A touch of flattery seems sometimes to be present in references to the Sovereign. While 'thy Servant Elizabeth our Queen' seems to me to strike exactly the right note, 'our most religious and gracious Queen' makes me feel embarrassed. If the Sovereign concerned is religious and gracious, God hardly needs to be told this; and, if in any instance this should not be true, God surely would not want to be told it. Were not such epithets intended more for human ears than for him to whom alone prayer is properly addressed? And, with all the years since 1662 in mind, must we not wonder whether the Prayer for the Queen's Majesty in Morning and Evening Prayer does not take rather too much for granted, when it asks, unconditionally and without qualification, that God may 'strengthen her that she may vanquish and overcome all her enemies'?

And is it only my imagination which senses a certain detachment, where the poor and needy are prayed for, a lack of warmth, an absence of empathy, even a suggestion of perfunctoriness?

The Prayer Book's theological solidity is not its most widely valued or most loudly celebrated virtue, but it is of fundamental importance. I certainly get the impression of great theological competence. The blame for the fact that English people are often quite outstandingly ignorant theologically cannot fairly be laid at the Prayer Book's door.

There is no need for me to draw attention to its literary graces. These are generally acknowledged. The majesty of its language and style, its wonderful combination of richness and variety with simplicity and directness, its pleasing rhythms and ubiquitous felicitousness, these are all well known.

That there are real dangers in the literary splendours of the *Book of Common Prayer* should be recognised. I mention just three: (a) the danger that the very beauty of the language may actually serve to conceal from those who use it the fact that all human attempts to express the grace and faithfulness and majesty of God are altogether unworthy and inadequate and broken; (b) the danger that the special grandeur of the language may somehow encourage the impression that God is confined to a world of Norman or Gothic churches, of choirs and organs, and is not near to us in our ordinary everyday life; and (c) the danger that those who come to church but rarely may be put off by unfamiliar language which they cannot understand. Each of these dangers is real and needs to be taken thoroughly seriously. But it seems to me unlikely that any one of these is best avoided by preferring a style which is flat and dull and commonplace. And there is also a danger that by insisting on using the most commonplace language in worship we may succeed in making it difficult for people to have a sense of the wonder and mystery and majesty of God. With regard to (c), while a certain amount of simplification and abbreviation may perhaps be appropriate in some places and for some occasions, it would surely be more to the point, if the Church were, even at this late hour, to exert its still not inconsiderable weight and influence in the cause of getting rid of the gross inequalities in educational opportunity which have marred our national life and in which the Church has so often complacently acquiesced, inequalities which there is reason to fear may in the near future actually be made greater. The corollary of the Church's use of the *Book of Common Prayer* must surely be determination on its part to make sure that all its members, however poor and lowly, are educated to share that use understandingly.

With reference to the contention about the respective merits of extempore prayers and a fixed liturgy, I would say for myself that, while I greatly value the freedom in conducting public worship to make prayers for the occasion as well as to use traditional prayers, I recognise that this freedom can be terribly abused, and that, if the person leading worship is not deeply versed in the Bible and the theology and history of Christian worship, the results may well be appalling. It is a dreadful thing for a congregation to be at the mercy of an ignoramus in these matters. And there are some, of whose ministrations I have had experience, whom I would heartily wish to see bound fast to something as salutary as the *Book of Common Prayer*.

There is one other general matter on which I should like to say something, the question whether the second person singular should continue to be used in church services in English, or whether the polite plural should replace it. This is an issue in other churches as well as in the Church of England. The question arises, it should be remembered, in two connections: where God is addressed and where an individual human being is solemnly addressed. (With reference to English translations of the Bible the question is whether the second person singular should be used (as in the AV and RV) wherever it occurs in the original, or (as in the RSV and NEB) should be retained where God is addressed but not elsewhere, or (as in some recent versions) should be dispensed with altogether.[2]

The use of the deferential plural in English in addressing a single individual goes back to the thirteenth century. Originating in the rigid class distinctions of a feudal society, the serf addressing his lord in the plural while the lord addressed his serf in the singular, it came to be used generally not only in addressing social superiors but also in addressing equals with whom one was not familiar. A similar phenomenon may be observed in other languages. But, while in German and French the second person singular is still regularly used in the family and between close friends, in English this use has largely been lost as far as ordinary colloquial speech is concerned. But I understand that in some languages there is now a tendency for the deferential plural to drop out, while the second person singular is being used more widely.

In addressing God the second person singular has been generally used in English until quite recently (though an exception can be cited from the fifteenth century). The clergy's enthusiasm for abandoning it I, for one, greatly regret: for it seems perverse to prefer to use in prayer to him, whose oneness is so specially emphasised in Holy Scripture (e.g., Deut. 6.4; Mark 12.29), a deferential plural, the historic associations of which are, at the highest, with conventional politeness and, at the lowest, with the forced servility of the down-trodden. The use of the singular surely agrees better with the intensely direct and personal quality of a man's encounter with God (people sometimes refer to an 'I - Thou relationship'). It is interesting that, when in eighteenth century Geneva the question whether *vous* should be used instead of *tu* in public prayer was raised, it was Voltaire who replied, when consulted on the issue by one of the pastors, that '*Tu* is the language of truth, *vous* that of compliment', and so encouraged the church of Geneva to keep to *tu*.[3]

With regard to the addressing of the individual human being in the context of worship it is interesting to observe how the *Book of Common Prayer* combines the use of the second person singular and the polite plural, as the Prayer Books of 1549 and 1552 had already done. In Holy Communion in the giving of the bread and wine the singular is used ('. . . given for thee, preserve thy body and soul . . .', etc). In the public baptism of infants the individual godparent is addressed, 'Dost thou, in the name of this child, renounce . . .?' and 'Dost thou believe . . .?': and, in baptising, the minister says to the child, '. . . I baptise thee . . .'. But in the Catechism there is

an interesting mixture, the polite plural being used in
the first three questions, but the second person singular
in the fourth and in the request, 'Rehearse the Articles
of thy Belief', and also in the question about the Creed,
while there is a further question in the polite plural
before the rehearsing of the Commandments and then
a return to the second person singular after it. There
is a similar, though less complicated, mixture in the
Order for the Visitation of the Sick. And in all three
services in the Ordinal, while the polite plural is used
in the solemn questions, the second person singular is
used in the form of words accompanying the laying on
of hands and the giving of the Book, except that in the
course of the short exhortation said by the Archbishop
to the new bishop, as he delivers the Bible, there occurs
a change from second person singular to polite plural.
Should I be right to think that this rather surprising
mixture is to be explained as the result of tension
between, on the one hand, the natural inclination to
conform to the current usage of ordinary social intercourse and, on the other hand, a strong sense that, in
those moments at least, when an individual is seen as
being, as an individual, most directly and particularly
the object of God's gracious action, it is more fitting,
more appropriate to the reality of the event taking
place, to address him or her in the true second person
singular?

Turning now to consider particular services in the
Book of Common Prayer, I can do no more than
mention just a few of the things which occur to
me.

Morning and Evening Prayer seem to me on the whole
splendidly satisfying forms of daily prayer, though the
absence of the element of prayer 'for all men' disturbs
and pains me. How right it is that both services begin with
Scripture sentences! But it seems odd that the selection,
from which the minister is to read one or more, comprises
only eleven; that of these eleven only three are taken
from the New Testament; and that the same selection
is given for both Morning and Evening Prayer. The

Alternative Service Book does make some improvements here.

The theological rightness of the significant 'but' in the General Thanksgiving ('. . . for all thy goodness . . . but above all . . .') was first made absolutely clear to me by a young German pastor in a prisoner-of-war camp in North Africa in 1943. I have often remembered him, when I have heard in extempore prayers a disastrous 'and' at this point, reducing God's redemption of the world to a sort of 'also ran'.

To the collects to be used throughout the year I am very much attached. I have found them a source of continuing help and refreshment. I wish that the *Alternative Service Book* could have left them alone, except when it had a real improvement to make as in the case of the Third Collect for Good Friday.

There are many outside the Anglican communion who recognise the Communion Service of the *Book of Common Prayer* as a precious treasure of the universal Church, and value it highly. Many of us owe it – some of us more, some less, directly – an enormous debt. To mention just one clause, there must be many non-Anglicans whose understanding of the work of Christ has been deepened and enlarged and whose faith has been strengthened by the words in the Prayer of Consecration, '. . . who made there (by his one oblation of himself once offered) a full, perfect, and sufficient sacrifice, oblation, and satisfaction, for the sins of the whole world . . .', even though they may never actually have heard those words in church.

With regard to the Order for the Burial of the Dead, I think that the best thing I can do is to commend to you a most perceptive appreciation of it by a former Senior Tutor of Cranmer's own college, Jesus College, Cambridge, B. L. Manning. His sermon on 'The Burial of the Dead', in his *More Sermons of a Layman* (London, 1944), pp. 124–37, is as relevant in the 1980s as it was when preached in 1941, and, if pondered attentively, would greatly increase the helpfulness of the funerals which take place in all our churches.

Lastly, I turn to the Ordinal. What struck me most forcefully when I re-read the forms for the making of deacons, ordering of priests and consecrating of bishops and then compared the equivalent forms in the *Alternative Service Book*, was the apparent weakening in the latter, of the recognition of the proper place of Holy Scripture in the life of a faithful Christian minister. In the Ordering of Priests in the *Book of Common Prayer*, the bishop's charge before the solemn questions includes:

> And seeing that you cannot by any other means compass the doing of so weighty a work, pertaining to the salvation of man, but with doctrine and exhortation taken out of the holy Scriptures, and with a life agreeable to the same; consider how studious ye ought to be in reading and learning the Scriptures, and in framing the manners both of yourselves, and of them that specially pertain unto you, according to the rule of the same Scriptures . . . .

In the *Alternative Service Book*, this has been reduced to:

> Pray that he will each day enlarge and enlighten your understanding of the Scriptures, so that you may grow stronger and more mature in your ministry, as you fashion your life and the lives of your people on the word of God.

The following paragraph of the *Book of Common Prayer* has been greatly reduced, and the words 'that, by daily reading and weighing of the Scriptures, ye may wax riper and stronger in your Ministry' (along with much else) have been jettisoned. No clear reference is left to the priest's duty, not only to pray for illumination, but also himself to work in the study of the Bible.

The second and fifth of the questions which follow the charge are, in the Prayer Book:

> Are you persuaded that the holy Scriptures contain sufficiently all Doctrine required of necessity for eternal salvation through faith in Jesus Christ? and are

you determined, out of the said Scriptures to instruct
the people committed to your charge, and to teach
nothing, as required of necessity to eternal salvation,
but that which you shall be persuaded may be concluded and proved by the Scripture?

and

Will you be diligent in Prayers, and in reading of the
holy Scriptures, and in such studies as help to the
knowledge of the same, laying aside the study of the
world and the flesh?

In the *Alternative Service Book* they have become:

Do you accept the holy Scriptures as revealing all
things necessary for eternal salvation through faith
in Jesus Christ?

and

Will you be diligent in prayer, in reading holy Scripture,
and in all studies that will deepen your faith and fit
you to uphold the truth of the Gospel against error?

In the *Book of Common Prayer* the bishop is to
say, when delivering the Bible, 'Take thou Authority to preach the Word of God, and to minister the
holy Sacraments . . .' This is – I think, significantly –
changed in the *Alternative Service Book* to 'Receive this
Book, as a sign of the authority which God has given you
this day to preach the gospel of Christ and minister his
Holy Sacraments.'
In the Prayer Book form for the consecrating of bishops the second, third and fourth questions ('Are you
persuaded . . .', 'Will you then faithfully . . .' and
'Are you ready . . .') all put great emphasis on the
importance of Scripture, whereas in the *Alternative Service Book* only the second and fifth questions mention
Scripture. Interestingly, along with this diminishing of

the stress on the Bible, there goes the jettisoning of the
surely salutary Prayer Book question, 'Will you shew
yourself gentle, and be merciful for Christ's sake to
poor and needy people, and to all strangers destitute
of help?' To conclude, consider these words from the
Alternative Service Book

Receive this Book; here are words of eternal life. Take
them for your guide, and declare them to the world.
Keep watch over the whole flock in which the Holy
Spirit has appointed you shepherd. Encourage the
faithful, restore the lost, build up the body of Christ;
that when the Chief Shepherd shall appear, you may
receive the unfading crown of glory.

Set alongside these the more direct and searching (to my
mind, at least) words of the Prayer Book

Give heed unto reading, exhortation, and doctrine.
Think upon the things contained in this Book.
Be diligent in them, that the increase coming
thereby may be manifest unto all men. Take
heed unto thyself, and to doctrine, and be diligent in doing them: for by so doing thou shalt
both save thyself and them that hear thee. Be
to the flock of Christ a shepherd, not a wolf;
feed them, devour them not. Hold up the weak, heal
the sick, bind up the broken, bring again the out-
casts, seek the lost. Be so merciful, that you be not
too remiss; so minister discipline, that you forget not
mercy: that when the Chief Shepherd shall appear you
may receive the never-fading crown of glory: through
Jesus Christ our lord. Amen.

Notes

This chapter is based on a talk given on 25 April,
1987, to the Durham Diocese Branch of the Prayer
Book Society to the members of which I am most
grateful for the invitation to speak to them.

1. E. Busch, *Karl Barth; his Life from Letters and Autobiographical Texts* (London, 1976), p. 399.
2. I have said a little more on this in *The Bible and Christian Life* (Edinburgh, 1985), pp. 218–20.
3. D. Buscarlet, *Genève, citadelle de la Réforme* (Geneva, 1959), pp. 141f.

XIV

The Prayer Book Outside England
Richard F. Buxton

A few days before writing this chapter, I was watching on television the bishops at the 1988 Lambeth Conference processing into Canterbury Cathedral. Seeing that procession, and contemplating this volume of essays, one could not but be struck forcibly by the contrast between the world and the church into which Thomas Cranmer was born 500 years ago and that of today. Had it not been for Cranmer's work four and a half centuries ago, those bishops would not in all probability have gathered in Canterbury in 1988, yet how ironical it is that most of them now use so little of his liturgical legacy in their life, worship and work.

Cranmer's legacy lies above all in the first two English Prayer Books, those of 1549 and 1552. The history of Anglican liturgy until about 1965 was very largely the story of the use and adaptations made of those two books by succeeding generations of Anglican Christians.

Cranmer produced the Edwardine Prayer Books to provide a uniform and universally used rite throughout the English monarch's dominions, specifically for the Kingdom of England itself. They differed in two other respects from the medieval service books, namely that they included in one volume all the necessary services of the Church, and were common to both officiating minister and people. As well as this, they were designed to be the service books of a Reformed and Protestant church. This is particularly true of the Holy Communion, where both books embody Cranmer's eucharistic theology of reducing the eucharistic action to what can only be described as a psychological aid to faith; this is made fully plain in the 1552 book.[1]

By the early seventeenth century things had moved on. With the union of the English and Scottish Crowns, questions concerning the extent to which worship in the two kingdoms was to be assimilated inevitably arose. But the Scottish Reformation had proceeded along somewhat different lines from the English and, in any case, eucharistic theology in particular had developed considerably both north and south of the Border since the middle of the previous century. The outcome of all this was the 1637 Prayer Book, the first Anglican liturgy produced specifically for use outside England. Both Scottish and English Caroline and Laudian influences may be seen in it in substantial measure. Classical Anglicanism should be regarded as a seventeenth century phenomenon, building on, adapting and developing the raw materials bequeathed by Cranmer, and the 1637 book is its quintessential liturgical expression.[2]

It is in the Communion Service that 1637 makes its greatest changes. The central eucharistic section of the rite is reconstructed along classical lines using 1549 materials. Thus Dialogue, Preface and Sanctus lead into a Prayer of Consecration where the institution narrative is preceded by an epiclesis of 'word and Holy Spirit' (this order is the reverse of 1549), and followed by the post-institution narrative prayer from 1549, which is now described as 'this Memorial or Prayer of Oblation'. The beginning of this reads:

Wherefore ... we thy humble servants do celebrate and make here before thy Divine Majesty, with these thy holy gifts, the memorial which thy Son hath willed us to make; having in remembrance ...

Whatever Cranmer intended the above sentence to express when he wrote it, it is quite clear that the authors of 1637 used it with the intention of giving expression to a eucharistic theology much richer and fuller than Cranmer's, one in which the reality of the action was contained in the rite itself.

This 'Prayer of Oblation' is followed by the Lord's

Prayer, the Prayer of Humble Access and the distribution of Communion, where the formulae are those of 1549. Compared with the forms of the English rite of 1604, the memorialist second sentences have been omitted. Again the intention of this is clear, the expression of a theology in which the body and blood of Christ are really received through reception of the consecrated elements. This is reinforced by the fact that the rite has a supplementary consecration rubric. An offertory of the bread and wine is inserted before the prayer for the church, a rather clumsy place for it, but it was no doubt felt impractical to insert it anywhere other than where the existing rite had its offering of money, or to move the latter.[3]

The changes in the rest of the book are far fewer and much less significant. Those worth noting include a very explicit blessing of the water, inserted in the baptismal rite.[4] The form 'presbyter' is used throughout. The book contains no ordination services.

Political circumstances at the time meant that the book did not come into use, but an important precedent had been set. Anglicanism could no longer be defined just as the religion by law established in England, nor Anglican liturgy simply a rite imposed by Act of Uniformity. It had started to become something that was to have an independent and definable life of its own.

The seventeenth was also the century of the beginnings of Empire for the British, and where the English went as colonists, many of them took the worship of the 1662 Prayer Book, even in some places to the extent of formal establishment. And with this came the first glimmerings of the idea of Anglicanism as a missionary religion; as the second reason for the inclusion of a rite of specifically adult baptism in the 1662 book makes plain:

and may always be useful for the baptizing of Natives in our Plantations, and others converted to the Faith.[5]

In the eighteenth century liturgical innovation in Anglicanism was confined to the Eucharist, and resulted from the researches of a comparatively small group of scholars, who had read in depth the increasingly available texts of the fathers, and become well acquainted with some of the great classical liturgies of the early centuries. In particular they discovered the Eastern anaphora, whose central section typically consisted of the institution narrative – anamnesis – epiclesis sequence. This, or something like it, they came to the conclusion, was the primitive pattern of eucharistic prayer.[6]

There was of course no opportunity to give liturgical expression to these ideas in the Church of England. However, among the very small body of episcopalians in Scotland these views became dominant, and the eucharistic parts of the 1637 rite were reshaped into this pattern, the definitive edition being published in 1764. The one verbal addition of significance is the phrase 'WHICH WE NOW OFFER UNTO THEE' (it is printed in capital letters) in the Oblation paragraph; this addition first appeared in the Scottish rite in a 'wee bookie' in 1735. In the epiclesis the phrase 'that they may be unto us' is altered to 'that they may become'. Both changes represent a significant strengthening of eucharistic doctrine. The intercessions have been moved to become the final part of the Prayer of Consecration in imitation of Eastern practice. The offering of bread and wine now immediately precedes the *Sursum Corda*. Just before this the money offering has been received, and a prayer composed from 1 Chronicles 29 said over it, thus appropriately and properly making this prayer refer only to the collection.[7]

The service as printed consisted only of the eucharistic part of the rite, the ante-communion being supplied from 1662. Presumably, too, the existing English Prayer Book was used for all other services as needed; there seems to have been no thought of producing a complete revised Prayer Book, nor would the resources of the tiny eighteenth-century Scottish Episcopal Church have been equal to such a task.

It was the American Revolution, and the newly independent United States of America that emerged from

it, that turned the Anglican churches of the American
Colonies into a Church, and one which needed a prayer
book of its own, at the very least if only to take account
in its prayers of the new political situation. In fact a
fairly thorough revision was made which, having been
ratified at the General Convention of 1789, came into
use in 1790. Marion Hatchett, in his masterly work *The
Making of the First American Book of Common Prayer*,[8] gives
a detailed account of the processes that led to this and
shows what an achievement it was to have produced a
book of enduring quality and usability in the difficult
circumstances of the time.[9]

The major difference from the English book was the
adoption of a consecration prayer in the Communion
Service following the Scottish (and Eastern) pattern.
Hatchett demonstrates that this was not only due to
Seabury, but to his influence combined with others in
the American Church at the time who advocated such
a style of prayer. The Prayer of Humble Access still
came between *Sanctus* and Prayer of Consecration; this
was not changed until 1928. A considerable number of
other changes were made in various places,[10] most of
which can be seen as adapting the services of the 1662
book to prevailing opinions, and to the needs of the time
and place. There were no Ordination services in the book
as published in 1790; these were added in 1792.[11] Thus,
for the first time, Anglicanism had produced a complete
version of the Prayer Book, alternative to that of 1662,
that came into regular use on a large scale.

A revised version of the American book was produced
in 1892,[12] and a further revision was made in 1928.[13]
For all their accommodation to changing needs and patterns of worship over more than a century, the changes
made are of detail rather than substance. The American
revisers of 1790 did their work well and it stood the test
of time.

Over the next century and a half, five further prov-
inces produced complete Prayer Books, namely Ireland,
Canada, Scotland, South Africa, and the Church of
India, Pakistan, Burma and Ceylon (whose book I shall

refer to as the 'Indian Book' for the sake of brevity).[14]
Each of these books has its own characteristics.

The Irish book is the most conservative in structure
and the firmest in its exclusion of the nineteenth-century
ceremonial developments in Anglicanism associated with
the Oxford Movement. This reflects a reaction to the
situation in England in 1877 when the first Irish book
was produced, a situation largely unchanged when the
1926 Irish book was published.

The 1922 Canadian version, though conservative, was
extremely thorough with numerous small alterations.
The 1959 Canadian book was more adventurous than its
predecessor, though retained its conservative character;
it does reconstruct the eucharistic prayer along classical
lines with wording that reflects an evangelical ambience,
and Cuming has drawn attention to the skilful and sensitive way in which this had been done.[15]

Though the Scots had been first in the field with the
revision of their eucharistic rite, they were comparatively
late in the day in the production of a complete Prayer
Book. In 1912 the Scottish Communion Office was
bound up with the 1662 Prayer Book, together with
other canonically permitted variations to the latter, these
being clearly distinguished by a vertical line in the left
hand margin of the pages concerned. A completely
revised Prayer Book was produced in 1929. As far as the
Holy Communion was concerned, the Scottish liturgy
was printed together with a slightly revised version of
1662. As a whole, the book reflects the Tractarian stance
that much of the Scottish Episcopal Church had adopted
from the late nineteenth century onwards.

The process of revision in South Africa took a long
time. It began in 1911, but the complete book was
not published until 1954, and reflects the strongly
Tractarian style of much of that province. The final
authorisation of its Communion Service dates back to
1929, and its eucharistic prayer contains both a pre-
institution narrative petition that those who receive
Communion may be partakers in the body and blood of
Christ, and a post-anamnesis epiclesis. It seems doubtful

if this should be described as a 'double epiclesis', since the pre-institution narrative material contains no mention of the Holy Spirit.[16]

The Indian Book, as the last to be produced, drew eclectically on many sources, as well as containing some distinctive features of its own.[17]

Since all the provinces of the Anglican Communion are autonomous, all these Prayer Books were independently produced and authorised for their own churches. But in this century provinces have had an awareness of belonging to the Anglican Communion, and two Lambeth Conferences in particular have paid attention to the question of liturgical revision, those of 1908 and 1958. The principles and suggestions these conferences made for liturgical revision were widely influential, and have given a cohesiveness to the whole process of producing these various Prayer Books that it might not otherwise have possessed.[18]

Apart from those provinces which produced complete Prayer Books, other provinces and dioceses produced new forms for some services, particularly the Eucharist. Some of these, particularly from some of the more advanced Anglo-Catholic areas, depart so far from the order and content of the Prayer Book as to pose the question as to whether they can be considered adaptations of it at all.[19]

Perhaps some mention should also be made of the use and influence of the Prayer Book outside the Anglican Communion. It has played its part in Methodist worship, John Wesley himself producing an 'abridgement' of it in the 1780s for use by Methodists in America. Much nearer our own day, it was one of the major sources used in compiling the liturgy of the Church of South India, though the *Book of Common Worship* of that church cannot be regarded as an actual version of the Prayer Book.

However, large parts of the Anglican Communion continued to use the 1662 Prayer Book just as it was, or with that variety of unofficial adaptation that characterised its usage in late nineteenth- and early twentieth-century England. Australia and New Zealand and large parts of Africa undertook no formal liturgical revision. To meet liturgical and pastoral needs in congregations whose first languages were other than English, the Prayer Book, or parts of it, was translated into many vernacular languages.

The translations of the *Book of Common Prayer* into languages other than English is an obscure aspect of the study of Anglican liturgy, and at first sight might seem to be a relatively unimportant one. But this is not the case, and the topic is one that deserves more attention than it usually receives.

W.K. Lowther Clarke devoted a short chapter to the topic in *Liturgy and Worship*,[20] and this is the only one of any of the major textbooks on Anglican liturgy that deals with the subject in any detail at all; it gives a good account of the matter as it had developed by the middle of the 1920s.

The definitive study of this subject was undertaken by D.N. Griffiths,[21] and this I have reviewed and commented on elsewhere.[22]

Griffiths identified three major reasons for translating the Prayer Book into languages other than English; first, to meet the needs of linguistic minorities in the British Isles; second, the apologetic purpose of commending Anglican ways of worship to other branches of the Christian Church; and third, to provide vernacular worship for non-English speaking congregations in the mission field – the Anglican principle that worship should be in the mother tongue made this necessary.

Of the linguistic minorities in the British Isles, the Welsh were the earliest and in many ways the best provided for, the first Welsh translation of the Prayer Book being produced in 1567. The first specific translation of the 1662 book was produced in 1665, and adequate supplies have been maintained in print ever since then.

In contrast, the Irish were very badly provided for. It has been conjectured that one of the uses of the 1560 Latin book was as an interim measure for Ireland, since many Irish clergy and congregations could not speak

English, and no books in Irish were available. They
did not become so until 1608, and even these were
little used. A further, and inferior, version was produced in 1712. This lack of Prayer Books in the Irish
language may be one reason why the Prayer Book made
so little progress in Ireland; how different subsequent
Irish history might have been if someone had regarded
the production of Irish Prayer Books as an urgent priority at the beginning of the reign of Queen Elizabeth I.

To turn for a moment from Ireland to Scotland, the
first Prayer Book expressly prepared in Scottish Gaelic
was not published until 1794; this included as an appendix the Scottish Communion Office in that language.[23]
Some eighty years earlier, in 1712, a consignment of
Irish Prayer Books had reputedly been dispatched to
Gaelic-speaking Scotland, in the mistaken belief that
the two languages were the same, a sad commentary
on English ignorance of their Celtic neighbours.

The first printed edition of a Manx Prayer Book
appeared in 1765. As a living liturgy this had a comparatively short life, for Manx as a spoken language began to
disappear from 1825 onwards.[24]

Both the Latin and the French versions may be
regarded as having been produced mainly for scholarly
and apologetic purposes, though the latter did have a
limited amount of practical use in the Channel Islands
and among some French-speaking refugee congregations in England. This need has died out in the British
Isles; in contrast, French-speaking Anglican worship has
grown in parts of the Western hemisphere.

By the end of the eighteenth century the Prayer Book
had been translated into six other European languages,
and into Arabic and Mohawk, which latter is the solitary
eighteenth-century example of a translation produced
for explicitly missionary purposes. In the nineteenth
century there was a massive expansion in Prayer Book
translation, the vast majority being produced in non-
European languages as a result of Anglican missionary
work. By 1900 the Prayer Book, or parts of it, had been
translated into no fewer than 127 different languages, of

which only seventeen were European. Griffiths' detailed researches stop at 1900, Lowther Clarke's account goes only as far as the mid-1920s. Doubtless the process of translation has continued in this century, though no one seems to have taken the trouble to document it.

It is now time to step back from the mass of detail with which this chapter has largely and necessarily been concerned so far, and to attempt to assess its significance. The first conclusion to be drawn is that all the complete Prayer Books produced by the churches of the Anglican Communion are very much versions of the original, recognisable members of the same liturgical family. The second is that one of the main trends in all of them is the provision of increasing richness and variety. The third is that most of them have been used accompanied by that great variety of ceremonial and presentation that became characteristic of the Church of England in particular in the late nineteenth century, though with each book the range of this is probably less than it is with the *Book of Common Prayer* in England itself, as many of the provinces tend to be more uniform within themselves than is the Church of England, in either a 'high' or a 'low' direction.

The fourth is that the greatest variety of form of liturgical expression and of doctrinal range is to be found in the various Communion Services, and it is with dissatisfaction with Cranmer's Communion Service that the pressure for liturgical revision in Anglicanism has usually started and often led to the most radical changes. This is a legacy of Cranmer's eucharistic doctrine, and of the 1552 rite which he composed so brilliantly to express it, a doctrine most Anglicans have not shared. This variety of expression is most apparent in the eucharistic prayer, though the great majority of these changes may be seen as variations on either the 1662 English tradition or the Scottish-American tradition, or an interplay between the two. Yet even in all this variety, they have been very largely composed from Cranmer's raw materials.

Thus the revised Books of Common Prayer, and the variety of ways in which the 1662 book itself has been used and unofficially amended, represent neither doctrinal nor ceremonial uniformity, for both these have operated within wide parameters. What does unite them is Cranmer's marvellous English; they have a uniformity of literary style and ethos, which is perhaps the strongest bond between them. (How, one wonders, does this survive in translation?) And though Anglican ceremonial varies widely from place to place, perhaps a certain dignity, calmness and sobriety is characteristic of it all. In this context it must be remembered that the standard of performance of Anglican worship in most places improved immeasurably from the early nineteenth century onwards. Cranmer provided the raw materials for a liturgical tradition which, for all its variety in detail, because of the use of these same raw materials and enrichment in harmony with them, had and retained a recognisable cohesion through four centuries. It was the use of this family of Prayer Books more than anything else that provided Anglicanism with its identity.

As a postscript one may ask, now that many parts of the Anglican Communion have largely abandoned worship in the Prayer Book tradition, for all the high quality of some of the new rites (this is notably so in the case of the 1979 American and 1985 Canadian books), how this cohesion is going to be maintained in the future. Will it be possible to say what the character and ethos of Anglican worship is, in brief and simple terms, on a worldwide basis at the end of this century?

Notes

1. Cranmer's eucharistic theology has proved notoriously difficult and controversial to interpret, and has given rise to a great deal of literature; see the standard textbooks and their bibliographies. See Chapter 3 of my own *Eucharist and Institution Narrative*, Alcuin Club Collection 58 (Great Wakering, 1975) for the detailed working out of my own conclusions on this matter.
2. Gordon Donaldson, *The Making of the Scottish Prayer Book of*

1637 (Edinburgh, 1954) is the definitive textbook about this, though some of his interpretive comments need amendment; see Buxton, pp.146–8.

3. Donaldson contains the full text of the 1637 Prayer Book, pp.97–247; the Communion Service, pp.183–204. See also W.J. Grisbrooke, *Anglican Liturgies of the Seventeenth and Eighteenth Centuries*, Alcuin Club Collections 40 (London, 1958), pp.165–82 for the text of the 1637 Communion Service, and pp.1–18 for a useful commentary upon it. I have just summarised the points of major importance here.

4. Donaldson, p.209.

5. Quotation from the latter part of the penultimate paragraph of the Preface of the 1662 Prayer Book.

6. Buxton, Chapters 8 and 9, *passim*.

7. Buxton, pp.188–92. For the text of the 1764 rite, together with useful introductory essay, see Grisbrooke, pp.335–48 and 150–9 respectively. See also B.Wigan, *The Liturgy in English* (London, 1962), p.38–51. The definitive work on this rite, which also includes a full text of it, is J.Dowden, *The Scottish Communion Office, 1764* (Oxford, 1922), seen posthumously through the press by H.A. Wilson. This is a magisterial piece of scholarship, and still essential reading for the detailed study of this topic.

8. Published by the Seabury Press, New York, 1982.

9. Hatchett, pp.144–8 in particular.

10. G.J. Cuming, *A History of Anglican Liturgy*, 2nd edn. (London, 1982), pp.145–6, gives a useful summary of them.

11. Hatchett, p.136.

12. For summary of changes made, see Cuming, p.161.

13. Cuming p.186.

14. See Cuming pp.159–61, 183–90, 201–6. For the texts of the Communion Services in all these books see Wigan; for the texts of the Baptism and Confirmation Services, see P.J. Jagger, *Christian Initiation, 1552–1969*, Alcuin Club Collection 52 (London, 1970). Twenty years ago it was possible to buy all these Prayer Books quite easily in Britain but, with newer revised liturgies having superseded them in their own countries to a considerable extent, this may not be quite so easy now.

15. Wigan pp.141–2; Cuming pp.201–2.

16. Wigan, pp.78–9; see Cuming, p.189.

17. Cuming, pp.203–4.

18. Cuming, p.184, 200.

19. Bernard Wigan collected together every extant Anglican Communion Service that had been published up to 1960 in his invaluable reference work already cited, *The Liturgy in English*. See this for the texts of these rites.

20. First published in 1932 and subtitled 'A Companion to the Books of Common Prayer of the Anglican Communion'. The relevant chapter is entitled 'Prayer Book Translations', pp.813–33.

21. Published in four articles as follows: 'The early translations of the Book of Common Prayer', *The Library*, 6th series, 3 (1981), pp.1–16; 'Prayer Book translations in the nineteenth century', *The Library*, 6th series, 6 (1984), pp.1–23; 'The French translations of the English Book of Common Prayer', *Proceedings of the Huguenot Society of London*, 22 (1972), pp.90–107; 'Four centuries of the Welsh Prayer Book', *Transactions of the Honourable Society of Cymmrodorion* (1974–5), pp.162–90.

22. 'Translations of the English Books of Common Prayer into Languages other than English' *Bulletin of the Association of British Theological and Philosophical Libraries*, 36 (1986), pp.5–9. Part of what follows is taken from this review article.

23. Lowther Clarke, p.815.

24. Lowther Clarke, p.714.

XV

Some Reflections on the Theology of Thomas Cranmer
Peter Forster

It might be considered presumptuous that someone
whose academic expertise lies in other periods should
tackle this subject. Yet I will attempt to capitalise upon
this weakness by taking a broad look at Cranmer's
theology, using the perspectives opened up from both
the patristic age and more recent theology. There are
two reasons why such an approach might commend
itself. Firstly, there can be little doubt that scholarship
advances by a combination of both large-scale and more
restricted approaches to a given subject. A good example is afforded by modern archaeology, where aerial
surveys reveal sites of possible interest, and these are
subsequently explored in painstaking and minute detail.
What is offered here, under but limited magnification, is
an aerial survey of certain important points in Cranmer's
theology. Secondly, although the link between theology
and liturgy has at times been somewhat overstated in
recent years[1], it is commonly agreed that the shape,
flavour and detail of the *Book of Common Prayer*
owe a great deal to Cranmer's *theological* convictions.
If the Prayer Book is to retain its liturgical and doctrinal
place in the Church of England, its theology needs to
enter into conversation with contemporary Anglican –
and ecumenical – theology.

It will be helpful to start with Cranmer's understanding of the atonement. The chief point of interest is
succinctly stated in the second of the Thirty-nine Articles (the clause being carried over unchanged from the
second of Cranmer's Forty-two Articles), which states of
Christ that he 'truly suffered, was crucified, dead and
buried, to reconcile his Father to us'. The idea that in

the atonement God is reconciled to the world is central
to the *Homily on the Salvation of All Mankind*, where the
purpose of the cross is to 'assuage God's wrath', and
to the argument of Book 5 of the *Defence of the True
and Catholic Doctrine of the Sacrament*, where a sharp
opposition is drawn between the propitiatory sacrifice
on Calvary, which 'pacifieth God's wrath' as 'the ran-
som for our redemption from everlasting damnation',[2]
and the sacrifice of praise and thanksgiving which we
offer in response. Such an understanding of the relation of the cross to the wrath of God was commonplace among the Reformers, who as heirs to a complex
and unresolved Western medieval discussion of ideas of
substitution and satisfaction in the theology of atonement attempted to present an orderly, reasoned view
of the atonement, from which they could present their
revised position on the soteriological relevance of the
church and sacraments. In his formative years as a theologian Cranmer had particular contact with Lutheran
theology, and here, although the theology of atonement embraced several streams of thought, Luther 'in
discussing Christ's work, places primary emphasis upon
its relation to God's wrath ... The satisfaction which
God's righteousness demands constitutes the primary
and decisive significance of Christ's work and particularly of his death'.[3] It is noteworthy that Calvin, although
equally holding that Christ underwent 'the severity of
God's vengeance, to appease his wrath and satisfy his
just judgment',[4] at least recognised that such ideas were
deeply mysterious: 'For, in some ineffable way, God
loved us and yet was angry towards us at the same time,
until he became reconciled to us in Christ'.[5]

In seventeenth-century Protestant theology this conception of the appeasement of God's wrath was to
become even more central to the understanding of
the atonement, as the nerve-centre of all God's dealings
with the world. The main developments here occurred
outside Anglican theology, although they have exerted
a considerable influence upon generations of Anglicans
who have been nurtured in the Evangelical tradition.

The sacrifice, oblation and satisfaction, for the sins of the whole world, at the centre of the Communion Service in the *Book of Common Prayer* have been largely interpreted, and not without justice, in terms of this way of understanding the atoning death of Christ.

Fortunately the Prayer Book does not quite give expression to this idea of the reconciliation of God to the world, and charitably we might suggest that Cranmer the liturgist had a surer touch than Cranmer the theologian. For the idea that in the atonement God is reconciled to the world is deeply alien to the New Testament, where the verb 'to reconcile' always has God as the subject, and the passive 'to be reconciled' is said only of man and the created world. 'God was in Christ reconciling the world to himself' (2 Cor.5.19): how would it sound if this verse were recast as, 'God was in Christ being reconciled to the world'? It is absolutely central to biblical thought that the atonement is from beginning to end the work of God, and in no sense can the atonement be conceived in terms of two parties, who had formerly been enemies, becoming mutual friends. Romans 5.1 states that through Jesus Christ we have peace with God, and not that God now has peace with us.

That Cranmer absorbed and gave expression to such a fundamentally flawed understanding of atonement was perhaps inevitable in the age in which he lived. He was by no means a leading exponent of such ideas. The development of a full-blown theory of penal substitution in the atonement was to come later. A difficulty under which contemporary liturgists and theologians alike labour is that so much discussion of the doctrine of the atonement since the seventeenth century has been marred by the contours of the idea of penal substitution, whether a particular writer has attempted to defend or attack this theory. While bearing in mind that the elucidation of the theory of penal substitution came later, and that features of the subsequent development cannot simply be read back into Cranmer's mind, we need to draw out a little more explicitly the nature of the problems which lurk in this understanding of atonement.

One aspect of the later development of the idea of penal substitution was the notion of the transfer of guilt from a sinner to the sinless Christ. This unfortunate notion is to some degree prefigured in Luther, but the full development came much later. It is a strictly nonsensical idea, because guilt, by its nature, cannot be transferred. In the later period the idea of the transfer of guilt from sinful man to Christ encouraged the antinomianism classically represented in James Hogg's *The Confessions of a Justified Sinner*. Nobody could read Cranmer's *Homily of Good Works annexed to Faith* and accuse him of fostering antinomianism. Another important aspect of penal substitution is the idea that Christ suffered on the cross the punishment which we deserved. This idea, which is present in Cranmer's thought, is true, but only up to a point. The biblical source of this idea is Isaiah 53. We can properly acknowledge that Christ suffered what we ought to have suffered, the punishment which we, with our guilt, deserved. He took our yoke upon himself. This idea has understandably played a prominent (perhaps too prominent) role in missionary and evangelistic preaching, but its limitation is that punishment as such cannot atone, cannot remove guilt and, most importantly, cannot make good what has gone wrong in the past. The idea that Christ's undeserved suffering prevents our deserved suffering is not a central theme in those parts of the New Testament which deal with the cross and atonement. The chief thrust of the New Testament is rather that by taking to himself, in the person of his Son, sinful humanity, God chose to take to himself the full reality of sin, and to deliver sin to death and destruction. What the death and resurrection of Christ thus represent is not merely the bearing of the punishment due to those guilty of sin, so much as the destruction of sinners and their sin as, to use Pauline language, the old man in Adam is replaced by the new man in Christ. As Christ trod the path of sinners to their death on the cross, he bore the anguish and punishment of the separation from God which is the most basic consequence of sin. He bore it in order to deliver it to death, to bear it away, so fulfilling and re-establishing the covenant between God and man, by making atonement. In this way the atonement represents both the objective destruction of the 'old' man of sin, and the objective, victorious establishment of the 'new' man in Christ.

The problem with Cranmer's view of the atonement can now be expressed more clearly. The heart of the atonement is the reconciling activity of God the Father, creator of all, becoming man as the second Adam, to re-found creation on a new, redeemed basis. In order for the restoration and redemption of creation to occur, the 'worst' thing possible had to happen to fallen, sinful man; quite simply, he had to be destroyed. But this was not due to any moral desire on the part of God for vengeance, retribution, punishment or for the satisfaction of his wrath. The only possible use for the idea that God was 'satisfied' by the Passion of Jesus Christ is that God – the true God – could be satisfied with nothing less than the radical destruction of sin, and the redemption of his creation. By speaking of the reconciliation of God to the world, Cranmer's vision, by comparison with that which I have just sketched, is significantly narrowed. In addition to the dubious projection into God of punitive human emotions, the older idea of penal substitution failed because it had a view of redemption which consisted in little more than the restoration of creation to its original goodness, and thus fell short of the wider cosmic and eschatological vision of the New Testament.[6] Although the theory in itself need not lead to a view of limited atonement, wherein Christ is deemed to have died only for some men, the 'elect', it did lend itself to such an interpretation. It is to Cranmer's credit that he did not develop this most unfortunate idea which, with seeds clearly visible in Calvin, forms a cornerstone of the Westminster Confession and some other confessions of the Reformed Church.

A penal substitutionary view of atonement tends to produce disastrous consequences in the life of the Church. Its legal categories spread a joyless legalism,

which was well illustrated in 1989 when the Lord
Chancellor, who is a member of the Free Presbyterian
Church of Scotland which adheres strictly to the Westminster Confession, was suspended as an elder, and
barred from taking Communion, simply because he
had been present at the requiem masses for of two
Roman Catholic colleagues. In milder forms the Evangelical movement in the Church of England, which has
paid particular respect and attention to the spirituality
and theology of the Prayer Book and the Thirty-nine
Articles, has also suffered from a persistent and, to fellow Anglicans, unattractive legalism.

The particular view of atonement which we find in
Cranmer, with its somewhat unbalanced focus upon
the world as fallen and sinful, and the reconciliation
of divine wrath, serves also to divert attention from the
overall divine purpose and glory in creation, to which a
properly conceived understanding of atonement should
point. It is significant that in both the Forty-two Articles
of 1553 and the Thirty-nine Articles of 1571, the sole
reference to the creation of the world occurs in passing
in the conventional description of God as 'the maker and
preserver of all things'.[7] There is more, much more, that
should properly be said at this point, and its absence has
dogged theology across the Reformed spectrum down
to the present day, when the thinness of our traditional
resources for confronting questions as diverse as the
ecological crisis and inter-faith relations has become
all too apparent. Negatively, we can applaud the manner in which Reformation and Renaissance thought
pointed to a freer relation between God and creation
than had obtained in much medieval theology, because
a proper independence of creation is presented in the
Bible from Genesis 1 onwards. Modern science depends
critically upon acceptance of the independent, contin-
gent rationality of the world, a rationality which must be
patiently and experimentally investigated. The contribution of Reformation thought to this acceptance, if sometimes over-stated, is now widely acknowledged.[8] The
difficulty was that because of the overall neglect of the

theme of creation, in its early formative phase modern science developed an ideological autonomy, which at a deep level has contributed to the ethical dilemmas of a modern society confronted with the largely autonomous onward march of science and its associated technology. As Professor O'Donovan has recently put it, 'If we wish to understand the phenomenon of liberal Protestantism as it emerged in the nineteenth century, there is no better way than to ask what was bound to become of a Christianity shorn of the doctrine of creation, confronted with self-confident and normless experimental science'.[9]

Another perspective on the idea of penal substitution is that it upsets a proper balance in the doctrine of atonement between substitution and representation. We should only conceive of Christ as the substitute for sinners if we also and at the same time conceive him as their representative. The idea of representation allows us to retain the necessary, indeed essential, element of substitutionary thinking in the theology of atonement, as part of the plot wherein God in Christ founds a new humanity in the resurrection, not as a substitute but as a representative, establishing for all mankind a new humanity, just as in creation itself Christ, as the mediator of the creative process 'through whom all things were made', founded the original humanity. If the idea of substitution is allowed to dominate, there is a problem in relating the (misconceived) reconciliation of Christ to God to the reconciliation of individuals to God. The chief strategy devised at the Reformation to achieve this is known as 'imputed righteousness', a concept accepted by Cranmer. The logic of this idea runs as follows. Only Christ as God and man was able to offer to God the Father the perfect offering or penalty for sin, which satisfied the righteous wrath of the Father. This creates in Christ a store of righteous merit (either sufficient for all men, or merely for the elect) which is fundamentally alien to sinful man. As sinners are brought to faith in Christ, this alien righteousness is 'imputed' or 'reckoned' to them, using the legal terminology which at

the time was dominant. The artificiality of this approach
was roundly criticised by contemporary Roman Catholic
theologians, and we must admit that their criticism had
a considerable degree of truth. It puts altogether too
great a burden on the role of faith, and detracts from
the objectivity of the atonement as the expression and
enactment of God's constant, perfect love.

I noted above that the type of atonement theory adopted by Cranmer saw redemption as little more than the
securing of creation in its original goodness. This problem is common to much Western theology, Catholic
and Protestant alike, where a legal interpretation of
atonement in effect is truncated to the beginning of
the Christian life. A Christian is given a forgiveness
which enables him to make repeated fresh starts in the
Christian life as he faces the reality of sin. The problem
is greater on the Protestant side, where righteousness is
'imputed' rather than 'imparted', and the example and
vision of the monastic life is largely discarded. The true
life of the kingdom, of the new age, is deferred to the
next life beyond the grave. In this life, the struggle
is to keep the effects of sin at bay: the kingdom of
God is on a 'care and maintenance' basis only. The
restriction in Cranmer's thought at this point is well
expressed in a neglected posthumous work of Oliver
Quick:

> Consider the words of the invitation in the Anglican
> Communion Service, the work of that greatest of
> Protestant liturgy-makers, Archbishop Cranmer. 'Ye
> that do truly and earnestly repent you of your sins and
> intend to lead a new life . . .' The suggestion is that
> the communicant is 'to turn over a new leaf' and begin
> again every time he communicates. Cranmer does not
> dare to write, as St Paul or St John would surely have
> written, 'intend to lead *the* new life', the life of God's
> new world inaugurated by Christ's resurrection. The
> full authentic note of victory is lacking, because the
> conception of the atonement is too narrowly juridi-
> cal.[10]

These observations may be supported by reference to Cranmer's *Homily Against the Fear of Death*, where it is said that nothing should trouble godly and faithful people who, despite the transience, anxiety and suffering of this life have the encouragement of the comfort and hope of a blessed state after death. As in the *Homily on Good Works* there is an insufficient sense that Christians may have in this life a real and progressive, if necessarily partial and provisional, experience of the life of the kingdom of God. The perfectly proper contrast between our present transitory life, and eternal life beyond the grave, is too strongly drawn. While one may wince at the shallowness of certain modern funeral rites,[11] even amid the sorrow of a funeral, we can doubt the aptness of the words which introduce the Prayer Book committal: 'Man that is born of a woman hath but a short time to live, and is full of misery.' Such sentiments have their proper place, but only when in tension with other affirmations, which are insufficiently recognised in the 1662 service. The 1928 revision of the burial service is a splendid example of the gains that would come from a sensitive revision of many of the 1662 services.

The somewhat exaggerated contrast between this life and the life to come reflects a broader contrast in Cranmer's theology between earth and heaven, creation and God. The roots of these sharp distinctions may be found in the Platonic tradition in the patristic age, beginning with the second-century Apologists and subsequently developed by such major figures as Origen and St Augustine.[12] There God had been defined and described very largely in categories antithetical to creation, and their sixteenth-century form is discernible in the familiar phrases of the first of the Thirty-nine Articles, where God is said to be 'without body, parts, or passions'. The impression with which these philosophically-based phrases leave us is one of the distance between God and creation. Such an emphasis is hardly without value, for, as Isaiah reminds us, God's thoughts are not our thoughts, and his ways are not our ways. The difficulty arises when this notion of God and his relation to the world is not properly penetrated with the complementary themes of incarnation and atonement, which, without denying a proper sense of the transcendence of God, would lead beyond the somewhat statically conceived and monolithic doctrine of God in Cranmer's thought, to a richer, and more thorough-going trinitarianism. This is not to suggest that Cranmer's God is himself trapped at a vast distance from the world, in a spatially conceived transcendent 'space'. Indeed, we find in Cranmer a strong assertion of divine omnipresence. But again, it is philosophical concepts of infinity and omnipresence, contrasted with finitude and location, which are employed. This leads him to assert a sharp distinction in the relation of the divinity and humanity of the ascended Christ to creation:

> For although Christ's divinity be such, that it is infinite, without measure, compass, or place, so that as concerning that nature he is circumscribed with no place, but is everywhere, and filleth all the world: yet as concerning his human nature he has measure, compass, and place, so that when he was here upon earth, he was not at the same time in heaven; and now that he has ascended into heaven, as concerning that nature he has now forsaken the earth, and is only in heaven.[13]

Cranmer's theology at this point lacks the directness and simplicity of biblical thought, which knows of no such distinction between the deity and humanity of Christ. The gracious and redemptive presence of Jesus Christ to our world involves both his humanity and his divinity, in the differentiated unity of his personal presence. Viewed from a perspective anterior to the incarnation, one could perhaps talk of the divinity of Christ apart from his humanity, as occurs in certain not wholly successful conceptions of a pre-existent divine Christ, but from a post-incarnational perspective, faith can only confess the one person of Jesus Christ, very God and very man. This need not lead us towards the Lutheran idea of the ubiquity of the body of Christ, against which, to some degree, Cranmer's views may

have been presented. Looking back at the Reformation disputes between Lutheran and Reformed theologians (Anglicanism here generally following the latter)
a strong conviction arises that false theses were met by
false antitheses.

The manner in which Cranmer develops his conception of the relation between the divinity and humanity
of Christ rests heavily upon his particular view of the
Ascension, a point to which he repeatedly returns. For
Cranmer it is axiomatic that a body cannot be in two
places at the same time, and since the body of Christ is
now in heaven, sitting at the right hand of the Father,
it cannot possibly also be present on earth. He seems to
have regarded this as something akin to a knock-down
argument, although, as T. M. Parker has pointed out, it
could by no means be taken for granted that Cranmer's
contemporaries would be accustomed to spatial views of
heaven.[14] The ease with which Cranmer, a cautious and
reflective man, well versed in the theology of the patristic age, could adopt the simplistic view of the Ascension
presented in Article Four, and repeatedly elsewhere in his
writings, reflects his rather uncritical adoption of spatial
concepts in his understanding of the relation between
earth and heaven, creation and God. Together with
his projection into God's sphere of being of worldly
conceptions of space, we see an associated problem with
Cranmer's view of time. In Article Four it is stated that
after Christ's ascension, he sits at God's right hand, pas-
sively waiting for the right time to return to earth. Such
verses as Matthew 28.20. 'Lo I am with you always, even
to the end of time' should warn us to avoid both an
undue distinction between the deity and humanity of
Christ, and also any suggestion that he is to be regarded
as inactive in our world today.

A better approach to the Ascension comes if we start
with such verses as Ephesians 4.10, which speaks of
Christ ascending 'far above the heavens, that he might
fill all things'. Even when the New Testament speaks
more simply of Christ sitting at the Father's right hand,
we should remember that this is to sit at the powerful,

executive 'right hand' of God. As Jesus explained to his disciples, he had to depart from them precisely in order that, in a new form, through the Holy Spirit, he would be able to return, in anticipation of his final definitive return at the end, completion, or fulfilment of time. Although we can readily understand how the language of presence of Christ through the Holy Spirit could be interpreted as a presence of his divinity alone, this would be far from the intention of the New Testament writers, for whom it is the crucified, risen, ascended and coming Christ who is so presented.

This approach need not lead to a crude notion of the ubiquity of the body of Christ. The concept of a 'body' is not in itself a material concept, even if there is necessarily a material element to it. We speak of our own bodies as recognisably consistent realities, despite the fact that we are constantly exchanging atoms and molecules with our environment. The mistake of defining with Article Four the body of Christ too narrowly in terms of its flesh and bones, although it has roots in the second-century defence of the resurrection of the body,[15] has a close association with the common Protestant mistake of interpreting the medieval concept of substance, as applied for example in the doctrine of transubstantiation, in too material a sense, thus underplaying the intended (if nevertheless rather artificially drawn) distinction between substance and accidents.

It may seem rather baffling to conceive of the Ascension as a real, historical event, the terminus of the appearances of the risen Jesus during the 'forty' days, and the prelude to Pentecost, yet also as much more than a movement from one place, earth, to a not dissimilarly conceived place, heaven. In order to do this we have to re-think the notions of space with which we are familiar on earth to render them adequate to describe God's place or space. It is helpful here to take the Incarnation and the Ascension together, because similar questions arise in each case. In respect of the Incarnation, we are concerned with the issues raised in the so-called kenotic controversy, the source of considerable acrimony between Reformed and Lutheran theologians. The Incarnation invites us to think both in accordance with the nature of Jesus Christ as the eternal Son of God, and as the fully human Jesus of Nazareth. Difficulties arise if we attempt to understand or picture the Incarnation using a narrow, or humanly conceived, concept of space as a physical area defined by its limits. Following such an approach soon confronts us with an awkward choice, between a unity in the person of Jesus which does not do justice to the dynamic, differentiated relation between his divine and human natures, and the Reformed approach, which tended to undermine the fullness of the Incarnation by allowing too great a separation between the divine and human nature. The clear tendency in Cranmer is to anticipate the Reformed position, with its associated difficulties.[16]

When we turn from the long-standing debates over the relation of the Incarnation to space to the Ascension, we meet a set of related, if different questions. Here we need to avoid Cranmer's over-localised concept of heaven, and to develop a more biblical concept of heaven, as a higher, mysterious aspect or dimension of creation, from where God rules the 'lower' visible universe. If we cannot draw a strict analogy between the relation between God and creation in the Incarnation and in the overall reality of heaven, a certain, qualified analogy can be suggested, at least in respect of the modes of thought appropriate to the apprehension of the connections involved. In the Incarnation we have the meeting of God and creation in the sphere of creation, whereas in the Ascension we have the meeting of God and creation in God's 'space' in heaven, a meeting which alters the very relation between earth and heaven as indicated in the event and reality of Pentecost. In the Ascension then, we have both to think of the ascension of Jesus Christ to a place, heaven, yet to think of this place not as a space with independent limits, but a place with limits defined by the ascended Christ; a place, in other words, which is constituted by the ascended Christ, and whose existence

cannot be conceived independently of the ascended, and
therefore coming, Christ, who ascended 'higher than the
heavens' (Heb.7.26) that he might fill all things.[17]

It is from the perspective of these observations that
I would like to turn to a brief consideration of the
well-worn topic of Cranmer's eucharistic theology. The
thread running through our discussion has been a certain dualism between God and the world. This is a
limited and moderate dualism compared with many
other theologies in the Western tradition, but one which
consequently has been less open to detection. The
essentially dualistic view of God presupposed by the
idea of penal substitution could only have developed in
the context of a prior dualism between God and creation. We have seen this dualism influencing Cranmer's
christology and in his interpretation of the Ascension.
It is little surprise, then, to find running through his
treatment of the Eucharist, and especially through the
controversial areas of eucharistic presence and eucharistic sacrifice, a recurrent contrast between notions of
the 'real' and 'symbolic' presence of Jesus Christ, between
the sacramental sign, and the reality signified.

It seems clear to me that this forms the basic inter-
pretative framework within which Cranmer's eucharistic
theology moves, even if it can be agreed that the
movement is at times more subtle than such a stark
framework might suggest. It affects both the development of Cranmer's understanding, and the view he is
able to take of his Catholic opponents. Even if some
were undoubtedly guilty of a rather crude theory of
transubstantiation as involving a miraculous physical
change of bread and wine into the literal, historical, body
and blood of Christ, many others in Cranmer's time held
to the much more careful concept of presence which we
see in Aquinas and the subsequent decrees of the Council
of Trent. This central strand of Catholic teaching maintained, and maintains even more strongly today (not
least in the ARCIC statement on the Eucharist) a careful distinction between the natural presence of Christ
in heaven and his real but sacramental presence in and

through the eucharistic elements. This Catholic teaching is certainly open to serious questioning,[18] but not to the wholesale condemnation provided by Cranmer.

In the presentation of Cranmer's own position, the location of the body of Christ in heaven precludes its presence upon earth, apart from such 'presence' as may be said to exist by virtue of a spiritual relationship in faith between the believer and Christ. We may agree, then, with the basic analysis of Cranmer's eucharistic theology provided by G. Dix, C. C. Richardson and T. M. Parker.[19] There is a basic shape to it which might loosely be labelled 'Zwinglian', inasmuch as Cranmer shared with Zwingli a certain underlying and influential dualism between the 'spiritual' and the 'physical' realms. This leads in turn to both Zwingli and Cranmer conceiving of the Eucharist basically as an *action*, the elements being of secondary importance, and almost incidental to it. For each of them, an undue focus upon the elements detracted from the command: *Do this* in remembrance of me, the eucharistic action being but one particular form, or sign, of the wider relationship with God established throughout the Christian life. Zwingli was well aware of the original meaning of the Latin word *sacramentum* as a military oath, and it was central to his understanding that in the Eucharist, Christians gave a public avowal of their faith in Christ and determination to live the Christian life. While Zwingli came gradually to accept that such ceremonial could strengthen as well as merely demonstrate a person's faith, for Cranmer this was always central to a proper understanding of the Communion, and in this regard it is clear that Cranmer is somewhat closer to Calvin than Zwingli had been. Towards the end of his life, Cranmer could use language practically identical to Calvin's, when he spoke at Oxford of the bread and wine 'as seals unto us, annexed unto God's promises, making us certain of God's gifts towards us'.[20] Calvin differs from Cranmer in repeatedly referring to the presence of Christ in the Eucharist as a *mystery*, which 'neither the mind is able to conceive nor the tongue to express'.[21] Calvin is able to express the matter in these terms because, despite his firm rejection of the idea of transubstantiation, he vigorously defends in the Eucharist a 'true and substantial partaking of the body and blood of the Lord', which, if by the Spirit, nevertheless 'causes us to possess Christ completely and have him dwelling in us'.[22] It was left to later Anglican divines such as Richard Hooker to establish this higher Protestant eucharistic theology in the tradition of the Church of England.

The contrast here between Calvin and Cranmer, although real, must not be overdone. For both, the key notion is the presence of Christ's benefits to the faithful recipient of the sacrament. For both there is a clear distinction between the signs of Christ's body and blood, and the reality itself. Yet we see in Calvin a much more careful attempt to avoid the separation between sign and thing signified. Cranmer only rarely refers to the Eucharist as a mystery, and when he does so, he is generally careful to extend such thoughts beyond the sacrament as such.[23] Although Cranmer makes considerable use of language of 'sacrament', the reference is to the use of earthly signs or symbols, rather than to a particular form of the presence of God.

Yet, if we grant a fundamental correctness to Dix's original thesis, we must also acknowledge that the many critics of his treatment of Cranmer have often had an important point to make. Cranmer wished to see a daily celebration of the Eucharist, but Zwingli was perfectly content with a quarterly celebration. In practice, if not to the same extent in theory, the Eucharist clearly meant a great deal to him, and the Communion Service of 1552, despite being shorn of all possible allusions to a real, substantial presence of the body of Christ, nevertheless has a strongly devotional atmosphere, as the believer is given a particular opportunity to be confronted with, and comforted by, the majesty of God. This comfort consists in the reception, through the Spirit, of the ben- efits of Christ's 'one oblation of himself once offered'. The divine presence is therefore a redemptive presence, a presence of the divine nature of Christ conditioned by what happened to Christ in the flesh. In this sense, and in this sense alone, can we speak of the 'true' presence of Christ in the Eucharist. But at best we can only speak of a partially conceived presence, corresponding to his rather truncated view of the atonement.

Karl Barth used to say that the greatest problem with the theology of the Reformers was their limited treatment of eschatology, deriving from their acceptance of the unfortunate equation between the kingdom of God and the church.[24] For Cranmer, the decisive action of God in Christ was too narrowly conceived in terms of the past event of the Incarnation, narrowed still further to the cross itself. But in the New Testament the life of Christ culminating in the cross is interpreted through the Resurrection, Ascension and Pentecost as the inauguration of a new age, determined as much by the 'coming' Christ as the 'past' Christ. Life in the present is shaped by the presence of this past and future Lord, who is the same yesterday, today and for ever. His presence with us is not a crass or literal presence of a past event, but it is a real presence as our coming Lord breaks into history, calling the Church to be his body on earth, as a partial, provisional, yet nevertheless genuine, symbol and form of the kingdom, a kingdom to which the whole of God's creation is called. The neglect of creation and the neglect of eschatology in Cranmer's theology go together; similarly, in the Bible these themes are closely related.

Finally, what relevance do these somewhat problematic themes in Cranmer's theology have for the future of the *Book of Common Prayer*? Although I have dwelt upon what I judge to be some unsatisfactory aspects of Cranmer's theology, my basic attitude to both the man and the book is one of great admiration. The problems with his theology are usually but mild illustrations of serious problems to be found here or there among his distinguished contemporaries and successors. That he was a liturgical genius, partly at least because of his thorough immersion in the writings of the Fathers, is not in question. The *Book of Common Prayer* served the Church of England well for an extraordinarily long time, but its usefulness in its present 1662 form for the worshipping life of most parish churches is today in serious doubt. Although the Prayer Book remains the standard for worship, its use is in steady, even rapid decline, and there is at present no sign of any slowing, let alone reversal, of its decline. Among many who had become saddened by its demise was Dr Gareth Bennett, whose perceptive comments upon the subject in his preface to *Crockford's Clerical Directory 1988* were overshadowed by other less important observations, and their tragic aftermath. It was left to Professor Henry Chadwick, in a memorable speech in the General Synod of the Church of England, to highlight the importance of Dr Bennett's comments:

> It was characteristic of the Anglican way of doing theology that our primary formulary of faith was a prayer book. We were the only communion in Christendom that had a way of praying as its primary formulary . . . I am not a member of the Prayer Book Society but I am not with a bad conscience. Perhaps one ought to be. Perhaps we all ought to be, because the Church of England is a Prayer Book society . . . No, we do not want to get locked into the past. That is not the point. But nothing is sadder than someone who has lost his memory, and the Church that has lost its memory is in the same state of senility – and it can be very tragic.[25]

The great majority of contemporary liturgical scholars believe that significant revision of the *Book of Common Prayer* is neither feasible nor desirable. With regard to feasibility, I hope, despite the inauspicious events of 1928, that they are wrong; with regard to desirability, as I observe and experience the rather limp theology and language of many parts of the *Alternative Service Book*, I am increasingly convinced they are wrong. A revision would be as much a theological as a liturgical exercise. It would have to take the many strengths of the

Prayer Book, including a proper focus on the majesty of God and the misery of man, but modify and augment them, in the light of the positive theological and liturgical developments of the past 300 years. But it would take a person of a genius approaching that of Cranmer himself to engage successfully in that breathing of new life into old forms of which Cranmer himself was assuredly the master.

Notes

1. Dix's influential comments (*The Shape of the Liturgy*, Westminster, 1945, p.672), when he attempted to damn Cranmer with faint praise, are misleading: 'Compared with the clumsy and formless rites which are evolved abroad, that of 1552 is the masterpiece of an artist ... the only effective attempt ever made to give liturgical expression to the doctrine of justification by faith alone. If in the end the attempt does not succeed ... that must be set down to the impossible nature of the task, not to the manner of its performance.' There were other important influences upon the Communion service, as I shall seek to demonstrate.

2. Parker Society I, p.346.

3. P. Althaus, *The Theology of Martin Luther* (Philadelphia, 1966), p.220. Althaus is here correcting a rather different view expressed by G. Aulèn, *Christus Victor* (London, 1931).

4. *Institutes*, II.16.10.

5. *Institutes*, II.17.2.

6. I am well aware of the possible objection that the Bible has much more to say concerning the wrath of God than I am apparently willing to allow. The subject could merit a careful and extended treatment, which would need to consider a range of very diverse texts. I cannot summarise a proper assessment of the material, but I will quote the important conclusion of C.E.B. Cranfield, from his magisterial commentary upon an important section of the *Epistle to the Romans*, chaps. 9—11, which speak so vividly of the wrath of God: 'We shall misunderstand these chapters if we fail to recognise that their key-word is 'mercy'. Paul is here concerned ... to show that Israel's disobedience, together with the divine judgement which it merits and procures, is surrounded on all sides by the divine mercy' (*The Epistle to the Romans*, Edinburgh, 1979, p.448).

7. The problematic nature of early Lutheran, Reformed and Anglican theology at this point has been well described by O. O'Donovan, *On the 39 Articles* (Exeter, 1986), chap. 5. It is

a pity, however, that Professor O'Donovan in an earlier chapter defends the unfortunate idea of the reconciliation of God to the world. As a result, his analysis fails to expose the full roots of Cranmer's problematic treatment of creation.

8. See for example, R. Hookyas, *Religion and the Rise of Modern Science* (Edinburgh, 1973).

9. Hookyas, pp.66f.

10. *The Gospel of the New Age* (London, 1944), p.88.

11. I have in mind, for example, the selection of verses from Psalm 90 in the *Alternative Service Book*, as compared with the full version in the *Book of Common Prayer*.

12. For the early development and its difficulties, see R.A. Norris, *God and the World in Early Christian Theology* (London, 1966).

13. Parker Society, I.p.97.

14. Review by T.M. Parker of C.W. Dugmore, *The Mass and the English Reformers* (*Journal of Theological Studies*, 1961, NS XII, p.140).

15. See, for example, the rather too literal discussion in Irenaeus' *Adversus Haereses*, Book 5, where there is little difference between resurrection and resuscitation, which contrasts with St Paul's more nuanced account in 1 Cor.15.

16. See, for example, G. Bromily, *Thomas Cranmer Theologian* (London, 1956) where, amid a generous assessment of Cranmer's thought, attention is also drawn to the 'Nestorian tendency' within it. See, for example, p.65, in relation to his treatment of Baptism.

17. For a further exploration of these questions of the interpretation of spatial concepts in theology, drawing upon important recent developments in natural science, see T.F. Torrance, *Space, Time and Incarnation* (Oxford, 1969), and *Space, Time and Resurrection* (Edinburgh, 1976).

18. As given, for example, by A.I.C. Heron, *Table and Tradition* (Edinburgh, 1983), pp.98ff.

19. G. Dix, *The Shape of the Liturgy* (London, 1945), Chap.16; C.C. Richardson, *Zwingli and Cranmer on the Eucharist* (Evanston, 1949); T.M. Parker, op. cit. (n. 14).

20. Parker Society, I. p.398.

21. Institutes, IV.17.7.

22. Institutes IV.17.19 and IV.17.12.

23. See, for example, the discussion in P. Brooks, *Thomas Cranmer's Doctrine of the Eucharist* (London, 1965), pp.94f. It is a fault in this interesting book that it fails to draw an adequate distinction between Calvin and Cranmer at this point.

24. *The Christian Life* (Edinburgh, 1981), p.244.

25. *Report of Proceedings of the General Synod, February 1988* (Church House Publishing, 1988).

XVI

Modern Ordinands and the *Book of Common Prayer*
Michael Vasey

In 1979, a petition was presented to the General Synod of the Church of England, which called the widespread abandonment of the *Book of Common Prayer* and of the Authorised Version of the Bible 'this great act of forgetting.'[1] There is much disagreement as to who is to blame for this corporate amnesia. The 1974 Worship and Doctrine Measure ensured that no parish could stop using the *Book of Common Prayer* without the agreement of its elected Parochial Church Council. In 1981 and 1984 attempts were made to bring in a Prayer Book Protection Bill which would have compelled a parish to use the *Book of Common Prayer* once a month at its main morning service, where twenty members or 20 per cent of the electoral roll (whichever was larger) so requested.[2] (These bills failed, not least because they would have overturned what Lord Beaverbrook, speaking for the Government in 1987, called the 'concordat . . . in effect codified' in the 1974 Measure.) Although the bill would have legislated for parishes, much attention focused on the theological colleges. In 1981 Lord Sudeley even spoke of adding a clause to compel the colleges to use the Prayer Book. On 22 January, 1987, Lord Sudeley again instigated a debate in the House of Lords, this time inviting the Government's response to a Prayer Book Society survey on the Theological Colleges and the *Book of Common Prayer*, a survey whose statistical validity was strongly criticised inside and outside the House.

The debates themselves reflected the power that Cranmer's liturgy, or at least his language, has over the imagination of many, even if Lord Glenamara's claim in 1981 that 'teenagers love the Cranmer Prayer Book language' seems overstated. The bishops responded with courtesy and sought to clarify many misunderstandings. They also pointed out that those who claimed to love the Prayer Book often seemed unwilling to attend its services, or to take their place in the councils of the Church. Assurances were given of a desire to ensure that ordinands were equipped to use all the authorised services of the Church. These have also been embodied in a House of Bishops resolution in 1981, and a specific question has been added to the questionnaire used when the Bishops' Inspectors review a college.

'Where does the blame really lie?' is one of the questions addressed in this essay. It is based not on statistical study, but one person's experience of thirteen years on the staff of a particular theological college, for much of which he has been responsible for the teaching of Liturgy (but not for the worship of the college). Cranmer Hall is part of a university college, St John's College, in Durham. It has an open Evangelical tradition and a gentle Anglican style; it draws its ordinands from many parts of the country and from a wide range of churchmanship. An earlier draft of this essay formed the basis of an extended session for ordinands and their pastoral fieldwork supervisors.

Given the personal and reflective nature of the essay, not to mention the controversial nature of the subject, it seems appropriate to begin by outlining the writer's own stance. I see the *Book of Common Prayer* as of great importance in the history and development of the Christian faith in England and in the Anglican Communion. It is an expression and distillation of the life of the Western Church, shaped, of course, by the discoveries and fears of the Reformation, and has been the main vehicle whereby the thought and faith of this tradition has been made available to ordinary English-speaking Christians. A significant part of my early Christian life was steeped in and nurtured by this book; with the Thirty-nine Articles, it provided the locus of my early exploration of Reformation and Evangelical theology; it formed the main content of such liturgy teaching as I received at theological college in the late sixties. Its prayers, like the landscape of Kenya or my mother's style of German–Jewish cooking, retain the integrating power of early formative experience. I am still captivated by the dramatic flow of Cranmer's Communion Service,[3] even though I am forced to view it as almost fatally flawed on pastoral, theological, liturgical and even dramatic grounds.

However, I live in another world, in which the *Alternative Service Book* itself is increasingly seen as too conservative to engage with the spiritual needs of the Church. The desire is not for weaker or more 'liberal' doctrine, but for bolder and richer contemporary Christian expression. For example, a recent report *For the Family*, from the Chelmsford diocese, shows that in many parishes Family Services are the best attended services,[4] and goes so far as to say of Family Services 'they have become another strand of Anglican worship'. Much of my own recent worshipping life has been with the *Alternative Service Book*, which I view as a very considerable achievement, for all its many weaknesses. As a recent appointee to the Liturgical Commission and to the ecumenical Joint Liturgical Group, much of my energy is taken up with seeking to build on the significant agreements embodied in the *Alternative Service Book* in a way that draws more richly on Christian tradition, and provides for the vitality and cultural contexts of contemporary church life. Hovering in the wings are new issues, arising from the growing together of the denominations. Conservation, inevitably, has a low priority.

The situation today

A number of elements can be identified in the situation today. Many ordinands begin training without ever having met a Prayer Book service. A sizeable number of them have come to a committed Christian faith since 1980, and have no knowledge even of the modern services that preceded the *Alternative Service Book*. When

the Council of St John's College discussed this matter in
1981, a diocesan bishop commented that no parish in
his diocese whose services were drawn mainly from the
Book of Common Prayer produced ordinands. Even
those who know and like the Prayer Book share an
assumption that the *Book of Common Prayer* is not
credible as a form of worship for the future. References to the 'colleges' often show considerable ignorance of the present training situation in the Church
of England. About a third of ordinands are trained on
non-residential courses, and not in colleges at all. About
a quarter of those beginning training are women. Many
are not graduates. Most are not 'young men' fresh out of
school or college, but have substantial experience as lay
members of congregations. Many concerns are tempted
to see the theological colleges and courses as a point
at which their particular vision of the church can be
imposed through programming the next generation of
the clergy. Ordinands are not unprogrammed robots.
They are Christians of experience, called by God from
many walks of life, who bring their own gifts and insights
to the life of the church. Of course, they have much
to learn, but responsible training takes seriously what
God is bringing to the Church through these people.
Manipulation is faithless and ineffective.

Many of the clergy of the Church of England are
deeply alienated from the *Book of Common Prayer*.
They have lived intimately with this book, sought to
use it as the basis of their pastoral ministry, taken its
services as the foundation of their daily prayer, and
found it wanting. Both Anglo-Catholics and Evangelicals have at times appealed to the *Book of Common
Prayer* for polemic or teaching purposes, but neither
have found it adequate, either personally or pastorally.
This clerical alienation does not simply come from ask-
ing of a particular liturgy something that no liturgy can
be expected to do. The experience of many clergy has
been that the services of the *Book of Common Prayer*
imposed on them an oppressive social and religious identity which has seemed on occasion to verge on fantasy.

Britain is no longer the centre of the English-speaking world. For example, in the production of modern language versions of traditional liturgical texts, British voices struggle for a hearing.[5] The missionary movement, with the resulting dramatic growth of the Church outside Christendom, has eroded the dominance of English Christian traditions.[6] The ecumenical movement has sought to discover a deeper theological unity behind the theological controversies of the sixteenth century. The liturgical movement has vindicated much of Cranmer's work, but has judged his Communion Service defective in not giving thanksgiving the place Jesus intended in the structure of the rite. When these considerations are added to the shift in centre of gravity in the English-speaking world, it is not surprising that the *Book of Common Prayer*, and the Authorised Version of the Bible, are fading from the scene. Even Shakespeare will be lucky to survive. The situation might just have been different if England had looked to the Christian church to give it ethnic and cultural identity in the twentieth century; but even that is doubtful.

A comparable marginalisation of the *Book of Common Prayer* and the Thirty-nine Articles has taken place in the study of systematic theology. Given the respect for tradition which characterises Christian thought, this ought to cause surprise. It may be symptomatic of a deeper intellectual and spiritual alienation from these documents than those who defend them in other contexts may be willing to admit. Or it may simply reflect the limited resources of a church struggling to adjust to its own sudden marginalisation. Oliver O'Donovan's *On the Thirty Nine Articles: a Conversation with Tudor Christianity* [7] represents a solitary modern exception to this neglect. If the *Book of Common Prayer* and the Thirty-nine Articles are to retain any vital place in the life of the Church, it must begin with a renewed respect for them in the study and teaching of theology.

The passing of the Alternative Services Measure in 1966, and the Worship and Doctrine Measure in 1974, have allowed a dam to burst. Before these, the authority

of Parliament over the services of the Church of
England had served to fossilise its worship. Until then,
the only lawful changes of any significance were those
allowed by the Shortened Services Act, 1872. Even the
very conservative changes proposed in 1928, and adopted in many places, were in breach of the law. This
externally imposed rigidity prevented the natural evol-
ution of forms of prayer in the Church of England. English piety and devotion were channelled, instead, into
hymns that were inserted, at first without the authority
of law, into the authorised services. When change finally
came, it is not surprising that it had the appearance of
revolution.

The 1974 Worship and Doctrine Measure sought to
protect the place of the *Book of Common Prayer*, both
as a doctrinal standard, and as a form of prayer, and
ensured that no changes could be imposed without con-
sent. The abandonment of the *Book of Common Prayer*
in most parishes must be seen as in accordance with the
wishes of most regular worshippers, even after allow-
ance is made for the insensitivity of some clergy and
the passivity of some laity. The 1974 Measure does not
distinguish between the *Book of Common Prayer* as a
doctrinal standard and as a liturgical book. In retrospect,
this may have been a mistake and probably hastened
the demise of the traditional services. Change might
have come more gradually if the Church of England
had bound new and old services in one book instead
of printing the lections out in full.

It is easy to overlook the effect of non-theological
factors in preserving the *Book of Common Prayer*.
Forms of prayer naturally evolve in the Church under
the pressures of popular piety, Christian teaching and
ecclesiastical oversight. In the sixteenth century this
process was hijacked and then frozen as the ordering
of Church life was transferred to the Crown and Parliament. Royal law cannot comprehend the respect for the
local and the pastoral which are an integral part of
Church law. In particular the *Book of Common Prayer*
was regarded as an important instrument in preserving

national unity. Henry VIII and his successors even sought to fix the wording of the *ex tempore* Bidding of the Bedes which from medieval times had been the primary form of public intercessory prayer and which continued, despite strenuous efforts by authority, into the eighteenth century. Printing also played a major part in sustaining a uniform and inflexible form of prayer.

Law and printing had the effect of preserving the prayers of the church unchanged. This allowed them to gain an aura of transcendent permanence. It may also have meant that they ceased to function as prayer for ordinary people. The alienation of the common people from the *Book of Common Prayer* received its most brilliant exposé from the chaplains in the First World War. E. Milner-White, in a wide-ranging essay in *The Church in the Furnace*,[8] wrote, 'Even the Prayer-book, august and beloved as ever, stands for judgement . . . it has been at best *semi-used and semi-usable*.' 'Hardly a soldier carries a Prayer-book, because there is little in it he can use.' Sadly, all this was forgotten after the war. The room given in the *Alternative Service Book* for unscripted prayer and local decision marks a return to the norm for Christian prayer. The explosion in computerised printing and microcomputers is likely to erode a uniformity maintained by a nationally produced book.

Some people imagine that it is simply a non-churchgoing establishment that bemoans the decline of the *Book of Common Prayer*. On the contrary, the Prayer Book continues to retain the allegiance of a significant group of English churchgoing laity, and also of some clergy. A number of factors obscure this reality and its significance. The Prayer Book is often defended with tremendous passion, but in a way that is easily dismissed as simple nostalgia, and as theologically and liturgically ignorant. (Compare Michael Foot's comment in *PN Review 13*, 'I would strongly support whoever it was who said "If the Authorised Version was good enough for St Paul, it should be good enough for anybody"' (p.10).) A number of churches, not least cathedrals, use the *Book of*

Common Prayer and have large congregations. These
include younger people, many of whom have been drawn
to the Christian faith through its expression in the forms
and music of Western Christian culture. Members of
these congregations often exercise their discipleship in
secular society and assert considerable Christian influence in so doing. At the same time they often find the
communalism of more 'gathered' congregations stifling,
shallow, and characterised more by bourgeois optimism
than by Christian faith. Little in their experience enables
them to understand why many congregations have
found such a style liberating and the prelude to growth.
Hard-pressed clergy, seeking to re-form some sort of
meaningful congregational life in 'post-Christian' England, often perceive the high-flown cultural harangues to
which they are subjected as unhelpful, and find it difficult to regret the departure of the 'awkward squad'
to cathedrals.

What place, then, does the *Book of Common Prayer* have
in a theological college today? I can only speak from my
knowledge of one college. Even this description may mis-
lead, if certain contextual factors are ignored. Liturgy as
a theological subject struggles for recognition in English
theology. Biblical studies and systematic theology are
treated as the serious and classic theological disciplines,
notwithstanding the claims often made for worship as the
basis of Anglican common life.[9] Liturgy is not properly
represented in English faculties of theology and qualified liturgy teachers are rare.

Morning and Evening Prayer and the Communion
Service from the *Book of Common Prayer* are used one
day each week in the college chapel. The Communion
Service is used once a term at the community's main
weekly Eucharist. Durham Cathedral is next door to
the college and uses the Prayer Book for most services. Ordinands have some freedom to choose which
services they attend, and can therefore minimise their
encounter with the *Book of Common Prayer* if they so
wish. It might have been more effective to have followed

the example of other colleges in using the Prayer Book for a month or a term each year. A desire to make chapel worship accessible to 180 non-ordinands in the college has mitigated against using the Prayer Book in this way. Each ordinand is given some guidance on leading the Prayer Book office on arrival. Some will encounter the *Book of Common Prayer* in fieldwork of placement parishes – possibly more than in other colleges because of the conservatism of the North. (It is worth noting the comment of the Bishop of Newcastle in the 1987 Lords' debate that it might be more effective to send newly ordained clergy to lead worship in local parishes where different rites are in use.)

The liturgy course has thirty-two hours staff–student contact time in which to introduce a whole way of thought and to prepare ordinands to understand the historical roots and contemporary forms of Baptism and the Eucharist. Twentieth-century developments, not least in the Anglican Communion, have made the *Book of Common Prayer* a liturgical blind alley; and within such tight time constraints it does not figure prominently in my teaching of the subject. Particular attention is given to the texts and structure of the 1549, 1552 amd 1662 Communion Services. Liturgy is jointly examined with the local Roman Catholic seminary, and the examination paper is shaped to encourage Anglican candidates to do one of their four questions on the *Book of Common Prayer*. The teaching of Reformation and modern church history, and systematic theology, naturally makes reference to the *Book of Common Prayer*.

It is difficult to assess the adequacy of all this. Some ordinands certainly gain a new respect for the *Book of Common Prayer*. On the whole, it feels less than satisfactory, but has to be set against many other priorities in training and against many other gaps in the Christian formation of those coming to college. Three factors mitigate against more effective introduction to the *Book of Common Prayer*. First, the Prayer Book seems no longer to be an accessible influence in the spirituality of ordinands or staff; it is losing plausibility as living liturgy. This is perhaps exacerbated when, for excellent reasons, staff are lay, women or non-Anglican. Second, the style of training is wary of building up a clerical persona that will inhibit clergy working alongside non-ordained Christians. Third, academic and practical training for mission and ministry in a non-theistic culture finds it difficult to give weight to liturgy at all.

Introducing Ordinands to the Book
of Common Prayer

Ordinands' difficulties with the *Book of Common Prayer* spring from more than ignorance of the text, and are not easily overcome.

Prayer Book use is much more than the text of the *Book of Common Prayer*; it is a style moulded by those aspects of the Evangelical and Oxford movements that gained acceptance for a period in certain sections of the Church. In normal use many rubrics are ignored, or texts adapted, in ways that are difficult to discover for those who do not know the customary use. Examples include: the omission or abbreviation of Exhortations; the use of the Collect of Trinity 21 as a non-priestly absolution; the use of the Shorter Commandments at the Holy Communion; the use of hymns and of prayers 'after the Third Collect'. Such uses are not easily grasped, except through regular participation in worship in a particular place. The usages of the 1928 Prayer Book are not printed in the ordinary copies of the *Book of Common Prayer*. One could mention also the objective and subdued ethos of the traditional Office, so alien to the style of much contemporary piety.

The *Book of Common Prayer* is a different genre from the *Alternative Service Book*, and this explains why those familiar with the one are often so bad at leading the other. The difference is between leading the customary prayers of the people, and helping a congregation to use a resource book in its worship of

God. It has been well expressed by Colin Buchanan: 'Cranmer', he writes, 'produced "meals-on-wheels" – i.e. he prepared the fare piping hot at the centre, and sent it out to the local parishes, where the clergy had to act as courteous waiters and simply lay out Cranmer's dishes to the waiting laity ... Nowadays the official services rank not as "meals-on-wheels" but as frozen peas.'[10] To use a different metaphor, leading a *Book of Common Prayer* service is somewhat like steering a liner; the minister needs to learn to work with, and use the momentum of, both form and congregational expectation. People often have difficulty grasping Cranmer's use of repetition and his evocation and channelling of strong emotion, as in 'spare us, good Lord, spare thy people, whom thou hast redeemed with thy most precious blood' (Litany).

Again, the formative influence of the *Book of Common Prayer* is not easily understood by those not nurtured by it. Good examples are:

1. The confession at Morning and Evening Prayer: 'devices and desires of our own hearts'.
2. The interpretive principle expressed in having an Old and New Testament lesson at each office.
3. The Holy Communion Prayer of Consecration with, for example, its 'who made there (by his one oblation of himself once offered) a full, perfect and sufficient sacrifice, oblation and satisfaction for the sins of the whole world'.
4. The exhortation and examination at the Ordering of Priests, often used in teaching about the life and responsibilities of the ordained ministry.
5. The first Exhortation in the Holy Communion service with its teaching about confession.
6. The Catechism and the collects, often learned by heart by older lay people.

Ordinands cannot discover these simply by intuition. Some examples may emerge in the teaching of spirituality or Church history. Others are only discovered through an unhurried process of listening and discussion.

The Spirituality of the Book of Common Prayer

Closely related to the formative influence of parts of the *Book of Common Prayer* is its overall ethos or spirituality. At the risk of offending by omission or generalisation, it may be helpful to identify some elements of this.

The holiness and sovereignty of God. This pervades the prayers and exhortations of the *Book of Common Prayer*, even in simple phrases like 'We have offended against thy holy laws', or 'who hast safely brought us to the beginning of this day'. Faith in a holy and sovereign God is harder to sustain in a more egalitarian and pluralist society, although it may be needed more. At the same time, these themes may be misheard as encouraging passivity rather than hope-filled action in confronting the hardships of life. The *Alternative Service Book*, like the New Testament, sees hope as springing from the resurrection of Jesus Christ. This is much more muted in the Prayer Book, particularly in the Communion Service. In the *Book of Common Prayer* the Resurrection signifies 'open[ing] unto us the gate of everlasting life' (Collect for Easter Day) rather than the 'living hope' of the New Testament.

Grace is an all-pervasive theme in the *Book of Common Prayer*, confronting human weakness and sinfulness with the active gift of God. This is combined with an equally Augustinian emphasis on human inward motivation and on self-deceit. 'Grant to us, Lord, we beseech thee, the spirit to think and do always such things as be rightful; that we, who cannot do anything that is good without thee, may by thee be enabled to live according to thy will; through Jesus Christ our Lord' (Trinity 9).

Eternity and mortality are never far from the surface: 'we may so pass through things temporal, that we finally lose not the things eternal' (Trinity 4). This emphasis on the eternal is accompanied by an almost worldly concern for right living. The *Alternative Service Book* more often focuses on the life of the Church and the quality of relationship within the Church. These last emphases may encourage introversion, but are hardly alien to the New Testament.

Monarchy and stability are major concerns in the *Book of Common Prayer*, as in the first collects at Holy Communion and the Catechism's injunctions 'To order myself lowly and reverently to all my betters: . . . To keep my hands from picking and stealing'. David Holeton comments, 'When compared with the inherited tradition of both Scripture and the Early Church, the Prayer Book language for God is extremely limited and is selected in such a fashion (either consciously or unconsciously) that it reinforces a Tudor world-view with all its limitations'.[11]

The Prayer Book is hardly the book to encourage active resistance to injustice! Professor Holeton compares the *Book of Common Prayer*'s Collect for Holy Innocents ('madest infants to glorify thee by their deaths: Mortify and kill all vices in us') with that in the Canadian *Book of Alternative Services* ('whose children suffered at the hands of Herod, receive, we pray, all innocent victims into the arms of your mercy; by your great might frustrate all evil designs and establish your reign of justice, love and peace . . .'). It is not hard to imagine which would appeal more to Rachel weeping for her children (Matthew 2.18).

Devotion to the suffering and death of Christ forms a less alien theme in the *Book of Common Prayer*. Cranmer retains, from the tradition of Anselm, many echoes of tender devotion to Christ and of awed gratitude at his atoning death, e.g. 'the most precious death and passion of thy dear Son'.

Austerity. In the essay already quoted, Milner-White wrote from his experience in the First World War:

> We never guessed of old how removed [the Prayer-book] was from common wants; nor how intellectual are its prayers and forms of devotion. Its climate to the simple, ardent Christian is often ice. The warm romance of man's pilgrimage to God is absent from it, because it takes early stages for granted and can only be used by those who have ascended many hills of difficulty. How we have blushed for the incomprehensibility even of the Collects![12]

Such a judgement may be hard to accept for those of us who value the concise piety of the Prayer Book. It is confirmed by observing the forms of service that are popular with many who are coming to worship for the first time, or after an absence of some years.

Theological Reflection

What are we to make of the alienation of many ordinands from the traditional prayers of the Church of England? No doubt, more could have been done in the past and could still be done. But it is clear that we are dealing with more than incompetent training or obtuse ordinands; we are meeting a symptom of something deeper in English Christianity. How are we to understand 'this great act of forgetting'?

It is interesting to observe who signed the petitions to General Synod. The long list of signatories includes many distinguished members of the educational, artistic, musical, legal, military and political establishments. Distress at the loss of the Prayer Book has been felt most by those who are most identified with the English cultural and religious heritage. Protest has felt most unreal in its failure to grasp that this anguish is not shared by the common people who have cared nothing for the *Book of Common Prayer* for at least most of this century. Public reality for them has been shaped by economic, political, educational, social and media concerns, which have had no serious place for Christian belief or prayer. Their native culture is now alien to that of the Prayer Book at many points, of which estrangement from the language and ideas of the Prayer Book is just one. Books and words have a different place in people's lives; television has led to a heightened appreciation of variety and the visual; there is a new sensitivity to creation and to symbolic modes of communication. The ambivalence of the clergy to the Prayer Book reflects a reality with which they have been confronted every day.

More profoundly, the decline of the Prayer Book is symptomatic of more than the Church's failure in the past to assert its right to adapt its liturgy or, in the present, to persevere in its use. It reflects a hardening of every part of English society against the God of the Prayer Book. This is something quite different from any so-called decline in moral standards. It is a deep and all-pervasive indifference to God. The Church may have contributed to this by ceding control of its worship to those to whom it did not rightfully belong, but many peoples overseas have kept the faith when their churches were far more corrupt or servile. No part of our society is exempt from a part in this failure or hardening, including those who feel themselves to be the guardians of its cultural and religious heritage.

St Paul in Romans 9 to 11 wrestles with a similar hardening, with what he calls the 'failure' of Israel. He recognised it as an unfathomable and terrible mystery. In part, he saw the blame as resting on a people who had made their spiritual privilege a source of pride. But ultimately he sees Israel's hardening as temporary and full of promise, and attributes it to God himself: 'through their trespass salvation has come to the Gentiles' (Romans 11.11).

The hardening of Christendom has been accompanied in the rest of the world by the greatest turning to Christ history has seen. My own view is that the hardening has come upon us through the love of money, with the loveless, prayerless pride that naturally accompanies 'trust in uncertain riches' (1 Tim. 6.17). Whether or not this is the case, the Church finds itself faced with the apparent failure of the word of God (cf. Romans 9.6.). It is natural that recrimination and despair often follow. Nostalgia for some religious or national past Golden Age is equally understandable. St Paul's great chapters show how testing such a time is to a person of faith.

In the midst of this trial the Church can be seen discovering again its identity as a pilgrim community, loosening its identification with an unbelieving nation, opening its heart to those outside the church, and finding again a solidarity with the marginal and the weak which has been part of the Gospel since God 'regarded the low estate of his handmaiden' (Luke 1.48). The Church may be temporarily blinded to theological themes to which the *Book of Common Prayer* bears witness; but it has been recovering from Scripture themes which are vital to its current task in God's providence.

Many New Testament writings reflect fierce conflict between those who saw themselves as the guardians of the religious heritage of God's people, and those who came to Christ from outside this historic tradition. St Paul saw any attempt to impose a venerable religious tradition on new Christians as a denial of the Gospel of Jesus Christ. It risked replacing the regenerative power of the Spirit of Jesus Christ with the merely human preservative of human tradition. When the conflict spilled over into human relationships, St Paul saw the characteristic vice of the traditionalist as 'passing judgement', and of the convert from outside as 'despising' (cf. Romans 14.3). St Paul's own writings show the better way of using the tradition as a resource, not a law.

What of the future?

If this analysis has any truth in it, the primary question is what will England make of Christ? How, if at all, will the 'hardening' end? From St Paul's great argument, it seems that we cannot know the outcome, but are to believe that 'failure' is full of promise and mercy.

It is against this backcloth that the future of the *Book of Common Prayer* should be set. Hopefully, the time will come when a more balanced and positive assessment of the *Book of Common Prayer* will be possible. Perhaps such a rich religious and musical heritage will not be abandoned forever in a society which prizes conservation so highly. Modern translations of the Bible, such as the *New International Version*, which stand in the same tradition as the Authorised Version, may help to keep this tradition accessible to Christians. Within the Church, there is need of a more deliberate attempt to understand the strengths and influence of the Prayer Book. Its best advocates will be those who, steeped in the spiritual tradition it represents, take their place in humility in a Church struggling to be with Christ in a new and uncharted vocation.

Notes

1. *PN Review 13* (Vol. 6, No. 5, 1979), guest editor David Martin, pp.51 ff.
2. A convenient chronicle, albeit critical, of these attempts can be found in *News of Liturgy* April 1981, June 1981, April 1984, April 1986, January 1987.
3. Brilliantly captured by Professor R.M. Hare in *PN Review 13*. 'We used, after the Minister had quoted the words "Do this as oft as ye shall drink it, in remembrance of me", to go and do it; now we are to have, instead, a lot of words, which anyone with any sense of drama could see would defuse the entire proceedings.' This dramatic force has been obscured in practice by Catholic and Puritan insistence on treating Jesus' words of institution as a formula of consecration; see C.O. Buchanan, *What Did Cranmer Think He Was Doing?* (Nottingham, 1976).
4. 60 per cent of those parishes which hold a Family Service, *For the Family* (Chelmsford, 1987), p.16.
5. E.g. *Making Women Visible* (London, 1988), paragraphs 17, 18 and Appendix 1.
6. Phillip Tovey, *Inculturation: the Eucharist in Africa* (London, 1988), gives some indication of moves away from Western traditions, including interesting improvisation on the *Book of Common Prayer* in a West African Church.

7. Oliver O'Donovan, *On the Thirty Nine Articles* (Exeter, 1986).
8. Ed. F.C. Macnutt (1917) p.177, p.184.
9. Cf. S.W. Sykes in *Anvil*, Vol. 5, No. 2 (1988), p.109: 'We have a deeply-laid instinct . . . that the realisation of fellowship must be a fellowship in common prayer.'
10. Colin Buchanan, *Leading Worship* (Nottingham, 1981), p.11.
11. *A Kingdom of Priests: Liturgical Formation of the People of God*; papers read at the second International Anglican Liturgical Consultation, ed. Thomas Talley (Nottingham, 1988), p.10.
12. Ibid., pp.184–5.

XVII

The Church of England and the *Book of Common Prayer*
Douglas R. Jones

The Church's liturgy, aside from the living witness of her adherents, is the most prominent public evidence of her beliefs and character. Doctrine in books, and even in the pulpit, is ignored by the vast majority of churchpeople. But doctrine incorporated in and diffused by shared worship cannot be ignored. It exercises a subliminal influence. In the *Book of Common Prayer* essential orthodoxy of belief and conduct has been conveyed to a large, if diminishing, proportion of the British people for centuries. The successful performance of this role has depended upon a widespread respect, sometimes love, for the liturgical forms of the Prayer Book, answering to the needs of the people, offering memorable phrases, nurturing new generations, particularly at home in the English country parish. The combination of the Prayer Book and the Authorised Version was powerful and magisterial, and became part of the fabric of English life. George Eliot understood Adam Bede to be representative of thoughtful country folk in the late eighteenth century when she wrote of him that 'the church service was the best channel he could have found for his mingled regret, yearning and resignation; its interchange of beseeching cries for help with outbursts of faith and praise, its recurrent responses and the familiar rhythm of its collects'. If the Prayer Book protected the English Church from the excesses of the Reformation and from the whims of private fancy, linking her inseparably with both Scripture and the Early Church, that was a bonus which looks better and better in the light of history. When Reinhold Niebuhr was asked what constituted the unity of the Anglican Communion,

he answered: the *Book of Common Prayer*. But now
the position is radically changed for both the Church of
England and the Anglican Communion. A few decades
have witnessed the dissolution of this inheritance in this
simple form.

The causes that have produced this result are complex.
The first is the gradual distancing of the *Book of Common
Prayer* from the language of the people, coupled
with the advances of scholarship. This was inevitable
and in the nature of things, the more so because the
Prayer Book was designed to be a contemporary manual
of the people. It is remarkable that it has held its place so
long. This is not in fact because it was riveted upon the
people by successive Acts of Uniformity, but because its
language always to some extent transcended contemporary linguistic fashions. Cranmer was a phenomenon.
At a time when the English language was a graceful
vehicle of communication, instrument of a magnificent
literary tradition, he rose above the complexities of its
idioms to produce a simple, rhythmical, memorable
expression of the people's worship. At the same time
he was a considerable theologian and liturgical scholar.
The combination is rare and many would say providen-
tial. In the seventeenth century the rhythms of the
Prayer Book remained simpler and more direct than
those of any contemporary writer. Compare a page of
Pepys. Even in the twentieth century not every revision
brings clarity. When C. S. Lewis asked a countryman what
'indifferent' meant, he supposed 'it doesn't make any
difference'. Of 'impartial' he said he had no idea! For
some, the images of sovereignty seem Tudor, though
they are more often biblical, and the emphasis upon
sin for modern liberal thought is overweighted, though
it be the obverse side of a perception of the divine
holiness. For many the 'thou' language has suddenly
appeared increasingly anachronistic. Indeed the change
from 'thou' to 'you' in modern services has been more
radical than is commonly realised. For it is not sufficient simply to substitute the one for the other. Whole
sentences have to be recast, often with marked loss of

rhythm. It is not surprising that the general verdict of liturgists has been that you have, for the most part, to start again from the beginning.

As to the Bible, the pressure to produce modern versions became irresistible. Chaplains in the world wars were acutely conscious that the biblical weapon in their hands was blunt. Moreover biblical scholarship had reached the point where the perceived inaccuracies of the older versions made new versions imperative. Only a kind of Authorised Version fundamentalism or, lately a recherché structuralist theory, could resist the process. It is sad and it is harmful that some, including scholars in other theological disciplines, have wished to ignore much biblical and liturgical scholarship. But the massive work of 200 years cannot be consigned to the dustbin. And the last person to whom they can appeal for approval and patronage is Thomas Cranmer.

The second cause of dissolution is the rigidity of parliamentary control. When air and space was required, particularly in the nineteenth century, it was not permitted, and there were those who went to prison rather than acquiesce. In the twentieth century, the one comprehensive attempt to revise (as opposed to replace) the Prayer Book was disallowed by an unrepresentative Parliament. The so-called 1928 Book was a magnificent liturgical achievement. Despite Parliament, the Church absorbed much of it, but its illegal status has dogged the Church's liturgical life until the present day. For a brief period there was freedom. The Prayer Book (Alternative and Other Services) Measure of 1965 made it possible to secure parliamentary authority for those parts of the 1928 Book which were widely used and had become customary. The result was *Alternative Services: Series I*. But these were never more than pamphlets and an ungenerous Synod declined to re-authorise crucial parts of the 1928 Book after the introduction of the *Alternative Service Book 1980*. Meanwhile in 1970 synodical government was introduced and the Church at last achieved the control of her own worship *except* in the case of the *Book of Common Prayer*. But then we were in the midst of a world-wide liturgical ferment which changed all boundaries. For the Prayer Book, freedom seemed to have come too late. Interest in its revision faded. Liturgical preoccupation was with the new.

The third cause of dissolution is the success of the *Alternative Service Book*. No one believes it has the linguistic felicity of the *Book of Common Prayer*, and some believe that any theological improvements are matched by theological shortcomings. But it is undeniably popular in the parishes, and this popularity is soundly based. By and large it meets present needs with a comprehensive versatility. Its eucharistic form owes something to the Prayer Book, but gives the aura of an older form deriving from the age of the Fathers. In this it provides a link not only with other revisions of the Anglican Communion, but also with those of the Roman Catholic Church. It has served to knit together the Evangelical and Catholic wings of the Church of England. If linguistically it is sometimes banal and rarely, if ever, poetic, it is nevertheless adequate, and has withstood the test of repetition. Vast numbers of worshippers have found it an appropriate instrument of family worship. One might say, without making extravagant claims, that it seems to have come into the kingdom for just such a time as this. For this is a time when a ferment of liturgical and biblical scholarship has reached a consensus on the shape of the Eucharist; a time also, when, as a result of a widespread movement of Christian thought, parish worship has become increasingly eucharistic. In comparison, many find the Prayer Book service of Holy Communion heavy, not so easy to adapt to the considerable element of congregational participation now common. If the swing to the Eucharist had not taken place, it is doubtful whether the *Alternative Service Book* would have achieved so dominant a role. Its revision of non-eucharistic services is less successful. Its revision of Evening Prayer gains nothing in clarity and tampers with a masterpiece of Christendom. Morning Prayer has vanished in many parishes. As to the text of the Bible, the plethora of modern translations has caused a confusion similar to that which preceded the publication of the Authorised Version in 1611. None is the obvious winner.[1] To return to the AV rendering of Genesis stories or Gospel parables or the Passion narrative, after long subjection to the other versions, is to realise afresh the magic of language which is full of echoes and overtones and memorable rhythms. And how important it is that the phrases of worship shall be such that they remain in the memory and become the sword of the Spirit! Nevertheless there is no turning back.

In this complex and often confusing context, the *Book of Common Prayer* has lost out. In so far as this is due to some of the causes sketched above, there is little reason to complain. The whirligig of time brings its changes and there is an element of inevitability in what has happened. But there are other factors where acquiescence is not so appropriate. One has to ask why what used to be called our 'incomparable liturgy' has become so widely displaced, when myriad voices have been raised to retain it. In almost every parish there are people who feel bereft. Where the *Book of Common Prayer* has been defeated is in *presentation* both in publication and in performance. The *Alternative Service Book* is published skilfully and attractively. It looks modern and efficient. The *Book of Common Prayer* remains in its heavy seventeenth-century form. It looks its age. The 1928 Book is still, as a whole, illegal. The Shorter Prayer Book of 1948 has been republished by the Cambridge Press, but discreetly lest its uncertain status should cause disturbance. The eight o'clock form of Holy Communion at Westminster Abbey was carefully edited by Dean Jasper, but is a peculiar of the Abbey. Pamphlets of some services exist. But there is no authorised, modern, attractive edition of the Prayer Book *as it is used*. No one uses it exactly in its seventeenth-century form. The *Book of Common Prayer* therefore, as it appears (decreasingly) in the pews, is an anachronism. The contest is unequal.

While all the Church of England's liturgical resources

were concentrated on the *Alternative Service Book*, little
or no attention was devoted to the presentation of the
Prayer Book services in the modern parish. At first
the intention was to offer *Lent Holy Week Easter: Services and Prayers* in two forms, one to accompany the
Alternative Service Book, the other to fit the *Book of
Common Prayer*. But a directive came to the Liturgical
Commission from the bishops to write no new services
in the 'thou' language. There was sense in this because
the 'thou' syntax can be an artificial creation in modern hands. But it meant that the *Alternative Service
Book* was seen to be versatile and flexible. The *Book
of Common Prayer* appeared restricted and inflexible
in contrast. How different was the unofficial and rich
adaptation of the *Book of Common Prayer* practised
by earlier Anglo-Catholic churchmen, as for example
in *The People's Missal* of 1916. Our forebears worked
hard at presentation. We do little. The most vivid proof
of this thesis is the publication in 1988 of the *Sunday Service Book*, with a preface by the Archbishop of
York. This is an effort of presentation, the *Alternative Service Book* and the Prayer Book services being
given roughly equal weight. The idea is excellent. Worshippers who like to thumb through their service book
would become acquainted with parts of the Prayer Book.
Parishes geared to use the modern services would find
it easier to present services in the older form, if only
occasionally. But it is arguable that this publication will
have exactly the opposite effect to that intended by its
sponsors. For the Prayer Book services are exactly as
published in 1662. Even the rubrics keep their quaint-
ness. As to Holy Communion, I am reminded of a
clergyman whom I heard boast publicly that, when he
encountered a request for the Prayer Book service, he
provided the 1662 form verbatim, including the long
exhortation, and did not receive a repeat request! The
Bishop of Leicester was not exaggerating when he spoke
of 'lay people who are being subjected to this legalistic
use of the *Book of Common Prayer*, which is very easy
for an incumbent to support if what he wants to do is to

kill the *Book of Common Prayer*'. The *Quicunque Vult* is
in its offensive version. The Litany, too, lacks those touches that have become customary. The prayers increase
misery by obtruding the theological and moral reservations which worry sensitive souls. Baptism is in the one
form which most priests of the Church of England have
never used. It is as though we have learned nothing.
This is not the Prayer Book *as it is used*. The modern
services are printed in the attractive form to which we
have become accustomed. The Prayer Book services look
what they are, dated and dusty. There is no doubt an
economic reason for this. Both will have been repro-
duced by photographic techniques, thus saving large
production costs. But however compelling the reason,
including of course the desire to avoid stirring contention, the effect is devastating. The *Alternative Service
Book* has the appearance of vitality, the Prayer Book
section the appearance of yesteryear. No doubt some
intellectuals will appreciate a classic. Most worshippers
look for the text of their worship. If the elderly see in it
the text they have been used to editing, the young will
have no such point of entrance. Were the editors themselves conscious of this? You would expect the Prayer
Book services to be printed first, and the *alternative*
services logically second. But the alternative services
are presented first, awakening expectation. The Prayer
Book services come second, extinguishing it. Have the
roles been reversed? Is the *Book of Common Prayer*
now the alternative service book? Did the editors suspect that to put the Prayer Book services first would be
to kill sales? If so, they were probably right. No doubt,
by this means also, arguments were avoided as to how the
Prayer Book services should be presented and awkward
questions of authority bypassed. No explanation over-
turns the basis judgment that this publication proclaims
aloud the success of the Church of England in its new
services and its pathetic ineptness in handling its liturgical heritage. There are some in high places who want the
Prayer Book to atrophy and die. The 1988 publication
presents it half dead already, and illustrates Professor

Roy Porter's accurate observation that 'supporters of the Prayer Book are being boxed into a corner where they do not want to be, with the only alternatives being the Prayer Book of 1662 as it stands and the ASB'.[2]

Why is it that the Church cannot, or dare not, publish an attractive edition of the Prayer Book *as it is used*?

The first reason is legalism. The history of worship in the Church of England since the Reformation has been dogged by legalism and it is with us still. In the use of the *Alternative Service Book*, for example in the intercessions at the Eucharist, anything goes, and the wide latitude is covered by the rubric which allows 'other suitable words'. In the use of the Prayer Book every variant word has been subject to scrutiny and argument, and the text is mandatory throughout. A publisher deciding to publish the Prayer Book in any revised form might well find himself in a legal maelstrom. But there is a paradox here. The parliamentary and other watch dogs, who have been ceaselessly vigilant to pounce on any action which changes the 1662 book, have thereby destroyed their own purpose. For the Prayer Book will survive on the basis of its present creative use, not on the letter of its 1662 form, embalmed and intact.

The second reason is the lack of foresight and the obduracy shown by General Synod. After the publication of the *Alternative Service Book*, a sustained effort was made to suppress as many alternatives as possible to the basic choice between the *Book of Common Prayer* and the new book. The *Sunday Service Book* is a fruit of this policy. But it must now be evident that what Prayer Book worshippers need is the text of the services as now used and in an attractive form. This would have been facilitated at a stroke if Series I had been re-authorised. For it must be asserted again and again that Series I was 'in no sense intended as a new rite, but rather as a collection of the variations from the *Book of Common Prayer* which were widely current'. Professor Porter has chronicled the fate of Series I at the hands of Synod.[3]

There were two main reasons why repeated attempts

to re-authorise Series I, supported vigorously by Archbishop Runcie and the bishops, were ultimately frus-
trated. There was the argument, beguiling to many,
that it was unnecessary. And there was the theological
argument, understood by few, that it contained heresy.
The pragmatic argument was the more powerful and
provided cover for theological caution. It was based
partly on Canon B5, partly on the view that the Series
I eucharistic form can, by the judicious use of permitted
variations, be wrested from Rite B in the *Alternative
Service Book*. The theological argument need not detain
us. The accusation that the eucharistic rite in Series I is
Pelagian does not stand up to inspection, and is so interpreted only by those who, in any case, have no wish to use
it. Professor Porter submitted this accusation to detailed
scrutiny in the article already cited, and in my opinion
wins the argument.

As to Canon B5, this has been exploited so constantly
that it must be set out before us.

*Of the Discretion of the Minister in Conduct of Public
Prayer*
1. The minister may in his discretion make and use
variations which are not of substantial importance in
any form of service authorised by Canon B1 according to particular circumstances.

Canon B1 refers to the *Book of Common Prayer* and
alternatives properly authorised by Synod. That means
the *Alternative Service Book*, the new lectionary, etc.
Another paragraph requires that any such discretionary
variation shall be 'neither contrary to, nor indicative of
any departure from, the doctrine of the Church of England in any essential matter'. And a last paragraph (4)
leaves decision as to what is 'of substantial importance'
to the diocesan bishop. This canon has been pressed
into much service. Its purpose is to free the Church
from the sort of text-tyranny which inhibits pastoral
sensitivity. The minister has his text but may adapt it
to pastoral need. The canon was never intended to be

the means of establishing a revised text. Beyond a certain point, cumulative small variations produce a revised text. That, nevertheless, is how it is being used. Here are four examples.

1. The Westminster Abbey eight o'clock service of Holy Communion is a revised rite. It is the *Book of Common Prayer as it is used*. It is explicitly justified by reference to Canon B5.
2. Bishop Dawes swung General Synod to the view that Series I was unnecessary by means of an appeal to Canon B5. Prayer Book worshippers have 1662 and Canon B5. Anything more is a waste of Synod's time and money.
3. The *Sunday Service Book* presents, as we have seen, services from the *Alternative Service Book* and the *Book of Common Prayer* side by side, and the Prayer Book Services are exactly as published in 1662. The Archbishop of York who commends the volume in a preface, knows well that no one will use it as printed. The minister and his congregation are expected to make considerable use of Canon B5, whether they know what they are doing or not.
4. The House of Bishops, within General Synod, carried the following resolution on 28 January, 1988:

The House of Bishops is agreed in regarding the continued use, where well established, of any form of service which has, at any time since 1965, been canonically authorised (notwithstanding the fact that such authorisation was not renewed after it lapsed) as not being of 'substantial importance' within the meaning of Canon B5.4.

This implicitly includes Series I, since its authorisation date was 1965. This must be regarded as a great and sensible gain. Nevertheless when one reflects on the antecedents of Series I, both immediate and distant, the liturgical skill devoted to it, and the sheer number of variations involved, there seems to be an exploitation of the innocent Canon B5 to achieve what an unwilling and ungenerous Synod would not authorise by open means. The suspicion must remain that the dust will settle providing the Prayer Book is not published and presented *as it is used*. The editors of the *Sunday Service Book* knew what they were doing when they avoided the duty of presenting worshippers with the text of their worship.

The Bishops may however be regarded as themselves exercising a proper discretion in so extending the scope of Canon B5. For what they have done is to acknowledge the existence of what might be called 'common law liturgical variations'.[4] These remain independent of their justification by Canon B5 or any other legal instrument. Bringing them within the scope of the Canon does, however, in present conditions, have the effect of making clear and public the will of the Church. This is close to the concept of 'economy' as practised in the Orthodox churches. The word itself has no resonance within the Church of England. In Greek theology it is derived (with an echo of Ephesians. 3.2) from the idea of God's management of his world and, in particular, the incarnation. St Irenaeus uses it of the divine plan of salvation (*Ign.* Eph. 20.1). From this it is used of God's dealings with his world as mediated in and through the Church. Economy is the Church's exercise of her stewardship, enabling the inflexibilities of law to be transcended without weakening the law. The *oikonomoi* or stewards of the Church's practice of economy are bishops, either in the diocese or in synods at various levels.

As with common law liturgical variations, so with economy, there are parameters within which it may be exercised. These, adapted to Church of England liturgical needs, are as follows.

1. We are concerned with what, over a reasonably long period of time, has become customary in the Church. In the spirit of the 6th Canon of the Council

of Nicaea, 'we wish the ancient customs of the Church
to continue'.

2. It is manifestly in accord with the doctrine of the
Church of England as defined by canon.

3. It is such variation as is necessary to adapt the
received text to contemporary needs. It is not therefore on such a scale as to overthrow the integrity of
the text. The intention is to keep as close to the text
as possible. Thus no derogation from law is implied
or caused. Economy does not supersede law: it transcends it. It has to do with that flexibility and tolerance
without which law breaks down.

4. It is such variation as has found general approval in
the Church. It is unitive, not divisive, promoting the
peace of the Church and the salvation and well-being
of souls.

5. It is such variation as the House of Bishops in Synod
can generally approve and encourage in their pastoral
oversight. This is in line with the mind of successive
Lambeth conferences.

The action of the bishops may be said to be entirely
within these parameters. Indeed it is a notable example
of the exercise of wise economy in the Church.

There is in fact an analogy to economy in the Western
tradition of moral law. Aristotle saw the limitations of
law and found the answer in the idea of *epieikeia* or epiky.
A more comprehensive discussion of this is to be found
in the article cited above. Here the point is to indicate
that Western lawyers need not be afraid of the Eastern
concept of economy.

There is therefore profound justification for the bishops' carefully judged extension of the discretion allowed
in Canon B5. They have used it to transcend the rigidities
in which we have been trapped by our legal system.
They have given us room to recognise time-honoured
custom. We have the *Book of Common Prayer* and the
Alternative Service Book coupled with the wise exercise
of economy in the Church.

But there is one further imperative need. Now that

the widely used variations in the Prayer Book are publicly and authoritatively acknowledged, with impeccable theoretical justification, it must be possible to publish a version or versions of the Prayer Book corresponding to the way in which it is used. Prayer Book worshippers must be enabled to have in their hands the text of their worship. The *Sunday Service Book*, a splendid idea ineffectively carried out, should be remodelled to ensure, before it is too late, that a new generation of worshippers will remain in touch with their inheritance and are not embarrassed by, or ignorant of, the devotional riches of the past, that, being trained for the kingdom of heaven, they may bring out of their treasure things new and old.

We await the imaginative, artistic, attractive, appropriate presentation of the *Book of Common Prayer* for the contemporary Church.

Notes

1. See 'The English Bible – Which version for worship?' by Gordon S. Wakefield in *The Word in Season* (Joint Liturgical Group), ed. Donald Gray (The Canterbury Press, 1988).
2. 'The Series I issue' in *Faith and Worship*, Winter 1984.
3. Ibid.
4. For a more comprehensive discussion see my article 'Customary Variations in Liturgy', in *Faith and Worship*, Autumn 1985.